D0915633

*Faith's Harvest*

# Faith's Harvest

## MENNONITE IDENTITY
## IN NORTHWEST OKLAHOMA

## Sharon Hartin Iorio

University of Oklahoma Press : Norman

Published with the assistance of the National Endowment for the Humanities, a federal agency which supports the study of such fields as history, philosophy, literature, and language.

**Library of Congress Cataloging-in-Publication Data**

Iorio, Sharon Hartin, 1922–
    Faith's harvest : Mennonite identity in northwest Oklahoma /
Sharon Hartin Iorio.
        p.    cm.
    Includes bibliographical references and index.
    ISBN 0-8061-3119-5 (alk. paper)
    1. Mennonites—Oklahoma—History.    2. Group identity—Oklahoma—
Case studies.    I. Title.
BX8117.05I57    1998
305.6'2870766—dc21                                                    98-38659
                                                                             CIP

1   2   3   4   5   6   7   8   9   10

*For my husband, Richard,*
*and for*
*Russell, Richard, Robert, and Stacey*

# Contents

# Illustrations

# Preface

Mennonites form a small fellowship of Christians. They number approximately 300,000 adult members nationwide* (Hostetter 1997). About fifteen hundred Mennonites are members of congregations located in the small cities and rural communities that dot the sparsely populated plains of Northwest Oklahoma, a region known for its fertile soil and abundant wheat crops. At the opening of the Cherokee Outlet on September 16, 1893, hundreds of settlers rushed across the state line and onto the grassy Oklahoma prairie to stake homestead claims on available government land. Among these

---

*On June 30, 1997, there were 302,256 baptized Mennonites in the United States (Hostetter 1997). More members are located in Africa, Asia, Australia, Europe, Canada, Mexico, Central America, and South America. As many as forty-six different bodies make up the total of Mennonite churches in the United States (Hostetter 1997). Some of the more distinctive groups in North America have been the Beachy Amish Mennonite; the Brethren in Christ; the Chortizer Mennonite Conference; the Church of God in Christ, Mennonite (Holdeman); the Conference of Mennonites in Canada; the Evangelical Mennonite Church; the Evangelical Mennonite Conference (Canada); the Evangelical Bible Churches; the General Conference Mennonite Church; the Hutterischen Bruder; the Mennonite Brethren Churches; the (Old) Mennonite Church; the Old Colony Mennonite Churches (Alberta, British Columbia, Ontario, and Saskatchewan); the Old Order Amish Church; the Old Order River Brethren; the Old Order Mennonites (Canada); the Old Order Mennonites (United States); and the Sommerfelder Mennonite Church. Groups in the United States with the largest membership are the (Old) Mennonite Church, the General Conference Mennonite Church, and the Mennonite Brethren Churches. More information about the various Mennonite churches can be found at www.prairienet.org/mennonite/MennoLink/organizations.

pioneers were Mennonites, many of whom had immigrated to the outlet by a circuitous route.

In the sixteenth century, Mennonite émigrés, Swiss and Dutch, had traveled from Switzerland and the European Low Countries, where their church had originated (Kauffman and Driedger 1991), to Germany, Prussia, and Poland. Then, in the mid-eighteenth century, many moved on to Russia, where their colonies were located for over one hundred years. Finally, in the 1870s and 1880s, they came to American shores and eventually to Oklahoma Territory. Mennonite farmer-immigrants seeking homesteads began to settle near Oklahoma in southern Kansas during the latter part of the nineteenth century. Most of them were drawn to Kansas because of the cheap farmland offered for sale along the route of the newly built Santa Fe Railroad and because the climate and geography of the area resembled that of their homelands in Russia and Poland. Some came by way of Canada and the northern plains states or from older Mennonite settlements in Pennsylvania and the Midwest, but most Mennonites who made the "run" into Oklahoma set out from Kansas, where they had located only a few years earlier. As a group, the new settlers formed a visible and distinctive part of Oklahoma's pioneer population.

For much of their history, Mennonite people in Oklahoma and throughout the world have been rural agriculturists. At present, the descendants of Mennonites who homesteaded the Cherokee Outlet are part of a large migration away from rural areas. Mechanization, increased production, and economic conditions that encourage corporate agriculture have greatly restricted family farming, once the principal occupation of Mennonites. A growing population, coupled with increased educational opportunities and diversification in employment, has resulted in the rapid urbanization of these Mennonites. The postindustrialized society has transformed the insular, rural lifestyle of the early Mennonite settlers almost beyond recognition.

Unlike the Amish, who reject almost all contact with "the world," many branches of the Mennonite faith today work cooperatively with the larger society. These Mennonites consider themselves "plain people" who no longer appear "plain." The story of Mennonite people in Northwest Oklahoma—the events that led them to Oklahoma, the forces that shaped their lifestyle, and, most importantly, their adaptation to the demands of a changing social world—is the subject of this book. It is a story of Mennonite life as it has developed over the past century, including the modes of communication that have transmitted and sustained the Mennonite heritage.

The underlying principle that provides continuity for the book is the idea that language is a powerful, if intangible, force in shaping the boundaries of group identity. The narrative is based on individual reflections that reveal both a collective, intergenerational memory and the memories of singular men and women. The book is intended to record how the past is preserved and the present shared by the group. The story of Mennonite life told here begins with the race for homesteads in 1893, then moves through the hardships of pioneer life to the growth of cash-crop farming. The intolerance shown toward Mennonites during World Wars I and II because of their German heritage and their belief in nonresistance is brought to light, as is the growth of the Mennonite peace movement. Ultimately, the text reveals a people who continue to evolve amid great social change, economic crisis, and escalating unrest throughout the world. In this telling are found two major frames of reference around which the Mennonite ethic revolves: (1) the concept of nonresistance to human violence and (2) the striving for a life separate from "worldly" society. Undergirding these two primary maps of group identification are the fundamental Mennonite values of work, piety, and family life that recur in the voices of individual Mennonites.

The book is divided into three principal parts according to major shifts in the group frame of reference for interpreting the past. Each part contains a set of chapters that both introduce and summarize one aspect or period of Mennonite society. These chapters are woven from primary and secondary sources and from descriptions of Mennonite life revealed in interviews, and each chapter ends with a personal narrative told in the words of the people who have lived the

Mennonite epic—the pioneers, their children, and their grand-children. The accounts of these individuals are, in essence, essays on Mennonite life. The language is intimate, and the opinions retrospective. While each first-person story illustrates a certain period in the social history of the group, none specifically locks into any one time span. Time shifts in the narratives of the storytellers, and the past is framed according to individual perspectives.

Much of the insight provided in the interpretations of these farmers and laborers, their wives, children, and pastors has been for years overlooked or ignored in history and sociological texts. Neither have communication studies attempted to understand how the voices of everyday people chronicle the past and bring it to the present. The narratives that follow proclaim a collective past and articulate a common Mennonite identity. They show the Mennonite ethnicity as it was and as it is perceived. Through them we look into ways Mennonites communicate their traditions, understand the changes they have experienced, and "keep faith" in a postmodern world.

# *Acknowledgments*

Many people helped make this book possible. I owe special thanks for support from my immediate family, to whom this book is dedicated. I also want to recognize family members Joe and Anna Belle Hartin, Pearl and Russell Hambleton, and Anne Langston, all of whom loved to tell stories of Oklahoma. Judge Alfred P. Murrah and Agnes Murrah encouraged my studies.

The idea for the research began at Oklahoma State University. It was there that the basic idea developed from discussions with Larry Perkins, who helped shape the concept, and with Charles Edgley, who helped shape the overall theoretical perspective. Maureen Nemeck provided invaluable early feedback on the work, as did Patricia Bell and Professor Emeritus Douglas Hale. Karen Randall and Marcia Scott, both of Enid, helped me set up the interview process efficiently.

Betty Evans and Louella Unruh helped me contact the interviewees. Kathy Janes spent many hours transcribing the lengthy interviews. An early draft of the book was reviewed by Marvin Kroeker, history professor at East Central Oklahoma University; Peggy Goertzen, librarian at Tabor College; and Wilma McKee, who has written about and edited a history of the Mennonite General Conference in Oklahoma. David Peters of Oklahoma State University also criticized the work with great care.

I want to thank Philip Gaunt, director of the Elliott School of Communication at Wichita State University, for his support of this research and Vernon Keel, the school's founding director. Special thanks go to the late Oliver Elliott and to Betty Elliott for their unwavering support of communication studies at Wichita State. A portion of the study was funded by the Eugene M. Hughes Endowed Faculty Development Award and a summer research grant awarded through the Fairmount College of Liberal Arts and Sciences at WSU, and I am grateful for that financial assistance. Aleen Ratzlaff worked for countless hours one summer as my graduate research assistant, and I also want to recognize Fran Majors, who edited an early draft of the manuscript, and Mary Thompson, Rita Pierce, Jolinda Ramsey, and Chris Power, graduate student researchers. Jan Toth and Bill Molash are thanked for their administrative assistance. Sarah Iselin, associate editor at the University of Oklahoma Press, graciously guided this book through the publication process, and Ursula Smith was a helpful and conscientious copyeditor.

Most of all, I am indebted to the Mennonite people of Northwest Oklahoma who welcomed me into their homes and shared with me their memories of the past.

*Faith's Harvest*

# Church Locations

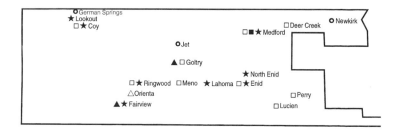

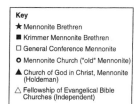

**Key**

★ Mennonite Brethren

■ Krimmer Mennonite Brethren

□ General Conference Mennonite

○ Mennonite Church ("old" Mennonite)

▲ Church of God in Christ, Mennonite (Holdeman)

△ Fellowship of Evangelical Bible Churches (Independent)

*Historical locations of Mennonite churches in Northwest Oklahoma*

# Rediscovering the Past and Interpreting the Present

This book began as research into group life. I wanted to understand something about continuity and change in groups over the course of time. I thought the best way to do this would be to study how individuals within a group understand themselves and their past and adjust to change in their own lives. My interest in these processes led me to a group of Mennonite people who live in towns and on farms in the northwestern part of Oklahoma. As a group, Mennonites are distinctive in the population mix that makes up Oklahoma's religious and ethnic community, even though they are a small minority.

The people and history of the state have been a long-standing interest of mine, in part because I am a native Oklahoman. After residing outside the state for a number of years, I returned to Northwest Oklahoma in 1975 and lived there until 1990. During that time, I became acquainted with several individuals who were of Mennonite heritage. My idea for this research began to take form in 1988. My goal was to develop an interactive approach to study communication and change in group life. I started by studying Mennonite church history, and a short time later I began to contact members of several Mennonite congregations. I wanted to center my work around the individuals who made up the group.

The Mennonite people of Northwest Oklahoma with whom I talked were descendants of early settlers who in 1893 homesteaded the area of Oklahoma once designated the Cherokee Outlet.* Opening myself to direct contact with the subjects of my research, I believed, was the most beneficial way to expand my knowledge of Mennonite people and understand the dynamics in their group. Many of the subjects revealed in this work have not been addressed in social-scientific accounts of religious-ethnic groups or in traditional histories of Oklahoma.

What I have written is a summary of group life augmented by in-depth accounts of personal experiences of some of the group members. This work is neither a history nor a social-scientific analysis of the group. While I do summarize the group's past, I do not attempt to record a detailed, sequential account of events or emphasize the date an event took place. I do not trace the history of particular churches or identify pastors or other influential individuals, either chronologically or in order of their significance. What I have done is to verify the accounts given me by individuals, using documents and other primary and secondary source materials. I have also used primary and secondary sources to expand and set in context the information gathered in my interviews. I follow the group's interpretation of events and issues in my presentation, and the group's inter-

---

*The Cherokee Outlet is the official term for an area west of the Cherokee Nation Reservation in Oklahoma that was ceded to the Cherokees by the United States government to be used for hunting and grazing purposes. The outlet was never home to large numbers of Cherokees. While it was traversed by a variety of Plains Indians who located at times in the area, neither was it the permanent location of large numbers of those tribes. Included in the land run that opened the Cherokee Outlet were the tribal lands allotted to the Pawnee and the Tonkawa tribes. The area opened by the run lies roughly between the ninety-sixth and one hundredth meridian and is bordered on the north by the Kansas state line and on the south by a line approximately fifty-eight miles south of the Kansas-Oklahoma border. This excludes the panhandle of Oklahoma, where Mennonite congregations formed, and Cordell, Corn, and other towns south of the outlet border where some other Mennonite congregations established themselves early in the history of Oklahoma settlement. The area that encompasses the Cherokee Outlet is known colloquially as the Cherokee Strip. The term "Northwest Oklahoma" is also used here in reference to that same area.

pretation does not always coincide with scholarly inperpretation. For example, Mennonites place a greater emphasis on religious discrimination as a cause for their migrations, whereas scholars view economic problems as playing a larger role in prompting relocation. My aim is to present a culture as viewed by the individuals who inhabit it. No effort has been made to present a summary or range of academic thinking on this particular topic.

The book is not intended to be a historical description. On the other hand, neither do I attempt a detailed sociological analysis or communication study of the group. I do not set up research hypotheses or operationalize concepts. I do not look for patterns of adult socialization, organizational structure, or group interaction, nor do I seek to understand the group's verbal, nonverbal, or mediated communication. What I have done is put together first-person accounts to describe from the point of view of the group their history and social identity. I have used in-depth interviews to highlight and personalize certain focal points in the group's past. I record an individual's perceptions of his or her life in the context of changes within the group and in the context of how these perceptions frame talk regarding the group's identity. My purpose is to preserve the collective recollections of these Mennonite people, to illustrate and personalize the Mennonite past by telling in detail a portion of the life history of certain individuals in the group, and to place this in the context of communication that now sustains the group's identity. My aim is to record and affirm the intellectual value of ordinary individuals' shared experience.

Although my research is somewhat of a pioneering effort in communication studies, it is indebted to a book about a farming community, *No Time but Place* by Jeff and Jessica Pearson (1980). I also owe something to the work of Studs Terkel (1970, 1984), who wrote social history by recording the words of a wide variety of people. The Pearsons wrote in the tradition of Terkel and added their own personal observations to the interviews they collected. Another book, titled *The Immigrants Speak* (LaGumina 1981), in which autobiographical accounts of Italian immigrants were presented as a study of ethnicity, also helped me form my ideas for this book.

Before beginning my own research, I prepared myself through a thorough review of what academic researchers had written about change in Mennonite life. I found that Mennonite identification covers a broad spectrum of religious doctrine and several ethnic subgroups (Barclay 1967; Fretz 1977). Of those Mennonites who entered the Cherokee Outlet in 1893, only three of the church divisions are represented in Northwest Oklahoma today. They are the General Conference Mennonite Church, the Mennonite Brethren Churches, and the Church of God in Christ. (Often referred to by the name of their founder, the latter are also called Holdeman Mennonites.) Among the Mennonites descended from those who originally located within the boundaries of the Cherokee Outlet, the Mennonite Brethren and General Conference Mennonites are the most numerous. These two groups also have become more acculturated than most other Mennonite subgroups nationwide. The third group of Mennonites, the Church of God in Christ—Holdeman Mennonites—is the smallest group. The Holdeman continue to this day to practice endogamy and to dress and groom themselves distinctively. They also cease formal education at the eighth grade.

Individuals associated with the Mennonite Brethren Churches and General Conference Mennonite Church were the general focus of my research. These Mennonites work and live cooperatively within the larger society. Most are tied to their faith by self-identification and shared beliefs rather than by dress, language, or insular associations. I chose these two groups because the work I wanted to do involved looking into group change, and they have undergone substantial change. Another reason for selecting General Conference and Mennonite Brethren Churches as the major sources for the subjects of my research was their accessibility to me by virtue of proximity. Most of these Mennonites live within a 100-mile radius of my former home.

Many studies have addressed the nature of Mennonite ethnicity. The demographic and social characteristics of the major Mennonite subgroups were presented in a pioneering work on Anabaptists published in 1975 by Kauffman and Harder. Their work then served as a benchmark for further research (Driedger and Kauffman 1982; Umble 1990). In 1991 Kauffman and Driedger issued an updated and enlarged version of the landmark study of 1975. Both studies offer detailed information on Mennonite norms and organization. Other analysts of Mennonite culture have also identified demographic characteristics of the various groups. These studies have touched upon type of community, location, family, and occupation (Driedger 1968); consumption of alcohol (Currie et al. 1979); trends in intermarriage (Driedger et al. 1983); and divorce (Driedger et al. 1985). But little of this research reveals how individuals conceive of their relationship to their culture. Through several survey studies (Driedger and Jacob 1973; Weinstein et al. 1988; Kurokawa 1969), information about attitudes has been generated. Surveys, however, are not designed to bring out information about underlying values, beliefs, and conduct, nor are they designed to provide adequate information on the processes that underlie and shape people's attitudes.

Sawatsky's research (1978) attempted to rectify those problems. His study found that denominationalization had resulted in progressive assimilation or blending of Mennonites into American society, but his study was criticized by Boldt and Roberts (1979), who offered a different explanation of how Mennonites were becoming like other Americans. Regardless of differences in findings, both Sawatsky and Boldt and Roberts assumed that assimilation into the larger society was positive, unidimensional, and linear. This view of assimilation as gradual and uniform was not a good fit with the essence of Mennonite identity, which rested not on integration but on separation from society. In contrast to this approach, other researchers have looked at how societies with many distinct groups operate (Eaton 1952; Erasmus 1981; Glazer and Moynihan 1970, 1975; Newman 1973; Novak 1971; Royce 1982). Of these studies, Heatwole (1974) looked at Mennonites as a part of a pluralistic society where distinct cultural divisions were ingrained. Separation of the group from society, he found, preserves the religion. This type of exclusionary relationship between Mennonites and American society in general has been pointed out in a variety of articles (Redekop 1974; Redekop and Hostetler 1977; Newman 1973), yet pluralist interpretations of Mennonites have their weaknesses as well. This body of work often overlooks significant movement toward integration.

An alternative to assimilation and pluralist approaches is built on a perspective developed by Barth (1969). Using a radically different approach, Barth considered the critical aspect of minority groups to be the expanding and/or contracting boundaries between groups. From Barth's perspective, it is not necessary for groups to depend on the absence of interaction to maintain identity. Furthermore, the tendency for some groups to merge with the dominant society and accept its culture is not a particular threat to their group identity. Assimilation is an important consideration; however, it represents only one of many types of boundary shifts that explain how groups can change yet sustain an identity (Alba 1988; Alba and Chamblin 1983; Fine and Kleinman 1979; Gans 1979; Yancey, Ericksen, and Juliani 1976). Studies of Mennonites emerging from Barth's (1969) perspective have noted the importance of individuals' personal identification with the group (Driedger 1975, 1977), individual and group links to the larger society (Kauffman, 1977), the ability of Mennonitism to meet all social needs for its members (Boldt 1979), and modern migration to urban areas (Rose 1988).

Barth's (1969) ideas concerning group-boundary maintenance and Goffman's *Frame Analysis* (1974) provide the theoretical orientation for my work. Goffman built his ideas from an interpretative orientation of everyday life (Cooley 1962; Goffman 1963, 1973; Park 1967; Perinbanayagam 1985; Schutz 1967). Barth's thinking is associated with Goffman (1974), who believed structures through which social boundaries are formed and reformed by individuals have to do with individuals' mental framing of what goes on around them. To Barth (1969), the unseen boundaries of people's perceptions were fundamental to ethnic group formation and continuation. Snow et al. (1986) and Snow and Benford (1988) supported this idea by showing the links in framing between individual orientations and larger social constructs, and others have built on their ideas (Tannen and Wallat 1987). Unfortunately, little research using Barth's (1969) and Goffman's (1974) theories has investigated the role formal and informal communication play in group-identity maintenance (Combs and Mansfield 1976; Davis and Baron 1981; Schramm 1983). No studies could be located at the individual level of analysis that used this approach to learn how Mennonite ethnic boundaries are changed or maintained. Almost all social-science research about Mennonites as an ethnic group has sought to interpret lifestyle change. The basic research question was, Are Mennonites losing their identity? The answer has been yes and no and, at times, both. The question this book addresses is not, Are Mennonites losing their identity? but, How are Mennonites constructing their identity?—a topic not addressed by any previous research.

My work is not located in a traditional research epistemology. The research that developed this book was guided by the theories of Barth and Goffman and centered on the premise that boundaries between groups are built from frames of reference that individuals hold and that these frames of reference may be stable but never static. In my thinking, ethnic group identity is conceived both by forming boundaries and by what goes on inside the boundaries.

Although an overall interpretative orientation shaped my research perspective, I entered into the project with no a priori theories of how the Mennonite social world worked. I wanted only to record the impressions put forth by members of the group about themselves and their group's past. I confined my study to those Mennonites who live in the area of Oklahoma that was once designated the American Indian tribal land known as the Cherokee Outlet, often called the Cherokee Strip. This part of Oklahoma is geographically and ecologically homogeneous. It is bounded by historical and legal description, and a substantial degree of continuity exists in the area's evolving economic environment.

My study was based principally on in-depth personal interviews; it was augmented by participant observation. More than sixty individuals were selected for interviews. They represented a wide range of individuals of Mennonite heritage. Some were active members of Mennonite congregations. Some were currently members of other Protestant denominations. Some lived in an urban area. Some lived on farms or in small towns. For purposes of verification, I completed interviews with persons of the same age group and locale who were not of Mennonite heritage. For purposes of verification I also compared interviews of several members in each of two congregations that were different branches of the Mennonite faith but located within the same city. I wanted to talk with those who had experienced change in the Mennonite way of life; I therefore concentrated on people who were from fifty-five to seventy-five years of age. I interviewed many who were older and some who were younger, about half of them men and half of them women. I conducted the interviews over a three-year time span and found the information gathered earlier to be consistent with that gathered during the final phase of the research. The interviewees represented a good cross section of Mennonites and a large sample for qualitative work, considering I was dealing with a total population of approximately fifteen hundred and was interested only in interviewing older adults from that population.

I began the interviewing process by using a technique described by Denzin (1970), which was to use my acquaintances in the Mennonite community to put me in contact with people they said would be "good" to interview. My friends introduced me to two ministers and one assistant minister of congregations in Enid. Each of these men was interviewed, and later they set up several additional interviews with other church members for me. In this way, I was sponsored into the group. Liebow (1967) and others have noted the importance of sponsorship into groups as a prerequisite to gathering meaningful information. Early on, at the suggestion of one pastor, I met with a Bible class for a group interview. At about that same time I began doing individual interviews. As word of my project spread about the area, the number of those interested in being interviewed increased. I found, though, that a few people who had been more than willing to make an appointment to talk with me showed some apprehension when I, a stranger, entered their homes. Ammerman (1987) encountered similar responses in interviewing members of another religious group. A few of those worried about whether they would know the "right" answers or why I chose them instead of someone who was a "stronger" church member or someone who knew more about the history of the church than they did or someone who just "knew more" than they did. After I assured them that the type of information I needed did not require any special memory for dates, names, or events and that, in fact, there were no "right" answers to my questions, most seemed reassured.

I presented myself straightforwardly as a researcher. If I fit in, possibly it was because of the Anabaptist influence in my own religious heritage or perhaps it was because of my lengthy residence in Northwest Oklahoma. I never really tried to become part of the group. My established marginality may have limited somewhat my ability to "get inside" the group; nevertheless, when word of my project circulated, the number of willing participants snowballed. My problem was not in getting entry to the group or in building rapport or in finding sufficient numbers of interviewees. My problem was selecting those best suited for the research task from the large pool of potential informants.

Some of the interviews were conducted at Mennonite churches, either before or after church services, but most were done in the homes of the interviewees. I found this beneficial because it allowed me to observe firsthand a respondent's environment. I conducted two group interviews. The rest were individual interviews or interviews where I talked to a husband and a wife together. Interviewing married couples was an advantage in that each seemed to feel more comfortable with a supportive ally present. These interviews were most often quite open and lengthy and produced large amounts of information. The couples would amplify each other's statements, question each other's memory of events, and even prod each other to reveal certain information or recount specific scenarios. Interviewing couples garnered much material, yet it presented a problem. There was no way for me to gauge how the comments of one partner may have affected the comments of the other. It is possible that, because of the influence each partner had over the other's communication, a couple's statements may not have reflected individual conceptions. This problem was mitigated, I believe, by the use of interviews done with only one participant.

My questions were general and open-ended. I sought to learn about everyday concerns, social and church involvement, religious beliefs, life stories, and the like. No predetermined set of questions was used. I did, however, ask all participants to talk about "changes" in Mennonite life they had experienced. Further, I asked each one to tell me why he or she thought change had taken place. There was no set interview schedule, although the sessions generally lasted between two and three hours. Many of the interviews were a source of information beyond the interviewee's own memories and thoughts. As a group, the Mennonites were quite interested in my project and in helping me as best they could. A good many people spent some time preparing for their interviews by gathering materials they thought might be useful to me. Family genealogical records, newspaper clippings, books on Mennonite history and customs, and magazine articles are examples of the materials interview participants often had spread out, ready and waiting for my arrival.

One further aspect of the interview process should be taken into consideration at this point. The project relied heavily on the self-reporting of Mennonites' perspectives. An assumption is thus made that members can provide accurate information about themselves and their group's history. This assumption has been called into question in the past by critics of direct-contact approaches to the study of social life. The major worry is that subjects will reconstruct their past to be consistent with their present outlook and experiences. Such criticism is less than justified here because of the purposes of this study. The object of my research was to discover how change was interpreted. I employed this plan because my study was concerned with self-identity. Nevertheless, despite the usefulness of in-depth interviews in getting to individual strategies in accounting for personal actions and beliefs, there are limitations to the reliability of this kind of investigation. The following work should be approached with a respect for those limitations.

I attended church services, study groups, and, on occasion, informal gatherings of Mennonite church organizations. I attended church meetings intermittently and for only part of the time I was gathering data for the research. My attendance at meetings was not regular because I was involved with studying more than one congregation and because, though I wanted to be approached by the group, I did not want to be considered a potential church member. I decided it was better in the long run to establish myself in a professional status, as mentioned above, than to gain acceptance for the period of the research and run the risk later of being considered a voyeur. This position may be considered by some a limitation of the research design. Despite that difficulty, the way I presented myself, as marginal to the group with a strictly separate life, did have one distinct advantage. Because I was never considered a member of the group, I never had to withdraw from it. I thereby avoided the often awkward situation that Maines, Shaffir and Turowetz (1973) and many other social researchers have faced at the end of fieldwork experience.

All interviews were tape-recorded. I took notes during the interviews as well. As soon as I could after the interviews were over, I took time to review my notes. I made additions and clarified what I had recorded for later reference. If I came away with any overall feelings about the interview, I put those impressions down in the notes too. All the interviews were transcribed in their entirety. Information and thoughts that developed from participant observations were also recorded in writing. I cross-checked the findings of the interviews to build concepts. Both during and after the information-gathering process, I employed the technique of "constant comparison" developed by Glaser and Strauss (1967) to organize and analyze the data. Once the data had been collected and relationships identified, most of which took place at about the same time, what remained for me was to organize the material and write up the findings. The observations I made about the group were drawn from the categories of data that arose from the interviews. In many instances I was able to refer to published authority to corroborate the accounts I heard; however, the statements I make about the group's framing of their perceptions were drawn from the interviews and participant observation alone.

I used primary and secondary sources of information, principally archival, as support for my research. These sources were used to cross-check data obtained from the interviews and participant observation for reliability and validity. I wanted to know whether the accounts I was recording from members' stories of their lives were similar to the notions others had recorded about this group or other comparable groups. Uniformity in accounts of independent sources verified my own collected data.

In addition, a good deal of information contained in the chapters that follow is drawn from primary and secondary sources. Much of the writing involved locating and synthesizing information on Mennonites from disparate sources. For confirming and structuring the overview of Mennonite history and culture, I relied on published and unpublished material. I used material provided me by the congregations from their local publications and Mennonite publishing houses. I used unpublished manuscripts provided by individuals I interviewed. I used published works from the personal libraries of the Mennonite participants in the research. I used library resources. I used newspaper accounts. I used census data. Wherever possible, I checked the accounts given me against published fact. On the whole, I found the Mennonites' descriptions of their group's past to be accurate if not always completely comprehensive. The accounts of the Oklahoma Mennonites appeared to be in sync with what had been written about them.

The first-person accounts are taken from the interviews or from written personal histories. Two of the personal stories are recounted by close relatives—a child and a grandchild—and three others are taken entirely from diaries or similar writing. The remainder are told in the words of the Mennonites who describe their own lives. The surnames of several of the people who appear in the book are the same. There are multiple explanations for this occurrence, which include (1) the small size of the group, (2) Mennonite rules of conduct that at one time forbade marriage to outsiders, and (3) the fact that most émigrés were from the same provinces in Russia and emigrated at about same time. Close kinship ties exist among several of the interviewees whose stories are recounted in the book. The relationships are as follows: (1) Abraham Ratzlaff was the uncle of Adam Becker, who was an uncle of Henry Becker; (2) Cornelius and Helena Heinrichs were grandparents of David Ediger and the aunt and uncle of Helen Ediger; (3) Harry Martens and Henry Martens are cousins; but (4) Abraham Ratzlaff and Adam Ratzlaff were not directly related.

Aside from the husband and wife interviews, none of the first-person accounts come from members of the same nuclear family. All except the last two first-person accounts are augmented by unpublished, and sometimes published, material relating to the personal and family history of the individual. All of the oral histories were condensed in deference to space. They were edited for continuity and for arrangement in a logical time sequence. About half of them were edited for grammatical errors because the persons interviewed made that request and I complied. In writing the personal accounts, I have tried at all times to the best of my ability to convey the exact words of the speakers in the context in which they were spoken; nevertheless, I do not claim complete objectivity. I recognize that my own perceptions have had some bearing on the inclusion or exclusion of material, and I wish the reader to be aware of that.

This book is a reflection of common knowledge. I wanted to construct a context that would help explain both the group's extensive transformation and its tenacious endurance. Emphasis was placed on turning points and transitions in personal and group life as identified from the vantage point of time. Two major frames of reference related to tenets of Mennonite theology were found: (1) nonresistance to violence and (2) separation of the group from worldly society. Each underlying frame of reference appears to have been "transformed" or interpreted differently at different time periods in the group's history. The strategies articulated by group members to support the two frames of reference were found to be linked with definitions of labor, religious life, and close community, and these definitions too were found to shift and evolve over the years.

The book is organized around three major shifts in the collective frame of reference. The time period covered in Part One extends from the origins of Mennonite life to World War I. From the language of the Mennonites interviewed, pacifism, the first self-identifying group reference, was thought of during that period as an inalienable—though taken-for-granted—constitutional guarantee of free expression and religion. Autonomy in religious and community life, the second self-identifier, was viewed not as an act of withdrawal from society but as a voluntary association of like-minded believers. Collectively the remembrances tell of Mennonites who viewed themselves as outside mainstream society yet who found some cooperative interaction with the mainstream necessary for business-related needs, primarily the sale of cash crops (mostly grains), and for public education. The collective accounts highlight the Mennonite contribution of introducing hard red winter wheat to plains states' agriculture. In addition to farmwork, other recurring themes that run through the personal narratives include community building with scarce social and material resources and the interrelationship of extended family and church life.

Part Two deals with the time span of World War I. During this era, immense pressure to support the American war effort clearly demarked and solidified hostile boundaries between Mennonites and the larger society. Ethnic heritage, use of the German language, church ritual, in-group association, codes of conduct and dress—all were points of contention, but at the center of conflict was the Mennonite doctrine of nonresistance. The period is framed in the voices of modern Mennonites as a struggle for legitimacy as Mennonite men of conscience held to their beliefs and congregational life came under severe attack. Working through the intense pressures to conform, social stigma, economic impediments, and even incarceration wrought by the First World War imposed an enormous strain. The voice of one Mennonite who was imprisoned for his beliefs illustrates the era.

Part Three reflects still another realignment in frames of reference regarding nonresistance and separatism. This realignment, which emerged during the post–World War I years and matured during the Ssecond World War, sets the frame of the current source of identity for the group. Visible barriers of social behavior that once held Mennonites apart from the larger society have fallen away. Instead of preserving identity by withdrawing from the world, integration with the outside world is now an accepted fact of Mennonite life. For the present, a code of personal responsibility rather than group sanctions shapes conduct. Attitudes toward military service have also been transformed. Now nonresistance is viewed as a personal choice rather than a standard of group conduct. Accompanying this revised frame of reference toward nonresistance is a proactive peace initiative. In today's world, visible barriers protecting Mennonites from "the world" have fallen, but invisible barriers of thought and communication maintain Mennonite identity.

The personal stories that conclude the chapters offer singular accounts of the Mennonite epic and describe the activities of everyday life. In this way, they give focus to the broad overview of Mennonite life offered in the chapter text itself. From the stories a certain sense of tradition and change emerges. These basic themes, or strategies individuals use to tell about themselves, recur even though the range of individuals' narratives is quite expansive. Through all these narratives the Mennonite values are interwoven: (1) productive labor as religious calling, (2) religious devotion enacted in day-to-day life, and (3) commitment to family and church fellowship. The individual accounts reveal unique personalities that are courageous and meek, hardheaded, exacting, austere, often quiet, occasionally jovial. Some life stories showcase strikingly personal identities; others, intimate personal struggles. Some reports are dominated by events: the family robbed and left destitute at the port of Constantinople, the marksman who won his land claim in a shooting match, the conscientious objector who risked his health in a medical experiment. Others are poignant in their response to the unrelenting rigors of farm life. Still others reveal distinction in the familiar. Glimpses of romance in the lives of devoted couples are disclosed, as is the artistry of a quilt maker. My study is developed as an overall description of the group's life, both physical and ideational.

# PART ONE

# Prairie Life

## BEFORE THE FIRST GREAT WAR

Draw a line on a map of Oklahoma north to south down the center of the state. Then draw one east to west. Lop off the panhandle from the northwest quadrant, and a little less than one-third of the southern half and the remainder will approximate the boundaries of what was once the Cherokee Outlet, the largest parcel of public real estate in Oklahoma to be opened for settlement by land run. More narrow north to south than it stretches broad in the other directions, the strip lies in what today is euphemistically called "flyover" territory—that central part of the United States that air travelers now glide above at thirty thousand feet as they journey east and west between the nation's urban centers

The fact is the strip has always been a place where "putting down" is out of the ordinary. At the dawn of civilization, mammoths passed through. Their remains surfaced as pieces of bone found largely on the Great Salt Plains near the strip's center. Millennia passed, and natives, at first on foot and later on horseback, followed herds of buffalo back and forth across the territory. Later on, drovers trailed cattle north through its grass and across its creeks to railheads in Wichita, Abilene, and Dodge City, crossing so many times that their routes, like Jesse Chisholm's, were identified by name. Title to the territory fell under the control of the Cherokee, who established their communities in the eastern part of Oklahoma and leased grazing rights on the strip to cattlemen. The cattlemen and their cowboys fattened steers and heifers on the bountiful pasture grasses, but few made their permanent home on the range.

Overlooked as a place for putting down roots, the strip was ignored until there was no other space for land-hungry settlers, and even then it was not the destination of choice for many of those who came. By the end of the nineteenth century the Cherokee Outlet, nestled between occupied Indian Territory and the Kansas state line, lingered as one small, unsettled parcel of what once had been a huge virgin expanse stretching west of the Mississippi to the Rockies. Where land once had been free to homesteaders almost for the asking, the strip was a prime candidate among the few isolated tracts that remained to be settled. At the same time, in the wheat-growing heartland of Russia, groups of Mennonite farmers, wary of a shift in government policy and fearing conscription into the expanding Russian army, began to flee their fertile farms and to look for asylum and new homes for their expanding population in the United States. Though their past was bound to agriculture, it was more coincidence than any organized plan that led these Mennonite refugees to Oklahoma. The would-be landholders who made the run at the opening of the Cherokee Outlet in 1893 were, for the most part, Mennonites included, a needy lot—those who had nothing, those who wanted a fresh start, those for whom the opportunity outweighed the risk.

Part One is a look at the origins of Mennonite life in the Cherokee Outlet. The collective memories of Mennonites who recall this time period communicate the exodus from Russia and early days in Oklahoma as a grand and arduous mission propelled by fear but built on great expectations of security in America's guarantee of religious freedom and manifest support for pioneer communities. Within the continuing story of the group, however, the voices of individual Mennonites tell of common ties among singular lives. Emerging within the context of early-day Oklahoma are the themes of family and community and religous devotion; they weave in and through the individual accounts of a Mennonite culture bound to farm labor as God's work. The individual stories share the basic themes of extended family and ethnic affiliation tied to agriculture as extentions of religious life, and they undergird, if not directly articulate, the broad frames of religious reference—pacifism and closed fellowship—that highlight the Mennonites' collective memories.

Chapter 1 deals with the roots of the Mennonite movement in sixteenth-century Europe and provides an overview of the Mennonites' history, centering on migrations that led ultimately to the resettlement of large numbers of German-speaking Mennonites from Russia during the 1870s and 1880s. The journey of one family from Russia across Europe and the Atlantic, and through the American heartland to Kansas, is detailed. Chapter 2 gives an account of the largest land grab in Oklahoma, the run into the Cherokee Outlet, and the story of a Mennonite who came into Oklahoma penniless and at his death left a 160-acre homestead for each of his seventeen children. Chapter 3 records hard times in early Oklahoma and chronicles the beginnings of one early church. Chapter 4 tells of the founding of various Mennonite churches in Northwest Oklahoma and describes Mennonite lifestyle during the early period of settlement. It concludes with the story of the fifty-year marriage of a Mennonite couple. The introduction of Turkey Red, the wheat that changed the nature of agriculture on the Great Plains, and the story or a young boy learning to work the land are the focus of chapter 5.

# CHAPTER 1

# The Heritage

We're very much like the Pilgrims.
—*Betty Evans*

The saga of Mennonites in Northwest Oklahoma begins in migration. On the move, migrating again and again, Mennonites, from the founding of their faith in the sixteenth century, have sought to preserve their beliefs by relocating their religious communities. The history of Mennonite migration, and thus the beginning of the story of the Oklahoma Mennonites, dates from the 1520s (Board of Christian Literature 1984), around the time the church was first organized.

In the past, the search for a religious home free from any outside influence was first and foremost in the minds of the Mennonite people. Mennonites were a part of the Protestant reformation movement begun by Martin Luther, John Calvin, and Ulrich Zwingli. The Protestants sought reform of many of the practices of the Catholic Church. Although agreeing with most major criticisms of the medieval church voiced by Protestants, some early reformists desired more thorough changes. These Christians were called Anabaptists. Their creed emphasized strict separation of church from state and rejection of infant baptism. Because virtually everyone in Europe in that age was baptized as a child, Christians who broke with tradition were called Anabaptist—people who baptize again (Board of Christian

Literature 1984). Anabaptists believed in membership through conversion and baptism of adult believers.

A group of Anabaptists, under the influence of Menno Simons (1496–1561), a priest who had converted to Anabaptist belief in 1536, came to be known as Mennonites. The Mennonites were without formal leadership. Instead, leadership came from within each group. No person was exalted above another. Theirs was a priesthood of the laity. Mennonites emphasized separation from the world and lived together in private communities. They opposed forming congregations and living as part of the larger social world as other Protestants did. In separating themselves, the Mennonites advocated a simple lifestyle and modest dress. They disapproved of displays of wealth, dancing, drinking alcohol, gluttony, and other forms of "worldly" pleasure.

Mennonites were basically apolitical (Urry 1983b). They avoided having any relationship to government, insisting on strict separation of church and state (Kauffman and Driedger 1991). Nonresistance was a major doctrine. Based on the biblical example of Christ's death on the cross at the hands of his enemies, the belief in nonresistance required Mennonite followers to "turn the other cheek" rather than return a blow. Beyond that, they were to pray for their enemies, comfort and feed them. The concept of Christian nonresistance went further than a simple belief in pacifism. It was more than a conscientious religious objection to engage in military service or a refusal to participate in war. Nonresistance required total passivism, that is, lack of retaliation to any use of force against oneself or another human. Mennonites rejected military service and the use of violence in private life, but they recognized the authority of the organized state, and most were willing to pay taxes. Because they shunned the "everyday world" and withdrew into exclusive communities, they were severely persecuted, as were other Anabaptists of the era who appeared to reject any type of national loyalty.

Fleeing the persecution of dominant cultural groups in western Europe, many sixteenth-century Mennonites relocated in eastern Germany, Prussia, and Poland, where the political environment was, at that time, more tolerant. The Mennonites in these settlements maintained a life in which their common identity was defined by dress, religious values, exclusive in-group social activity, and self-sufficient farming (Smith 1927). While they spoke standard German in religious services, Mennonites commonly used a local "Low German" dialect in day-to-day interaction with one another.

For some years all was well, but by the mid-eighteenth century Mennonites again began to experience difficulties. Mennonite farming settlements had prospered, and the Mennonite population had expanded. With their advances juxtapositioned against economic decline in the larger public sector, ill will stirred in the general population and created a climate of fear in both of the groups. Tension grew when Prussian authorities supported the disgruntled majority by passing laws that threatened military conscription of Mennonites. Some time later, both Prussian authorities and the Lutheran Church imposed restrictions on Mennonites, forcing them to pay taxes to the more populous and dominant Lutheran Church and prohibiting them from purchasing land without special permission (Bender and Smith 1964; Rose 1988).

The Mennonite response to the political pressure in Prussia and to an upsurge of social discrimination in other eastern European countries was a new wave of migration, this time to Russia. Throughout the reign of Catherine the Great (1762–96) and continuing during the reign of NIcholas I (1825–55), emigration to Russia was encouraged by the Czarists. Hugh tracts of unproductive, unoccupied, and/or uncultivated land were opened to settlement, and colonists were encouraged to relocate in the new territories. Russian peasants were moved from more heavily populated regions to the new areas, but colonists were sought outside Russia as well. Mennonites were among those recruited to relocate in Russia, principally because European farmers' skills and their knowledge of agricultural techniques were more advanced than those of the Russian peasants (Hale 1980).

The call to resettle in Russia appeared to be a godsend to the Mennonites. The offer included free transportation to Russia, 175 acres of free land per family, a loan of $250, religious freedom, freedom of language, freedom to educate in their own schools, military exemption, and no taxes for ten years. The first group of Mennonite pilgrims left Danzig in the fall of 1788 (Wenger 1949). In all, about nine thousand European Mennonites, many from Prussia, Poland, and eastern Germany, made the move (Kroeker 1989). Although there was no mass exodus from Mennonite communities, a good many groups of families and individual Mennonites began to leave eastern Europe and form settlements in southern Russia, the Caucuses, and Siberia.

Here, through hard work, frugality, and the willingness to adopt innovative advances in farm practices and technology, they enjoyed phenomenal success. The Mennonites flourished in Russia. Their farms prospered and their settlements grew. They sought cordial contacts with their Russian neighbors, but they were culturally insular. They kept to themselves socially and followed the traditions of the past. They practiced self-government within their settlements and operated their own educational system. The two forms of German language persisted, church doctrine directed social relationships, and Mennonites lived very much the same simple life they had before in eastern Europe, dedicating themselves to hard work. New crops, including wheat and other grains were planted, and new methods of farming were employed. Milling and other technological advances related to agriculture were developed. The economy expanded (Remple 1974). The once-unproductive land produced greater and greater yields.

Mennonite institutions grew as well. An extensive educational system developed, and Mennonite-supported hospitals and asylums were founded (Bender and Smith 1964). As time passed, the Mennonites in Russia maintained their distinct lifestyle, dress, language use, and religion. Their successes in farming and industry were held up by the Czarist government as models for the Russian peasant. Russian authorities allowed the Mennonites almost complete autonomy. The Mennonite identity was clearly affirmed.

Then there was crisis. A tide of Russian nationalism swelled, in part from a sense of uneasiness. Widespread uncertainty as to the effects on Russia of the political unification of German states in the 1800s fed the public's fear (Dyck 1981, 201–2). As the tide of nationalism rose, political policy shifted. The favored position of Mennonite emigrants eroded during the later part of the nineteenth century. Although most Mennonites felt no allegiance to Germany, the fact that they spoke a German dialect and continued to use forms of German in religious services and in their schools made them targets of suspicion. Fear of Mennonite ties to a rapidly expanding Germanic nation on Russia's western border grew. Public anxiety, coupled with the belief that the Mennonites' near-absolute legal autonomy was the basis of their economic gain, fostered a growing resentment toward Mennonites on the part of Russians in general. After 1880, Russian was required as the official language in Mennonite schools, and special political privileges were revoked. Pressure from rising land prices and other economic constraints mounted outside the group. Inside the group, a growing population with little access to new arable land in the established Mennonite colonies set off a different chain of economic pressures. Then conscription was reinstated, and emigration again became an option for many Mennonites (Reimer and Gaeddert 1956; Francis 1955; Urry 1983b).*

The German-speaking Mennonites who settled in Russia to escape persecution were now to suffer once more the same persecution they had so often in the past sought to escape. As their life in Russia became less tolerable, the Mennonites considered alternatives to their situation. Scouts were sent out to look for a new home. Twelve men were designated to travel to North America to investigate opportunities for

---

*Most individuals interviewed attributed migration from Russia to religious persecution; however, other Mennonite scholarship has placed greater emphasis on the economic aspects of migration. For that perspective, see Dyck (1981), Urry (1989), and Remple (1973, 1974).

relocation. They returned with favorable reports of farmland in the western Unites States and Canada (Dyck 1967). The land available for homesteading was free or very inexpensive and, in terms of soil composition and climate, was similar to their homeland in Russia. The governments of Canada and the United States welcomed skilled farmer-immigrants to settle the open prairies of the West and guaranteed freedom of religion. The time was right for moving on once more.

# *Abraham Ratzlaff*

The following account is of the trip to America made by one Mennonite family who gave up their home in Russia to look for something better. The Ratzlaff family left Russia in 1874. Their first destination was Kansas; their second Oklahoma. The Ratzlaffs' story has been taken from a diary of Abraham Ratzlaff, the family patriarch, who led his kin nearly halfway around the world to a distant new land. Abraham Ratzlaff lived out the remainder of his own life in Kansas. Later, some of Ratzlaff's nieces and nephews and his own children were among those making the run into Oklahoma in 1893. Written in German, Ratzlaff's diary was translated into English, and, more recently, it was edited by his granddaughter. The excerpts begin with the family still in Russia.

> Our parents lived God-fearing lives. My father was the mayor of the village. We were raised by Father, who was always exact; the work was to be done precisely as he had instructed. This was something that has remained with me and become part of my flesh and blood.
>
> My father was ill for two years before he died. [During his illness] he had a great many visitors. In the winter, when there was snow and rain, the counsel often gathered in our house. [What I mostly remember of this is that] after everyone had left, the floors were dirty with snow and mud.

Children should scatter flowers along their parents' way while [the parents] can still see and enjoy them. When it is all over, we cannot undo these things [that we have done or failed to do]. Flowers are not to put on the coffin.

With my father gone, our family's great migration to America took place in the summer of 1874, in the month of July. My wife's parents had already sold their farm; therefore, it was necessary for us to move.

We cleaned our trunks and toasted them inside and out with flames so they would not become moldy and they would keep our supplies dry [during the long trip]. Then we loaded the trunks with zwieback [a sweet, dried toast] in preparation for the trip.

[Four months earlier] on March 3, the Lord had given us a young daughter. We named her Maria. She was born healthy, but my dear wife was unable to nurse this baby. My wife's breasts were very painful, swollen, and hard. In spite of the help of doctors, her breasts became severely infected and had to be treated surgically. The milk she was able to give [contained] poison which could have killed an innocent child feeding. Though I don't know how it could have killed it. We were at wit's end, and the only road was to the One above us.

Our help came. It was from dear ladies in the community. They who also had babies would offer to take our baby for a few days and nights. The mothers had enough milk for two babies. We gladly accepted these offers. I immediately carried my baby to those mothers, but our job in this matter was short-lived. When two babies are nursing, the milk does not last long, in spite of the great sympathy [from the first group of mothers willing to help]. Others then continued to offer their help, and the baby was carried to them until we realized we could no longer impose on these mothers. I then brought little Maria home again, and Grandmother and I took care of her.

The time for our journey was coming fast. We were ready. The ship was going to leave, and how were we going to take care of this baby on the trip? On the ship across the ocean? What were we going to feed the baby? We had no more advice to follow, except one. It was given to us when a Russian woman came to call. After she learned of our problems, she said, "Why don't you get a young puppy from us? This will solve the problem." At this time of year there were a great many puppies with the Russian people, so that we accepted the advice. I went immediately to a nearby Russian village and begged a puppy, and [its owners] gave the puppy gladly.

I need not say that my dear wife very reluctantly permitted this innocent little animal to nurse. It lived only one day. We accepted its death, then I got a second; it also died. The third also died, and the fourth survived and grew and was healthy and happy. We could see it thrive each day. It ran and scampered around the room and curled its tail as if the whole world belonged to it.

After this time, dear Lena's breasts healed, and she had enough healthy milk to nurse Maria, so that we were relieved of our problem, so we thought. But not so. The baby had not been taking breast feeding for so long that she refused to nurse. This was a big problem. We were all overjoyed when, at last, she nursed.

It is at times a blessing that the Lord lets us be in situations with problems we cannot easily solve.

Our time for departure was nigh. We left our home in July. Our friends and neighbors drove us to the railroad station. Here the actual farewell took place for all travelers. Father, son, mother, and daughter alike. Friends and acquaintances said farewell with many tears, calling to each other. Maybe we'll never see each other in this world again [we thought]. Those who remained behind followed us with tearful eyes and waving handkerchief till the train was no longer in sight. We traveled by rail, my mother, my wife's parents, my brothers, as well as my [own wife and children] and I. [The train took them through

Russia, across eastern Europe, north to Hamburg to depart through the North Sea to America.]

Our ship departed Hamburg August 12. Hundreds of people stood at the edge of the sea waiting for the small ship to take us to a larger one to cross the ocean. While we were waiting, we listened to a very powerful sermon, which brought tears to the eyes of men. Many, if not all, entered the ship for the long voyage with heavy hearts and apprehension. Perhaps many would have returned to their homes, if it had been possible. [Although it was not impossible to reenter Russia, the return trip was long and arduous and many had sold their land and possessions for passage.]

I didn't like the *Teutonia* especially. It was not very desirable. In addition, it was overfilled so that comfortable travel was not possible. One thousand Mennonites and eight other families of another nation were taken on board. The ship was at sea eighteen days. On the second of September we heard a joyous shout, "Land in sight." About noon the ship was docked. Physicians came aboard for examinations, and by evening all were able to enter the much longed-for America. We got lodging for the night at Castle Garden. In the morning, somebody gave us a New Testament. After two days we were ready for the remainder of the trip. [The time was spent exchanging money, buying tickets for the train, etc.] We left Castle Garden Friday towards evening. One hundred families were going to Kansas, some to Nebraska, others to the Dakotas, to whatever place the families had chosen. Topeka, Kansas, was our first stopping place. [There the entire group spent about three weeks quartered in an empty factory building.]

In the afternoon of October 3, we arrived with all of our belongings to the section of land that was to be ours [purchased at auction for three dollars an acre]. Since this was our home, my wife's parents, my brothers, as well as my wife and I all tried to make the place as homelike as possible. We brought along boards, wood, and nails from hutches. With these, we made huts in which we lived until we could have a house, equipment, and cows. Johann [his wife's brother] built on the other side of the north line. The grandparents [his wife's parents] build on the northeast quarter of section 17. The other brother on the opposite side of his parents. Thus we all lived near each other. Love ruled among us. If at all possible we saw each other almost every day.

CHAPTER 2

# The Great Rush
# for Land in Oklahoma

It was a good place for farming, and
this was the principle on which the
Mennonites really, really lived.
                    —*Helena Toews*

Beginning in 1873, as many as eighteen thousand Mennonite pilgrims eventually found their way out of Russia to the plains states of Nebraska, North and South Dakota, Colorado, Kansas, and Oklahoma or to the western grasslands of Canada (Haury 1981). This migration of German-speaking Russian Mennonites during the 1870s and 1880s came to be the major determining force in the settlement of Mennonites in Northwest Oklahoma. The history of Mennonite settlement in America, however, is much older, and it too bears on the distinctive mix of Mennonite ethnics in Oklahoma.

Historically, the Mennonite migrations across Europe and eventually to North America were begun almost simultaneously with the organization of the church. These migrations, set in motion during the late sixteenth century, eventually reached across the world and have continued throughout the life of the church. As early as 1683, about a hundred Mennonites and Quakers established a settlement in the New World at Germantown, Pennsylvania. Later, at various times during the colonial and federal period of the nation's history, other Mennonite pilgrims, seeking religious asylum and economic opportunity, left their homes in Switzerland, Germany, Holland, and other European countries. Some relocated to the United States.

These same waves of migration brought large numbers of the group to Canada, and still others found their way to Central and South America. The largest groups of Mennonite immigrants entered the United States coincident with particular political and economic events worldwide. Driven by cycles of religious persecution, political discrimination, and economic hardship, as many as eight different waves of Mennonite migration from Europe and Russia to the United States have been identified by historians (Dyck 1967, 154–68). The migrations of the 1870s and 1880s resulted in bringing the greatest numbers of Mennonite settlers to the central United States. The pattern of Mennonite migration before entry into Northwest Oklahoma at the time of the 1893 land run is important to the story of the settlement of Mennonites in Oklahoma.

Throughout the history of the nation, Mennonites have entered the United States from areas outside the country's boundaries, joined established Mennonite communities, or founded their own congregations as westward expansion opened new territories for settlement. Population growth and the never-ending search for productive farmland encouraged the descendants of the early Mennonite settlers in Pennsylvania to move westward to found communities in Ohio, Indiana, and other midwestern states. It was some of the descendants of these Mennonites who, in turn, moved farther west and joined the Russian émigrés in establishing homes and congregations in Minnesota and the plains states of Nebraska, North and South Dakota, and Kansas.

When the large numbers of German-speaking Russian Mennonites entered the United States in the late 1870s, they went West, for the most part, upon disembarking. About ten thousand of them traveled directly to Kansas (Hiebert 1974). Another four hundred from Galicia in Poland and Volhynia, an area near the Polish-Russian border that is today a part of Lithuania, also emigrated to Kansas and Nebraska at this time (Hiebert 1974). The Kansas climate and geography were suited to the type of farming practiced in Russia and eastern Europe (Jenkins 1986), and good land was cheap to buy. Another important attraction of the Mennonites to Kansas was the marketing efforts of the Atchison, Topeka and Santa Fe Railroad. Part of the effort to encourage economic development along the path of the railroad during the late 1800s was the Santa Fe management's shrewd use of German-speaking agents to promote settlement in Kansas. As pro- moters, the railroad representatives proved very effective publicists who handled the business of "selling" Kansas extremely well (Smith 1927). These agents met boats carrying immigrants as they arrived in America and were among the first to welcome the travelers by extolling the glories of Kansas and attempting to persuade the newly arrived Mennonites to choose land along the western Santa Fe route. As a result, a good many Russian Mennonites made their homes in central and southern Kansas near the Oklahoma border.

When the Mennonites arrived in Kansas, they attempted to trans- fer their former lifestyle intact and located almost exclusively among others of similar ethnic background and religious tradition. For example, the Dutch Russians found homes among other Dutch Russians, and those from the Volhynian area found homes among others from Volhynia (Haury 1981). This type of settlement preserved the regional ethnicity of the immigrants and the various religious practices among the groups. Over the church's history, differences regarding doctrine, ritual, and personal behavior had set groups apart and created several branches of the church. A good number of the Russian immigrants to Kansas were Mennonite Brethren. The Mennonite Brethren Church had emerged in south Russia amidst a great revival that took place in the early 1860s. The group was given the name Mennonite Brethren in part because they addressed each other as "brother" in their daily interaction. Influenced by neighboring Baptists in Russia, they took up the ritual of baptism by immersion (Dyck 1981, 270–73; Bekker 1973) but retained their Mennonite identity (Dueck 1995, 454).

General Conference Mennonite Church members also were found among the Kansas settlers. The General Conference was formed in 1861 by a union of congregations in Iowa. The conference differed from the (Old) Mennonite Church established in Pennsylvania. The newly formed conference emphasized missions, education of members, and evangelism (Sawatsky 1987, 6). It grew rapidly in the Midwest. Among its membership was a large constituency of German émigrés of the 1860s and 1870s; thus the new Russian Mennonite immigrants found a kinship among General Conference members that stemmed from mutual heritage and experiences (Dyck 1981, 262).

Other immigrants belonged to branches of the faith who called themselves Krimmer Mennonite Brethren. They took their name from their geographic region in Russia—the Crimea. They practiced "rigorous austerity in dress and life" and baptized their members by leaning them forward from a kneeling position for their immersion (Dyck 1981, 284). Members of the (Old) Mennonite Church also were found in Kansas. These Mennonites were descendants of members of the original Swiss Mennonite colonists who settled in Pennsylvania in the early 1700s* (Dyck 1981, 208–9). Still other branches of the Mennonite faith with smaller membership were represented as well. Mennonite settlement followed exclusive ethnic and conference-affiliation patterns, and there was little mixing of those from different backgrounds in communities formed on the Kansas prairie (Haury 1981).

---

*As other Mennonite groups began to settle in America, the title "Old" Mennonite Church was used to refer to this group. Later, when some members broke away from the group and called themselves Old Order Mennonites, members of the original church began to refer to themselves simply as the Mennonite Church and stopped using the term "old" in conjunction with their name. But despite requests from church members to abandon its use, the term is still often connected to this group of Mennonites (Dyck 1981, 208–29). Because so many branches of the Mennonite faith exist, writing the term "old" in parentheses is a way to refer to the group as a branch of the church while distinguishing it from the Mennonite fellowship in total. In this text, the group is referred to as the (Old) Mennonite Church for that reason. The church continues to this day. Members enjoy simple worship services (Dyck 1981, 229) and support higher education, foreign missions, and participation in mainstream society.

A few Mennonites who hoped to settle in Oklahoma may have come from established communities in Pennsylvania and the Midwest (Kroeker 1989). Others came from Nebraska and the Dakotas; many of these were the children of Mennonite pilgrims who had only recently arrived in those states as emigrants from Russia, Poland, and Germany, but the overwhelming majority of the Mennonites who came to make their homes in the newly opened territory crossed over the border from Kansas (Hale 1980). About 85 percent were from Marion County in east-central Kansas, or from near there. Moreover, many of the Kansas Mennonites who made the run or purchased property in Oklahoma shortly thereafter had been born in Russia (Haury 1988).

By the time the federal government began plans to open territory in Oklahoma, Kansas had ceased to be the land of opportunity for which the Mennonites had hoped. Land was in short supply and Mennonite families were large, often having seven or more children. The price of farmland had risen to twenty dollars or more an acre (Hale 1980). Larger farms were more economically viable, and farms divided among children of deceased parents were often too small to sustain a family. On the other hand, in Oklahoma, for a modest fee, anyone could homestead on government land, or land could be purchased for about a dollar and a half per acre (Roark 1979). Thus the poorer and younger families were drawn to Oklahoma. For the young, the territory offered an opportunity to build a future; for others, the territory offered opportunity to rebuild a past. Historically, almost all Mennonite migrations had been launched to escape political persecution, but the escape to Oklahoma was escape from economic destitution.

The "run" of 1893 was the biggest and most spectacular land run in the history of the nation. It opened a large portion of land in Oklahoma Territory to individual homesteaders. At the same time the Cherokee Outlet was being opened to public land claims, the Pawnee Reservation and the Tonkawa Reservation were also released from tribal assignment (Morris, Goins, and McReynolds 1986). When the territory was opened to settlement at noon on September 16, 1893,

Mennonites making the run found themselves among the huge crowd of 100,000 (Kroeker 1989) to 150,000 (Dale 1949, 338) that surged across the lines marking the northern and southern borders of the strip. The settlers rode on horseback and in covered wagons, buggies, buckboards, carts, even surreys. Some walked. All were intent on staking a claim to a 160-acre homestead. Within two hours, the tides from the north and south had swept across the prairie to meet near the middle of the strip (Kroeker 1954).

Many of the Mennonite pioneers laid claim to a quarter section of land during the run, but others lost choice parcels because they were not willing to fight for their land when challengers falsely asserted prior claims to their staked locations (Kroeker 1954). By the end of that September day, settlers' claims dotted all areas of the outlet, and Mennonites were associated with the settlement of various communities, including Meno, Deer Creek, Goltry, Orienta, Fairview, Lahoma, Jet, Lucien, Manchester, Kremlin, Medford, North Enid, Newkirk, and Ringwood (Kroeker 1989).

Mennonites had discovered Oklahoma. The pilgrims had at last found a home.

# *Adam Ratzlaff*

The life of Adam Ratzlaff is related by his grandson, Alvin, and by Alvin's wife. It is also told, in part, through newspaper articles, family records, and a story about Adam as a child that was published in a Kansas elementary school textbook. Alvin Ratzlaff had finished cutting his wheat the day before he was interviewed. He was still busy with farmwork but was able to spare some time for this recollection of how his grandfather, whom he knew well, claimed land, then success, through the great run of 1893.

There were no school buses for us to ride in those days [Alvin begins]. In the afternoon when high school let out, the other kids in my family would stay after and practice their typing, but I would run uptown to the grocery store where you could almost always find my grandfather. In those old stores, there would always be a row of chairs lined up for people just so they could sit and relax.

My grandfather would be there with a sack of peanuts and he would say, "Sit and help yourself." I liked to sit there with him. I know now what he was doing—learning what was going on in town. He was always interested in business and looking into what was happening. My grandfather believed in work.

My grandfather was a farmer and a banker, and he set my uncles up in the grocery store business. He was the father of seventeen children. He had seventeen children, and when he died, he left each one of them a 160-acre farm. In those days, that was a pretty good inheritance.

When I knew him, he was always on the managerial end of the business. He owned farms and equipment, and his boys did the work. I don't think his family saw much of him. He and his boys farmed six quarter sections with horses. He built a barn to take care of nine teams of horses. In that barn there were eighteen horses to get ready and harness at any one time. My father's place was next to my grandparents'. So, in the evening, quite often, when my grandfather came home from work, he would stop by our place just to see how everything was going. I would go out to meet him. I knew my grandfather very well.

When Grandfather Ratzlaff was seven years old, his parents and six other Mennonite families left Russia for the Holy Land, hoping to find religious freedom and a new home, but when no land was available, they went over to Turkey. My grandfather wrote down that they were in Constantinople for six weeks and then went to north Turkey to a German settlement. That is where he heard his first Christmas program. The seven families were divided then, and those folks in Turkey kept the Mennonite families from Christmastime until spring.

My grandfather's family and the other families were in Turkey for seven years altogether. Not very long after they arrived a war broke out, and there was a terrible famine. With so very little to eat for days and days, all of the fathers and mothers eventually died except for the Ratzlaff family. Only [my] grandfather, Adam, who was fourteen, his father, his mother, and old Grandmother Voth survived, that is, along with thirty-one orphaned children who had lost their parents to starvation. The youngest child was three years old. Knowing they must have help, they wrote to Mennonites in Kansas. Finally Mennonite friends sent them money to get to America.

It was a terrific undertaking, bringing those thirty-one children to a new world to live among English-speaking people. It took two weeks to get across Europe to Antwerp, where they would meet their boat. They found a place to rest in Antwerp, got tickets on a Red Star Line ship, and just when they were ready to start [boarding the boat for America], Grandmother Voth fell down a stairway and broke her hip. After that, she had to be carried everywhere.

They had a terrible time crossing the ocean. The boat was caught in a big storm and floundered around for ten days. The captain and crew tried to have the passengers leave the boat because they thought it would sink, but the people would not leave. The passengers kept pumping water, and many of them prayed aloud. Three times the captain thought they would all have to leave the boat, but the people refused. Finally, they were sighted by a passing ship, and everyone was rescued. After twenty-nine days at sea, they reached New York City.

When they landed in New York on January 1, 1880, a stranger helped them get on the right train. [In preparation for the train ride], Grandfather Ratzlaff's mother tied the children together with a long rope. She didn't want to lose any of them. The rope was tied to the left arm of each child, and the right hand was left free to carry a small bundle.

They arrived in Topeka without money or food. Letters from the Kansas Mennonites had told them someone from the church in Newton, Kansas [where there was a sizable population of Mennonites], would be there to meet them, but [when they disembarked] they were unable to find the person from Newton. He had not arrived. They waited and waited in the train station. When no one arrived, young Adam was sent out to find something for them all to eat. For two days, he wandered around the town searching for someone who spoke German. "Sprechen sie Deutsch?" he would ask everyone he saw. At last, the search ended when he happened on a Mr. Miller. This fellow, who was a butcher, understood German. After Mr. Miller learned there were thirty-five hungry people at the train station, he and his wife brought them all home and called in their neighbors to help. It must have been quite a sight when the Ratzlaffs came walking up to the Millers' home carrying old Mrs. Voth, bringing with them the thirty-one children tied together with the long rope.

In no time, everyone had plenty to eat. The Millers found places for them all to stay that night and the next day helped them go to Newton and on to Halstead [a town with a large Mennonite community near Newton]. Not long after that, the Mennonite people of Newton found good places for every one of the children to live. That's where all the children lived, where they all grew up and married. My grandfather was fourteen at the time he came over. He and his parents stayed there in Kansas too, and after a number of years he married his first wife, whose name was Sarah.

The day came when there was a very severe drought in Kansas and the grasshoppers destroyed what few crops remained. Things were very hard, and Grandfather heard about free land in Oklahoma. Grandfather made the run [into the Cherokee Outlet], and he got a claim. He lined up on the border at Hunnewell, Kansas, and when the signal was given he rushed across and staked his claim near [what is now] Medford, Oklahoma. After he staked the claim and saw that everything was okay, he decided to go back to Kansas to get some supplies.

When he returned from his trip someone else had taken possession of his claim and was there on the land he had staked. My grandfather was forced at gunpoint to give up his claim. He had to move on, and so he went.

He came clear on down to Fairview [about 50 miles south and west] near where his wife Sarah's father had staked a claim. Now Grandfather and Sarah's father were homesteaders together in the same section. Sarah's father staked on the northwest quarter of that section, and Grandfather staked on the northeast quarter.

Then Grandfather Ratzlaff discovered someone else had staked on that claim too. He hadn't known it. Maybe neither of them did. One of them staked on one side of the claim and one on the other. It could have happened that way, you know. There's quite a distance there. It's possible neither of them knew the other was on the claim. [When the circumstances were discovered] there was some contesting back and forth. So to settle the argument, they decided to shoot it out. But they didn't shoot at each other. They chose a knothole in a cottonwood tree and agreed that whoever could shoot and get the closest to that knot, that person would get the lease. Grandfather stepped back, took his aim, and Grandfather shot right into the knothole.

Naturally, he got the claim, and the other fellow had to move on. It's not here where we are [near Orienta]. It's where the trailer park in Fairview is now. He built a little soddy house there, and, after finishing the house, then he went back to Kansas to bring his family to Oklahoma. They came in two covered wagons packed with supplies and, among other things, a bag of Turkey Red wheat seed, some farm animals, and a Bible. When he could, he built a frame house.

Right after he had staked his claim and started farming, my grandfather saw the possibility of making money by buying the neighbors' broomcorn and hauling it to the nearest railhead in Enid. In those days, the trip was three days by wagon. He and some other fellows would make the trip, sleep out under the stars at night, ford the Cimarron River, and resell broomcorn for a profit in Enid. He always said, "Buy when everyone's selling. Sell when most want to buy." And he always gave the Lord the credit for whatever good fortune came to him.

They raised broomcorn and feed crops the first years of farming because the soil was not adapted to wheat growing. One bad experience they encountered was flooding. One time the water came up so high from the creek it flooded the farm, and they lost all their possessions. But even with the flood, he said the Lord watched out for him. After the water went back down, Grandfather Ratzlaff found a pair of overalls that had caught in a treetop and inside the pocket was a five-dollar bill. He had lost most everything, and that money got him started again.

Grandfather was always looking for opportunities. He found an opportunity to sell the homestead, and he did. He took the money and bought a farm northwest of Orienta and built a large frame house. All of his children except the three oldest were born in that house.

His wife Sarah died in 1909. It was about a month after she gave birth to her ninth child. Later, Grandfather married Bena Frantz, and she had eight more children, making a total of seventeen children in the family. The house was so terribly crowded that they had beds under beds; they pushed mattresses under other beds to make more room. This was such a family— I can remember as a kid watching Bena, the second mother, literally running between the washhouse and the main house, running, running back and forth, back and forth, on a dead run, running like that because she had so much work to do with all those children.

Grandfather always worked hard and drove a hard bargain. He accumulated most of his farms through second mortgages. But he didn't just make money to keep money. The depression came on, and people would come to him for a loan. They thought if they could take a second mortgage on their place to keep them going maybe they could hold their farm together. Grandfather would make them a loan, but so often he was disappointed. They wouldn't be able to hold it together. I knew he had some disappointments along that line. He was always willing to give people a chance, especially his own church people.

Grandfather wanted the church to have a paid preacher, but how to finance the pastor was a tremendous hurdle. He had to convince the other wealthy landholders. Grandfather wanted to bring J. B. Epp, the father of Theo Epp who wrote the *Back to the Bible* radio broadcasts, to town to be the preacher. He was able to do it, but it took some doing. He put Epp on one of his own rental places, and then he went out to find a way to get him some income.

Grandfather did it by talking another farmer into renting a quarter section of land to the church. The deal was that the church members would go together and farm the quarter section and the profits would go one-third to the church, one-third to Epp for his support, and one-third to the owner of the property. How he accomplished that, I'll never know. I knew my grandfather, but I never could figure out how he talked that man into renting that quarter section. That farmer was known to be the tightest person alive. But Grandfather did it.

[Adam Ratzlaff, his grandson related, sometimes had difficulty reining in his talent for shrewdness in business, an ability valued by Mennonites, and placing it in harmony with other Mennonite virtues, for example, avoiding worldly pleasures—in this particular instance, gambling.]

In 1933, the town of Fairview put on an "old settlers" day. There was going to be quite a celebration. Lots of things were

planned—games, contests, and a raffle for a brand-new Chevy
coach. My grandfather bought a ticket. After Grandfather
bought the ticket, he felt uncomfortable with it, because buying
a raffle ticket was a form of gambling, you know. He decided
to get rid of it. He tried to sell it to my dad, said he'd let him
have it for a dollar. Dad wouldn't take the ticket. He asked other
people, but they said no. He tried, but he just couldn't get rid
of the thing. Then, when they had the drawing, it was Grandfather's ticket that won. "I won it fair and square," he said then,
after the winner was called. "It's the lucky ticket, and I get the
car." [With this, Alivn smiles and adds], he used the car to haul
the kids and grandkids back and forth to high school in Fairview
[implying that using the car to benefit the children legitimized
the method of its acquisition, thus soothing his grandfather's
troubled conscience].

My grandfather had made a large donation to the Oklahoma
Bible Academy in Meno when the school needed money to build
a dormitory. As a result, they said any of our family could stay
in the dorm and not pay room. But it didn't matter, because the
children didn't want to go to school in Meno; they wanted to
go to the high school in Fairview. Most of them did eventually
spend some time at OBA. I roomed with Benton, the youngest,
when I attended OBA. After I graduated [from] Fairview High
School, I enrolled and graduated from OBA's two-year Bible
course. My wife was there at the same time, and that's how we
met.

My grandfather loved to sing in church. You could hear him
above anyone else. I loved to sit with Grandfather in services
because I could sense how he loved the Lord and singing, and
how emotional he would become in his singing. . . .

Alvin breaks off here. He has been monitoring the farmyard around
his circular drive through the large plate-glass window in his living
room as he talks about his grandfather. Now something out there

has attracted his attention. He goes out to investigate and does not come back. His wife holds the family history book in her lap. She finishes the sentence for him. She can do that. Her life has been a counterpart to her husband's, and she too knew Adam Ratzlaff very well.

CHAPTER 3

# Hard Red Loam
# and Hard Times

A Mennonite can look at land and tell.
—*Wesley Kroeker*

The geography of the 160-acre homesteads allotted by the federal
government and the land-run method of site selection forced a breakup
of the system of closed community life that Mennonites had practiced
in Russia. The grid pattern of property allocation placed the group in
a new situation when they moved into Kansas, but Mennonite customs
and community life remained relatively stable. Circumstances, however, changed dramatically for those who relocated to Oklahoma.
Mennonite life as it had been known in Russia and later Kansas was
subjected, in Oklahoma, to a different model of community settlement, a different type of church life, a different farm environment, and
living conditions more difficult than these Mennonites had experienced
in either Russia or Kansas.

The run that opened the Cherokee Outlet was not coincident with
the initial habitation of the western areas of Oklahoma for either the
general population or the Mennonites. Prior to the run, the outlet
was protected from settlement by treaty, even though cattlemen had
used it for grazing purposes and a few "boomers"—unauthorized land
squatters—had slipped unchallenged into the outlet. Areas just out-

side the boundaries of the outlet had been opened to the general population earlier, and some Mennonites had come into parts of Oklahoma prior to the run. They had been drawn to Oklahoma several years earlier, at about the same time Mennonite missions were established south of the outlet at Darlington, and near Clinton, and at other sites accessible to the Indian population (Hart 1988).\*

General homesteading by Mennonites and others in the outlet, however, had its beginning with the great land run of 1893. The Mennonite migration to Oklahoma, once begun, continued and even increased after the outlet was opened. The run swelled population. But the land claimed in the run was not free. Those who successfully staked claims paid $1.50 to$2.50 per acre for the privilege of ownership (Gittinger 1939). Most of the Mennonites settled near the middle of the outlet, where the price was set at $2.00 per acre (Kroeker 1989). Almost all the land in the eastern sector, which was better suited to farming, was claimed by settlers on the day of the run or shortly thereafter. The population of the territory grew rapidly, but at the turn of the century there was still a certain amount of unclaimed land in the more arid, less productive western sections.

---

\*The first Mennonite mission in Oklahoma was established at the Darlington Agency by the General Conference Mennonite Church in 1880. It was the first missionary program begun by any Mennonites in the United States. Eventually eleven missions to the Oklahoma Indian tribes were established and more than 100 missionaries sent into the field (Kroeker 1989). The relationship of Mennonites to the Native American population in Oklahoma will not be addressed in this text. Information about Mennonites and their missionary efforts among two of the Oklahoma tribes can be found in Lawrence H. Hart's (1988) "Arapaho and Cheyenne Meet the Mennonites," published in *Growing Faith: General Conference Mennonites in Oklahoma*. Marvin Kroeker's article, "Die Stillen im Lande," published in *The Chronicles of Oklahoma* (1989), and James C. Juhnke's article, "General Conference Mennonite Missions to the American Indians in the Late Nineteenth Century," published in *Mennonite Quarterly Review* (1980), discuss the early Mennonite missionary efforts among Native Americans. Other information on the subject of Mennonites and Native Americans is found in Calvin Redekop's "Mennonite Displacement of Indigenous Peoples: An Historical and Sociological Analysis," published in the 1982 journal of *Canadian Ethnic Studies*.

For many years, this land had been only a vast, open cattle range (Roark 1979).

Pioneering in the state was encouraged for years after the run, bolstered by the railroads' publicity and the boosterism of local newspaper announcements and editorials. *The Mennonite*, a widely distributed periodical, also supported the migration of Mennonites to the area. Large advertisements offering available farms in Oklahoma were printed continuously in a variety of publications, even after statehood in 1907. The ads did not stop appearing until around 1920.

The Mennonites who had migrated to Kansas had found land there apportioned by the one-mile-square method, to be purchased by the acre. The same system applied in Oklahoma, but with a difference. In relocating to Kansas, often an entire community had migrated almost intact from eastern Europe or Russia (Haury 1981); but migration to Oklahoma, with a few exceptions, was not the transportation of intact communities or groups of extended families. It was, instead, a stream of mostly young families, or couples, or even single men. Mennonites who were unknown to each other found themselves thrown together in new congregations.

In many instances, the people making up the initial groups formed in the new territory met in each other's homes and were not formally organized as churches. The Mennonite settlements in Northwest Oklahoma were formed around those who shared similar religious beliefs and practices, but not always the same genealogical heritage or cultural tradition. In locating in Oklahoma, the reshuffling of congregational membership introduced an internal heterogeneity to what had been a very close-knit biological and social ethnicity.

Families and kin were distanced from each other. Homesteads were scattered and isolated. The loneliness that ensued was eased somewhat by the Mennonite practice of settling on farmland adjacent to other Mennonites, but the way farms were claimed and new churches established caused a reordering of community life. Nevertheless, an attempt was made by the settlers to find their own kind, to create a sense of community by settling in areas where other Mennonites of the same branch of their church were known to be homesteading (Roark 1979). A few families of Krimmer Mennonite Brethren; some Church of God in Christ, or Holdeman, Mennonites; and one or two of the (Old) Mennonite Church (Kroeker 1989) made the run. Many of the Mennonites coming from Kansas into Oklahoma Territory, however, had been associated with the sizable Mennonite Brethren group and the General Conference Mennonite Church, which were active in that state. It was natural, then, for many of the new congregations formed in the territory to be Mennonite Brethren or General Conference.

On the day of the run into the Cherokee Outlet, a few Mennonite settlers had been fortunate enough to find claims on the rich farmland in the eastern section of the territory, near what is now Ponca City. Most, however, pulled up stakes shortly after the run, when they learned of the Mennonite community being established near Meno. The idea to resettle farther west appeared, even to those new to the territory, to be less advantageous. The soil was simply not as fertile nor water as plentiful farther west, but the proximity to other Mennonites was greater, and the Ponca City Mennonites moved west.

Shortly after the Cherokee Outlet was opened, several Mennonite Brethren families from farms around Henderson, Nebraska, moved down to Oklahoma together. They were too late to file for homesteads but were able to purchase homestead rights east of Enid for not much money (Fiftieth Anniversary of the Mennonite Brethren Church 1947). They erected a church near North Enid in 1896. Within a year or two after the run, General Conference Mennonites living in Moundridge, Kansas, recognized the opportunities others from their congregation had found in the Meno area and also began to trickle south, family by family, finding farms and settling into sod houses put up with the help of their Mennonite neighbors. The Mennonite settlement pattern of homesteads, churches, and communities eventually radiated outward north and south along an uneven east-west line from Enid to Fairview. One of the oldest organized congregations in Northwest Oklahoma to have a recorded history is the Church of God in

Christ (Holdeman) church at Goltry, founded in 1893. The second, also a Holdeman congregation, was the Fairview Mennonite Church, founded at Fairview in 1895. Both of these churches continue to remain active to this day.

The appeal of homesteading was strong, and the efforts of businesses enticing. The churches were encouraging, but making a life on the prairie was risky. Economic and weather conditions, both equally important, were equally uncertain. Homesteaders lacked money for seed, farm implements, and machinery. Lending sources were scarce and distant. For dirt-poor farmers, raising collateral was next to impossible. To stabilize the situation, the Rock Island and Santa Fe Railroads offered "seed money" in the literal sense by providing wheat seed at cost to the hapless settlers (Johnson 1977, 15). But the years 1893 to 1895 were dry and crop yields therefore restricted. As a result, many Mennonites and a considerable number of other early settlers moved back and forth between Kansas and Oklahoma in the years that followed the opening of the Cherokee Outlet, continuing the pursuit of livelihood and a home.

In Northwest Oklahoma, as it had been earlier in Kansas and still earlier in Russia, Mennonite life revolved around family, farming, and faith (Hale 1980). The early years in Oklahoma were difficult ones for all the pioneers. Many new homesteaders in Northwest Oklahoma had never before done farmwork, but this did not hold true for the Mennonites. Mennonites knew agriculture. They were aware of crops suitable to the area—apricots, peaches, watermelon, beans, and grain (Stucky 1973, 27–32). They were prepared for cultivation of wheat. They also knew how to work. For centuries, Mennonite families and individuals were devoted to farm labor. For Mennonites, farming was preordained as a virtuous occupation. Work was considered a tenet of the religion, idleness a sin. Mennonite communities were organized around farming. The Oklahoma Mennonites proved no exception to this tradition.

If the Mennonites were willing to spend long hours in the fields, they were willing to devote still more time to learning about and implementing new farming techniques. A good deal of their prosperity in Russia had been built on a willingness to adopt innovative agricultural practices and newly introduced farming equipment (Hale 1980). This fusion of religious and economic values and agriculture practices was transported by the group from Russia and implanted in the Mennonite social organization that developed in Oklahoma Territory.

Mennonite life was not easy. The Mennonites were frugal farmers. Their tradition called for plain living. They did not hesitate to invest in fencing, outbuildings, and the latest in implements, but they spent little time and money on themselves. On the whole, they followed conservative business practices and reinvested profit in their farming operations rather than using it to enjoy the extras in life. The agricultural skills they had developed colonizing in Czarist Russia led them to select land on the basis of soil composition, drainage, and elevation. Many were shrewd judges of land values who prided themselves on the ability to hold out until the best deal was made. To their pioneer neighbors, the Mennonites seemed to be blessed with a skill to select good farming land for their home sites and produce high crop yields from their labor. They were acknowledged to be among the best farmers. After all, they had accumulated more than three hundred years' experience in the endeavor. Yet despite their expertise, frugality, and diligence, Mennonites endured great hardships in Oklahoma. The thick prairie grass still had to be turned, sod broken up, and fields plowed, planted, and harvested.

The Cherokee Strip was sun-baked, flat, and virtually treeless. Only a few settlers were able to build frame houses after the run, and most of those houses were very small. Many people lived temporarily in tents or dugouts burrowed into eroded ridges or riverbanks. Abandoned railroad cars became a primitive form of mobile housing. The settlers quickly learned that sod could be loosened, dried, and used for building. Free and plentiful, it was the most common construction material used during the first few years in the territory (Erb 1974). Later, when lumber was available, the Mennon-

ites adapted the construction of their prairie dwellings to the require-
ments of their traditional farming priorities. It was not unusual to find
a Mennonite barn raised prior to construction of the family's frame
house.

Pioneer living was crude. The diet of the settlers was simple and
extremely limited, consisting mostly of beans and potatoes and fried
"cracklins," a lardlike substance that contained bits of bacon. Bread
was baked daily except Sunday, the day of rest, when little cooking
was done. It was customary to bake zwieback, a divided or double roll
shaped in two parts, on Saturday and prepare other simple dishes,
sausage and cheese, for example, so that food needed only to be put
on the table on the Lord's day. Dried zwieback stayed fresh almost
indefinitely and was a common staple in the Mennonite diet, as it had
been earlier in Russia. Coffee and flour, but little else, were purchased. Hunting provided wild game for the table. Mennonites were
opposed to violence among individuals and nations, but they were not
opposed to the use of firearms on the frontier. Shotguns kept skunks
and possums away from the chickens, protected other farm animals,
and provided a supply of fresh meat. Gardens grew fresh vegetables,
some of which were canned for use during the winter months.

Kleeta Mus, made from lumps of dough cooked in milk, offered
nourishment and a way to stretch an insubstantial larder. Pluma Mus,
a pudding made from plums, was sugary and good to eat. The pudding
base could be made with prunes, cherries, or other fruit and was a
favorite treat for Mennonite homesteaders. Fresh fruit was scarce, but
bitter, wild sand plums grew in thickets along low ridges and in
pastures. Gathered, sweetened, and cooked down to make preserves,
sand plums were a familiar accompaniment to homesteaders' meals
(Suderman 1987).

Often food was prepared on a cooking range fired up by "cow
chips," dried pieces of manure that burned odorless. Some Mennonite
stoves, patterned after those used in Russia, were made of brick with
several levels of hot-air chambers that radiated warmed air to the
entire house (Haury 1981). Cow chips were the major source of fuel

for cooking and home heating during the first, bitter-cold winters the settlers spent in Oklahoma Territory. Temperatures often dropped well below freezing, and high winds swept across the near-level fields, increasing the severity of the weather.

With homesteading opportunity came backbreaking labor, meager living conditions, inclement weather, and trials difficult to endure. There were plagues of grasshoppers, epidemics of diphtheria and scarlet fever, and prairie fires. There were tornadoes and drought and sandstorms. In summer, the temperature could soar well beyond 100 degrees. Gophers turned up yearly to attack gardens, and prairie dogs tunneled through newly planted fields. The sod houses were dusty and drafty and leaked when it rained. Water from wells often was tainted with foul-tasting alkali and gypsum. The Mennonites were tenacious and industrious, but many were not able to overcome the adversity. Some Mennonite families who came to Oklahoma gave up and went elsewhere. A few even returned to Russia (Hale 1980). Those who remained measured prosperity in terms of economic survival. The hardy did survive. For centuries the Mennonite value system had been geared to thrive on adversity.

## Adam Becker

The Adam Becker family life in early-day Oklahoma was compiled from memories written down by Becker's son, B. A. Becker, and provided by a great-niece, who had torn the story from an undated copy of the *Mennonite Weekly Review*, published most likely twenty to thirty years ago.

On September 16, 1893, when the Cherokee Strip opened in Oklahoma, my father, Adam Becker, and his brother Peter made the run. Each staked out 160 acres of land close to a dry creek and timber seventeen miles west and two miles south of what is now Enid. After the run, they went to Alva, then the county seat of Woods County, to file on the land. From there they traveled back to their homes in Moundridge, Kansas.

The first thing Father did when he got home was to look for a buyer for the [Kansas] farm and make arrangements to move to Oklahoma. This took some time. On March 7, 1894, everything was ready. The farm had been sold, but the 14 horses, 12 milk cows, 5 young heifers, 250 chickens, and all the implements, farm machinery, and household goods were kept and loaded in three railroad cars. Uncle Pete [rode] with the stock to take care of [them]. Father took our two families part of the way by railroad, leaving from Moundridge and riding south to North Enid, Oklahoma. There were eight of Uncle Pete's family and ten in the Adam Becker family. We got to North Enid at eleven that night. My brother Peter and four others drove by horse and wagon to North Enid to meet us there. They helped unload the stock and other things.

The next morning, it was decided who would drive the covered wagons. I think my oldest sister, Susie, drove one covered wagon, with a spring wagon pulled back of it. My cousin Andrew, brother Kurt, and myself drove the cattle on foot. It was twenty-two miles from where we started at North Enid to our claim. Those who had been there before told us about the place, which was marked by a lone elm tree. We started fairly early that morning.

There were no roads and no bridges. Everything went all right until we got to Turkey Creek, which had about three to four feet of water in it. The cattle and horses all drank of the good water. We had a big barrel along and filled it with water, which we had to boil for our use. The milk cows, however, got tired and wanted to lie down, although we still had seven miles to go. We milked them quickly, got them up, and kept them going until a little after sundown. We got to that elm tree and camped out there all night.

The next morning we went to the edge of the creek, which was dry when it did not rain. Here Uncle Peter made a dugout, about twelve feet by sixteen, high up on the creek bank. In there we set up three bedsteads and a little stove. That is where we camped until the rest of the things arrived from Enid. We children were always hungry, so the women had to bake bread and cook all day long. There was plenty of milk to drink and eggs to eat, along with cured salt meat or pork.

The next evening, four big loads of household goods and a hayrack full of baled hay came. We boys built up a four-bale-high wall and put a long pole and a cover over it for a roof. We piled all the best furniture under it and had just enough room left to sleep. Then the next morning four or five wagons were sent to get more stuff. Father stayed home and took us boys along with him to locate a place to build our house. Father already knew about where the line of the place was, so he said to us, "Boys, here is where we will dig." We dug about four feet deep into a bank about sixteen by twenty-eight feet altogether, and we built a house to live in temporarily.

Before we started on the sod house, we plowed a fire guard several rods wide all around the ten-acre patch where we made our house. The grass was about two to three feet high [on both sides of the plowed strip], and we set fire to it. [The area inside the plowed strip was allowed to burn away in order create the fire barrier] to have a safe place for our lumber and household goods and to keep them from danger of [prairie] fires.

Father told us, "Let's get the plow and slip [a type of plow blade] and use the horses to slip the dirt down the ravine and make a crossing [dam] right away so when it rains we will have water for our stock." It rained in a few days and that dry creek got to be a river.

We [the young brothers] kept digging while Father drove to Enid to get the lumber for the house. The three of us older boys and Father worked early and late, and, in just three weeks from the time we started to dig, the family moved into the new house. Uncle Pete's family still lived in the older dugout where we had first moved in. His claim was a mile to the south. All of us got together and dug into a sandy hill there and made a house for him. We split logs for the roof and plowed prairie sod to cover those half logs. Uncle Pete's family lived in that dugout six or seven years.

Other neighbors moved near us that fall and winter. All in all, about twelve to fourteen families moved in. Father was always busy helping put up sod houses for the new neighbors, but he had one of us boys busy plowing prairie all the time so that we could put out crops. After we got an acre of sod disked fine, mother and the girls made a garden. We raised good crops and garden—more than we could ever eat—potatoes, cucumbers, onions, and watermelon by the wagonloads, planted in with kafir corn on sod. Some of the neighbors did not have horses or plows and thus did not raise any crop that year and had a hard time making it. From time to time someone would come and say, "We need help." Father never refused to help.

As things settled down a bit, neighbors and others began asking to come together on Sundays and have Sunday school. Since we had the largest place and plenty to eat, Father invited them to our place. My father had been deacon of the church north of Moundridge, so he called the neighbors together to talk about starting a church. In the course of time, a church was organized.

We also needed a school as there were about twenty children scattered about the countryside. One morning at breakfast, my father decided to go to a place nearby called "the timbers" and cut down trees to build a log schoolhouse on the southeast corner of our place close to that lone elm tree that we first camped by. He said we would call it the Lone Elm School. The three of us boys, Father, and some neighbors got the schoolhouse ready in the fall of 1895. Father drove to Alva, the county seat, to get the charter for the school. The county superintendent accepted the name "Lone Elm Number 24 School." A teacher was hired who taught a three- or four-month school term. Even though he had a wooden leg, he and his daughters, fourteen and sixteen years old, would walk four miles to and from school, morning and evening.

We were having Sunday school at our place and after several months it was decided to ask the Reverend Johann (John) Ratzlaff from the Emmanuel Church north of Moundridge, Kansas, to come and help us get a church organized. We had no railroad and the little town of Meno wasn't even there then. Father drove to Enid to meet Preacher Ratzlaff and bring him out to us. After a few meetings with the group, it was decided to name the church New Hopedale. More Mennonite families moved into the area [near Meno] about this time, since there was a large amount of land that still could be filed on and some that could be bought cheap. When our house got too small for the services, we decided to use the log schoolhouse, but after several meetings, we found that it also was too small. We found a larger schoolhouse to meet in. Later we built a sod church, but we still needed a better meeting place.

About the same time that the Reverend Ratzlaff moved to Oklahoma to be our preacher, his oldest son, Pete, came up from Fort Sill and bought the half section where the church and cemetery are now. Reverend Ratzlaff and his son donated two or three acres to the church. A house was built for Reverend Ratzlaff eighty rods east of the church. The church members farmed the quarter section where the church sat and whatever that farm brought was the minister's salary.

The first church building was completed in 1897.

# CHAPTER 4

# Living for Jesus

I was baptized outside in a creek just
south of the church. The sun was so
bright. It was in November. There was
a layer of ice on the water, and they
broke it.

—*Tina Kusch*

At the turn of the century, the Mennonites and other settlers in
Oklahoma Territory lived a hand-to-mouth existence in an almost
literal sense. Cattle and hogs were butchered, gardens raised, wheat
and other grain grown and harvested. Farming was labor-intensive,
tools and machinery scarce, and harvests unpredictable. The largely
self-sufficient homesteads required almost constant attention. There
was little time for relaxation and recreation. Sunday was virtually the
only day of rest, and rest on Sunday, for Mennonites, was mandatory.
Farming and family—all of life—revolved around the church, just as
it had for centuries in Russia. The church was the center of community
for Mennonites in Oklahoma.

Although it is difficult to generalize about the religious practices
found among the immigrants since the Mennonites in Oklahoma were
divided into so many different subgroups and Mennonitism varied even
within those subgroups and among congregations, some general observations about church and home tend to hold among most of the groups.

Shortly after the opening of the Cherokee Outlet, Mennonites began to gather together to form religious congregations. Within only eight months after the run, T. M. Erb and R. J. Heatwole, itinerant preachers, had visited eighteen different groups of Mennonites in the eastern part of the strip. They traveled eight hundred miles to do this, half of it by wagon (Erb 1974).

The Mennonites who worshiped together at first in members' homes were active, and their assemblies grew rapidly. They soon built houses of worship and formed alliances with Mennonite conferences and parent organizations. Within three years of the run, permanent church structures began to dot the countryside. One of the most viable early Mennonite communities established in the northwestern part of Oklahoma was a Mennonite Brethren group located at Fairview (Kroeker 1954). In part, because of the time it took for members to travel to church meetings and in part because of the growth of the congregation, the church divided in 1896 into two separate congregations: Nord Hoffnungsfeld (North Fairview) and Süd-Hoffnungsfeld (South Fairview). Not far away, the Saron church organized at Orienta and joined the General Conference in 1897. Like other early Mennonite church groups, Mennonites near Orienta first met at a homestead then later in a sod schoolhouse until a frame church structure was erected in 1905 (Orienta 1958, 1). A Mennonite Brethren church was established at Medford in Grant County in 1896 (Goertzen 1990).

Another early church, New Hopedale, near Meno, held meetings in a member's sod house before moving to a new schoolhouse. The church's first structure in Meno was dedicated March 6, 1897 (Koehn 1949). At its present location since 1904, the church affiliated with the General Conference the same year it moved to its present location (Haury 1981). In 1897, a second Mennonite congretation was formally established at Medford. That group joined with the General Conference in 1898 (Haury 1981).

The group that settled around North Enid just after the run called themselves the First Mennonite Brethren Church. The group organ-

ized in 1895 and 1896 and by the end of two years had constructed a
one-room frame meetinghouse north of the city (Fiftieth Anniversary
of the Mennonite Brethren Church 1947) to house its meetings. Also
in 1898, Mennonites formed the Zion church at Lucien and
Friedensau at Perry. Both of these churches affiliated with the General
Conference (Haury 1981). There were two (Old) Mennonite Church
congregations established after the run—Milan Valley at Jet, formed
in 1897, and German Springs in Kay County, established in 1895 (Erb
1974).* Two Old Order Amish communities (Erb 1974; Kroeker
1954) may possibly have existed. The Deer Creek church in the town
of Deer Creek emerged in 1899 and joined the General Conference
in 1901. The plurality of early churches is supported by the demographics of the era. There were as many as forty-one hundred German
people who had been born in Russia living in Oklahoma at the time
of statehood (Hale 1980). Not counted in this number were the children of immigrants born in the United States. Certainly, all of these
native Russians were not Mennonite, but a substantial number in
Oklahoma at the time of statehood were.

Basically, the relocation of Mennonite immigrants to Oklahoma did
not disturb the general patterns of church worship. The Mennonites
were a community of faith. Life was organized through the church.
Pioneer Mennonite families would be considered pious by today's
standards (Haury 1981). For individuals, the daily routine as well as
the cycle-of-living customs revolved around religious practices.
Typically, father, mother, and their children held devotions daily.
Congregations held regular worship services on Sundays. German
was the language spoken.

---

*By 1800 churches associated with the original Mennonite settlement in German-
town were being identified as "Old" Mennonite. As time passed, however, the name
came to be considered inappropriate and inaccurate. At present the original title is
still used by some and is written sometimes in references as the (Old) Mennonite
Church. A study that compared "plain" and "not-so-plain" groups is that of Fretz
(1977).

The church houses were built plain, with little decoration, in compliance with the Mennonite ethic and members' limited financial resources. There were few architectural amenities or decorative trimmings. Most Mennonite houses of worship consisted of one large room. The basic design and decor were not unlike those of many early-day territorial churches. The pattern of construction did differ in one respect from most of the other churches in the territory, however. About half of the Mennonite churches were built with two major entrances: one door for women and one for men. The custom was for men and women to enter church services separately and, once inside, sit segregated, opposite each other, in pews divided by a central aisle that ran the length of the sanctuary (McKee 1988a).

The sermon often went on for an hour or longer, and services could last most of the day on Sunday. In at least one community, sheds were built behind the church to protect the members' highly valued horses from nature's elements during the all-day services. As time passed, the horse stalls were converted to parking garages for members' automobiles. Since travel was slow and services lengthy, members often arrived at church with sausage, cheese, and other food packed in baskets. After morning worship, the women would get a noon meal ready and serve their families. After dinner, worship was taken up again. In the afternoon, German Sunday school was taught for the children in many of the churches. As the years passed, the religious instruction in German was, for many children, their primary training in the use of the German language.

The churches were served by lay preachers who usually received no pay for their work. The preacher's income was supplemented only marginally by what small donations members could give. On occasion, church members would help the preacher by assembling at his home to plant, harvest, or perform other farmwork. These ministers supported themselves and their families by farming or other labor during the week. Oftentimes, rural ministers served more than one church, traveling from congregation to congregation in the territory.

In the church services, singing was led by the Vorsänger, a man from the congregation who set the pitch for the a cappella singing. Few churches owned pianos or other instruments to accompany the congregation's voices (McKee 1988a). The hymns were often sung from memory and in German. The entire service was conducted in what church members referred to as High German. It was called High German by Mennonites because it was the official German language used in printed texts, and it differed from the Low German, or common dialect, spoken in many of the members' homes.

Foot washing, communion—or partaking of the Lord's supper—and holidays, especially Christmas Eve services, were sacred, faithfully observed rituals (McKee 1988a; Haury 1981; Erb 1974) in Mennonite churches. According to the Anabaptist doctrine, baptism was concomitant with church membership and performed for Mennonites individually. Baptism usually occurred in early adulthood; for most, the rites were performed during their late teens or early twenties. A young adult was baptized before he or she was married.

Weddings, funerals, and baptisms were chaste observances. The groups that baptized by immersion performed the ceremony in farm ponds and creeks. Funerals were commonly held in the home (Kroeker 1988). As for weddings, the bride often wore black (Kroeker 1988). Weddings were frequently held during the regular Sunday worship services, and the lengthy sermon was not abridged for the occasion. There was rarely need of wedding invitations, since the entire community was almost always present at the Sunday services.

The Martin Luther German Bible was studied. Other sources of church literature, when available, were almost always printed in German and were extremely limited at this time. One publication, a Mennonite German-language newspaper, carried local news and religious articles. At twenty-nine, J. F. Harms, a farmer and minister in Medford, was its first editor and publisher. The paper became a weekly in 1889 and was mailed beyond Oklahoma Territory to subscribers in other American Mennonite communities and in Russia. Russian Mennonites regularly sent articles and information back to Harms for publication. For a year's work at his business, Harms was paid as much as fifty dollars by the Mennonite Brethren. Some years he received no remuneration for his services (Mennonite Brethren Publishing House 1960). Harms's work as a Mennonite publisher in Oklahoma was not permanent. When he left Medford in 1906, the newspaper and printing press were relocated to McPherson, Kansas (Kroeker 1954).

Reading printed information was usually resrticted to Mennonite-produced publications. Other daily activities were ordered around bibical prescriptions as well. To faithful Mennonites, following the Bible meant following a call to withdraw from all worldliness. That meant withdrawal from the influence of individuals or organized groups outside the church. It was customary for Mennonites to practice simplicity in every aspect of their daily lives. This included plain dress. Jewelry, colorful or fancy clothing, gold watches—adornment of any kind—were prohibited. Couples did not practice the exchange of wedding rings until the 1930s. Among religious teachings important to the group, thrift, self-denial, and pacifism were the basic prescribed values undergirding the social organization of the church (Hostetler 1983).

The state constitutional convention and the fanfare accompanying the arrival of statehood in 1907 were largely ignored by Mennonite people. Mennonites were bound by religious precept to avoid participation in governmental affairs. Beyond that, the fledgling state government appeared a seemingly extraneous authority when juxapositioned against the Mennonites' daily struggle to eke out a living on the Oklahoma prairie. Mennonites paid their taxes but refused to participate in local civic activities. Just as life on the farm isolated the Mennonite families physically from neighboring communities, church life protected Mennonite families from other outside public influences. For the Mennonite residents of Northwest Oklahoma, the political maneuverings at the state capital in Guthrie and later in Oklahoma City were remote indeed.

The Mennonites and their families were "quiet in the land" (Keim and Stoltzfus 1988). They held themselves quietly apart from the community at large. They spoke little to outsiders, and the very nature of their close and closed social organization encouraged restraint and brevity in dealing with their own kind. Lengthy periods of silence among companions and families at work were not considered unusual.

Although the Mennonites did not live communally, their collective life during this period was exclusively in-group. The sharing of farm tasks was an opportunity for socialization as well as an expedient way to accomplish large undertakings. Harvest time and the slaughter of hogs and cattle were two occasions that called for the gathering of relatives and Mennonite neighbors. During harvest, the males of the family, together with neighbors and hired hands, worked from sunup until sundown, while the women of the family spent most of the day preparing as many as five meals to be carried to the fields to refresh the exhausted, hungry crews.

Slaughtering, another major undertaking for Mennonite farmers, was reserved for cooler weather. It usually lasted only one or two days and required highly specialized labor. Tradition in some communities called for inviting the volunteer crew of helpers to a huge, early-morning breakfast served at the site of the activity. Butchering was a festive occasion, with women, children, men—everyone in attendance—participating. Butchering was labor-intensive. The process involved killing the animals and cleaning, cutting, and preparing the meat. The making of sausage; of head cheese from the edible parts of the head, feet, and organs of the pig; and of cracklings was also a part of the process. Mostly fat, cracklings were used for flavoring and frying and as a substitute for bacon. Little of the butchered animal was not rendered edible in some way.

A great deal of skill was required to accomplish butchering correctly. Special training and attention to detail were required for the proper cleaning of intestines to pack the sausage and for gauging the precise amount of boiling time needed to cook cracklings. Women were often assigned both of these chores. Women also cooked and served meals to the men workers. The socializing took place during the work. When the work was completed, the families returned to their respective homes. After butchering day, the prepared meats were kept cool during the winter months by hanging them in an unheated shed. Meat also was canned for preservation.

The isolated rural lifestyle of family farming was the style of life of most Oklahoma settlers. At statehood about 70 percent of the total population was rural (Gibson 1984). For Mennonites, the pattern of insular farm life was reinforced by church-dominated activities based on strict rules of behavior and patriarchal control. Overall authority for the family belonged to the father, but the line of authority was not rigid. Mennonite women were expected to do their share of the work, and they accepted their share of the responsibility. Sex roles did divide farm labor, yet the magnitude of mutual effort required for successful farming also required respect for the economic input of women. Family roles, nevertheless, were well defined, with leadership and decision-making power assumed by the husband and father.

Strict discipline was kept in many Mennonite homes. Much of the discipline centered on the precise and exacting demands of farm labor. Training and punishment hinged on the stern willpower of the fathers, who exercised authority over the children. Mothers too expected their children to be obedient. Fathers and mothers were both known not to have spared the rod with their children. Despite this, anger and harsh words in the administration of punishment were discouraged by church teachings. Mennonite children learned to respect the authority of their parents and to conduct themselves in the Mennonite way of life. They were included in family devotions and worship services from infancy.

Mennonite families were quite large. It was not unusual for mothers to bear as many as twelve or more children. Because children were an economic asset, an additional source of farm labor, large families were also the norm for the general population in the early days of Oklahoma settlement.

Just as the male was the head of the household, church leadership rested in the authority of the deacons, bishops, and elders (Haury 1981). These men enforced the rules of living for the congregation. In general, there were rules of conduct against gluttony, alcohol consumption, tobacco use, card playing, dancing, and public amusement of any kind. Reading "worldly" literature was strictly prohibited (Haury 1981), but newspapers, some classical literature, and other publications were acceptable reading material. Reading the Bible was considered essential, and reading whatever Mennonite publications were available at the time was encouraged.

Those who deviated from the norms were sanctioned in one of several ways, depending on the severity of the offense. Sometimes the sanctions took the form of indirect censure. For minor offenses, the wrongdoer might be chastised by community "talk" about the improper deed or the unseemly behavior. For some infractions, an offender might be asked to stand and apologize before the congregation for his or her misdeeds. Doing any kind of work, especially farmwork, on Sunday was strictly forbidden and punishable by the group. Serious infractions of the rules—for example, divorce—could be punished by excommunication, which Mennonites sometimes called "being canceled" (McKee 1988a). The exclusive use of the German language in church and at home served to reinforce the Mennonites' separation from society. Interaction with the community at large was frowned upon and in-group marriage considered essential to preserve the close-knit group.

The Mennonites quickly learned, nevertheless, that they did not exist in a vacuum. In Europe and Russia, they had preserved their ethnicity through completely closed, self-governing cultures that were economically viable and virtually autonomous. In Oklahoma, the situation was entirely different. The homestead method of land distribution had broken up the old closed-community patterns. The Mennonite settlers were few and scattered in remote areas. It was practically impossible to exist for long without needed supplies from the outside world. Mennonites found themselves in a new situation.

The need for cash and the economics of American agriculture demanded a market for Mennonites' farm products.

Still, the Mennonites made efforts to shun society. In their calm and quiet way, they continued to support a social organization centered around their religious orientation. The individual, the family unit, the extended family, and social relationships and activities—all operated under the auspices of the church, and the church operated on a rationale of exclusion from society. Mennonite congregations fostered self-segregation. On a day-to-day basis, Mennonites engaged only in limited transactions with outsiders, whom they referred to as "Englishe."

# Cornelius C. and Helena (Heinrichs) Heinrichs

The lives of Cornelius Heinrichs and his wife, Helena, are examples of the extended-family relationships and close fellowship of Mennonites and show the importance of mitigating precarious economic situations that not infrequently befell members. The couple's story has been taken from the writings of Cornelius Heinrichs, letters, and other papers that were incorporated into a memoir written by their grandson, David Ediger, whose own story will appear later in this text.

"In the village Liebenau, when I was six months old, my loving mother died, so I was reared by Mr. and Mrs. Heinrich Nikkel in the village of Liebenau, where I also received my schooling." Thus begins the story of my grandpa, Cornelius C. Heinrichs, born February 20, 1852, in the Molotschna colony in Russia. Grandpa Heinrichs was given to his mother's sister to be raised, and he grew up in Russia east of Molotschna in a newly formed colony, Kuban, the adopted son of Heinrich and Katherine Nikkel.

Throughout his life, he never wanted to discuss the circumstances of this event, and so it remains a mystery. Cornelius grew up working for his adopted father, Heinrich Nikkel, learning the art of milling. This man was a miller who had a well-situated flour mill, which generated considerable income.

As my grandpa grew to be a young man, he saw many people were being persecuted because of their faith. He wrote in his journal, "Brother Heibert was put in a Russian jail for two years even though he was innocent. One Sunday morning I visited him. We prayed together. I on the outside of the window and he on the inside." At age twenty-three, still a bachelor, my grandpa decided to emigrate to America.

In 1876 Cornelius came to Nebraska, making the long journey with his cousin. His adopted mother had died earlier that same year. He wrote she caught a cold, became ill, and passed away within a week. "Mother Nikkel reached the age of fifty-five years and five months," he wrote. "She did not need to make the long trip to America." But his adopted father, Heinrich Nikkel, came to America about the time my grandpa came and was one of the ministers in the Henderson [Nebraska] Mennonite Brethren Church.

In 1877 Cornelius was saved. He was baptized on April 29 and became a member of the Mennonite Brethren. Shortly after joining the church, he felt a call from God to go into the ministry. He wrote a letter to the conference officials expressing his desire. After they considered it, they wrote back that, according to their findings and evaluation, his personality makeup was too charismatic or emotional. They advised against it. So he followed their advice and gave up on the idea of becoming a minister. But he continued teaching young people in Sunday school classes throughout the rest of his life. He taught Sunday school for thirty-eight years.

When he began to think seriously about marriage, a Heinrichs family, unrelated to him but [members of] the Henderson M. B. church, invited him over for a Sunday evening visit. They had three daughters in their twenties. When he arrived, the three daughters were seated on the divan according to their ages, and the father suggested that the oldest girl would be available for marriage. Then and there Cornelius made it clear that the youngest, Helena, was the one he had his eye on. Fortunately, the deal was worked out, and Cornelius and Helena, the youngest, were married.

My grandmother, Helena Heinrichs, was twenty-two years old when she married. She had come to America six years earlier. She was saved at the age of twenty-one. Like my Grandpa Cornelius, she made her decision for Christ after she had come to the United States. The wedding took place on November 28, 1880. Grandfather wrote, "Father Nikkel read the marriage vows and spoke briefly about them. He united us in marriage, but before that, Peter Regier read Proverbs Chapter three and brought out wonderful thoughts."

[During the first nine years of married life, the young couple farmed, and Cornelius managed a mill near Henderson on the Blue River, which was a fairly large and deep river and a place where Mennonite baptisms were sometimes held.] The first two of their children died at birth. Next was a son, Abraham C. The fourth born was my mother, Helena Heinrichs.

As I mentioned, Grandpa Cornelius farmed eight acres and managed the mill. He knew all about different kinds of grain and milling techniques. My grandpa milled wheat and rye. A farmer would bring his wheat in and have it milled for a fee or trade some wheat for the expense of the milling. My grandpa thought there was an art to milling: how fine to grind and how the germ should be screened out. After milling, the hulls that remained became horse and cattle feed. He also fed this offal to his dogs. He always kept dogs around the mill to protect it when he was gone.

Milling was heavy work, and when my grandpa saw his sons trying to drag the big 100-pound sacks of flour around, he thought they should leave milling and get into farming. By this time, all the land around the Henderson area was settled, and land prices were high. Although he himself was not the pioneering type, he decided that the only way the boys would ever be able to get started in farming and own their own land would be if the family moved where there was cheap land or land for homesteading. Several other families in the area were thinking the same way, and so in 1892, Cornelius, Helena, and, by that time, their five children, sold the farm and moved to Joes, Colorado. Joes was about 100 miles east of Denver, and it was in flat farming country. There were about twenty-five Mennonite families in the area then.

[Cornelius and Helena homesteaded and farmed near Joes, but rainfall was sparse, and farming was not particularily successful. They had two more children during their four years in Colorado.] Joes was never a big, prosperous town. My mother, Helena, went to school in Joes during those years, and when she was ten years old she was saved and baptized. Some thought that maybe she was too young. In the Mennonite Brethren Church at that time, ten years old was considered very young to make a decision for Christ.

Finally, after four dry years, Grandpa decided they must try somewhere else. He wrote, "Our income was so sparse we decided, together with the other families, to move to Westfield, Texas." The family moved in a wagon. It took seven weeks to make the trip to Westfield, a community north of Houston. Now it is a suburb. The lumber was very cheap, since there was so much forest. "We all built houses right away," Grandpa wrote.

In Texas, they got the rain they lacked in Colorado, but, as it turned out, it rained so much as to almost ruin Grandpa and his family. Malaria and similar diseases plagued them and their livestock. In the three years they were there, their horses developed sicknesses they could not get rid of. Finally, they were done in by a great Galveston hurricane in September 1899. In Grandpa's words, "When the flood came, we lost everything but our lives."

So they moved again. "We had only 15 cents when we finally got to Enid," he wrote. Had it not been for the help [from other Mennonites] to get to Oklahoma, they would never have made it. [The family's move from Texas] happened only seven years after the land rush and settlement of the Cherokee Outlet in Oklahoma, and the Mennonite Brethren community near Enid was struggling to get started. When the Enidites heard of this group of families in Texas who were looking to move somewhere, they wrote to them and begged them to come to Enid. In one letter they said that they—the Enid Mennonites—would take the bridles off their horses when they came through so the Texas bunch would have to stay.

All of the Mennonite families in Westfield headed north, again moving by wagon train. When they forded the Red River, quicksand was a threat, and so they had to hook all of the horses to one wagon at a time and pull each wagon through separately. [After arriving safely,] Cornelius and Helena settled north of Enid, renting a farm for six years. In 1906, they bought a quarter section and started again from scratch, building their house and all the barns. Their son Abe was a good carpenter, and he supervised the work. They dug into the hillside and built a two-level house. The basement opened to the south and west, and the top front was to the east. It was a nice big house with a well-landscaped yard. Grandpa had a big cattle barn, a granary, and also a shop. All the buildings are gone now, but the drive and the yard are still there.

During those years, they had all four of their boys at home working for them. In those days, you didn't go to high school or college. When you got out of grade school, you came home and worked. Abe was the oldest; he was good at everything, especially carpentry and construction—then Corney, then John, who liked church work more than farming, but, as it was then, he farmed anyway. The girls were Helena, Marie, and Tina, who became ill with dropsy, a liver ailment, and died at age fifteen.

Jake was the youngest. Altogether, there were nine children born to Cornelius and Helena. Six survived to be adults.

During the years from 1900 to 1917, the boys did most of the farming, and that left time for Grandpa to do the things he enjoyed the most: teaching Sunday school, reading, writing, and ministering to and visiting the neighbors. Many times, even on weekdays, he and Grandma would hitch up their favorite horse, Colie, take their Bible and their little songbook, and go visiting. They would go see a widow or a family who needed encouragement, inviting themselves in for vespers and a time of devotions. Grandpa had Scripture [readings] and thoughts that were ready for such occasions. I know a lot of people really appreciated it. Of course, a lot of it was just visiting with friends, and my grandparents were visited in return. The church was more of a family or community back then, and it was spontaneous, not something set up by the church. You just went visiting, but to be invited for Sunday dinner, that was something pretty special. For those times, a couple of chickens would have to be killed.

Grandma Heinrichs was a good homemaker and enjoyed working in her garden and growing flowers. She was a very pretty, very nice looking lady. She wore her hair in a bun. She had real black hair before it turned salt-and-pepper-colored. She was very strict on keeping the rules, like keeping her head covered for prayer. She always kept her head covered in church. The ladies wore homemade caps; some were fancy, others plain. They fit down over the back of the head with strings to tie under the chin. Her house was meticulously kept, inside and outside. She had very beautiful handwriting, and we still have some of the things that she wrote. She had a good voice and loved to sing. She was a rather quiet lady. When I was a teenager, I sometimes thought maybe she took life too seriously.

On the other hand, Grandpa was outgoing and very interested in world affairs and politics. [For most Mennonites of this era, an interest in world affairs meant an interest in Mennonite affairs worldwide.] He liked to keep up on what was happening in Russia. Grandpa talked a lot about Russia, and he was fluent in Russian. As a young man there, he had picked it up in conversations with Russians. He had met lots of people while working in the mill. The Mennonites in Russia then spoke German exclusively; only a handful knew Russian.

In 1915 Grandpa and Grandma were naturalized as U.S. citizens at the Garfield County courthouse in Enid. Grandpa was anxious to become a U.S. citizen. Until then they were Russian citizens, but as the Communists took over in Russia, Mennonites suffered greatly. Of course, all of this was of great interest to him. He was very thankful to be in America with the freedoms we have here.

In the evenings after supper, Grandpa would talk about what he had read in the newspaper, and what they were doing in Poland and in the village in Russia where he had lived, and what was going on in Washington. He was unusual in this. Most farmers didn't have any use for knowing or talking about these kinds of things. But he kept up on all the news, and he remembered it too. When Grandpa and Grandma would go around and make these house visitations, they took time to visit in addition to the devotional times, and then Grandpa would discuss the news. People were usually interested, even though they didn't know much about it.

In the community, Grandpa was very well liked because he loved everybody. He wasn't considered very industrious because, in those days, the thing that counted was getting out there and working from before sunup until after dark. You saved your money, and you bought farms—that was what was worthwhile. One time, someone asked me how my Grandpa Heinrichs was. I said, "He's just as fine as ever," and I was told, "Well, he ought to be fine, because he has sure never strained himself." Grandpa was not a lazy man, but he was more interested in his reading and writing than in spending all day behind the plow.

In 1917, when the United States began to fight in World War I, my Uncle Jake and quite a few other men from the Enid area were drafted. Our family and other church members encouraged Jake to find a noncombatant role in the army. Before he left, they said over and over to him, "Don't take the gun, don't take the gun."

The Mennonite men from Enid and three carfuls of other draftees were all put on a troop train headed for army camp. The train derailed in southern Oklahoma. One man was killed, and many were injured. When Jake regained consciousness he was lying on a hillside, bleeding. Jake's hand was torn up. My grandpa wrote about the incident, saying that with "the hand of God and the doctor's fast work, [Jake] was soon home again in his beloved wife's arms. Many tears of happiness were shed and thankful prayers were made to the Lord." By the time Jake recovered, the war was over.

In 1918 Grandpa retired. He put his house on wooden rollers and pulled it with horses to a smaller, forty-acre place. Jake took over Grandpa's farm, and the brothers helped Grandpa fix up his house on the new place and build a barn. Our barns at home had dirt floors, but he had a wood floor with a cement feed trough in his barn. Grandpa had an orchard and garden at the new place too. He kept about 100 chickens and raised baby chicks.

In those days, everyone had setting hens to raise baby chicks. He kept the setting hens in a separate place in front of the laying hens [those that produced eggs for the table]. He had a row of wooden boxes on the floor for them. In the spring, the baby chicks would grow to be fryers. We had fryers just in the spring, not all year 'round. He butchered the fryers and kept the young hen chicks for laying and then butchered the old laying hens for chicken noodle soup. Everybody did it that way.

Grandpa still had his buggy with a top and his good driving horse, Colie. We had cars then, but he preferred to drive the six miles to church in that buggy. When it was cold, he and Grandma would wear a warm laprobe, made from the skin of a horse. The church was built with a heater grate on the middle aisle, about halfway to the front. By the time Grandpa and Grandma would get there, the church would already be full and everyone singing hymns. He would walk up the middle aisle and stop there on that grate, rub his hands, and get warmed up real good; if everyone was singing or whatever, that didn't bother him. He just waited until he was warmed through, and then he would sit down. The men and women sat on separate sides then, and he always sat on the front bench. Grandma sat on the front bench on the ladies' side.

In 1924, when I was thirteen years old, Grandpa got a letter from Russia, from one of his brothers. When the letter came from Russia, everyone made a great to-do over it. It came from Siberia. After Grandpa left Russia, he had never known what had become of his brother. His brother had lived through the Communist revolution and had ended up somewhere in Siberia. Grandpa wrote back to him but never heard a reply. He never had any more contact with this brother after that one letter. He figured that his brother probably never received his letter.

Grandpa and Grandma celebrated their fiftieth wedding anniversary in 1930, one year before Grandma died. The anniversary celebration was pretty unusual because, in those days, people generally didn't live that long. We held a special service for them in the church on Thanksgiving evening. Their son Abe opened the festivities by leading the singing of three gospel hymns, reading Psalm 100, and [offering a] prayer. After a sermon, the children and grandchildren presented a program of many hymns and readings.

When Grandma died of a stroke the following year at age seventy-two, Grandpa wrote in his journal: "The last words she said that were plain enough to understand were 'Jesus, Jesus.' Her wish was to go home to her redeemer. . . . She leaves me, with who for 50 years, five months, and 21 days, she shared joy and sorrow."

Grandpa then moved in with us. Dad had built a little shed and corral for his horse, Colie, and Grandpa still kept his buggy. He loved feeding that horse and brushing it, and sometimes maybe he brushed it more than it needed. Then Colie died. He had colic or something, and that was a tragedy. Abe had a gray, gentle horse for Grandpa then, but, of course, he wasn't near as pretty as Colie. That horse had to take the place of Colie, but it was never quite the same to Grandpa. But he still took care of his horse as long as he could.

My sister, Bertha, had married Abe Buller, and they lived in Grandpa and Grandma's house and Grandpa stayed in what had been Bertha's bedroom in our house. He had a writing desk in there and some shelves for his writings and books. He got a Mennonite newspaper that covered a lot of world news. It was printed in Canada and was a week or two old when he got it, but it had world news and news about Mennonites in Europe and Russia.

Grandpa died on January 25, 1940, less than a week after suffering a stroke. He was one month short of his eighty-seventh birthday. At his funeral the choir sang "He Took My Sins Away" while the casket was brought in and family members took their places. The obituary was read in German and English. Reverend John Siemens spoke in German; his text was from Philippians 1:6 and 4:6. The Harmony Quartet sang a German song, after which Rev. Seibel spoke in English. His text was taken from Psalm 17. Reverend Seibel was the pastor of the Enid M. B. church at that time. Reverend Seibel wrote a memorial for Grandpa that said Grandpa was "a friend of the Bible and a man of prayer. He enjoyed speaking of philosophical questions. We will no longer hear his prayers or of his good experiences, nor feel his warm handshake, but his influence lives on. We say with him as he did to us on Thursday evening, 'auf Wiedersehen, what a hope.'"

# CHAPTER 5

# *Turkey Red*

The Turkey Red was wonderful wheat.
It would grow tall—as high as a man's
waist.

—*Abe Janzen*

The wave of Mennonite immigrants that swept over America in the late nineteenth century eventually wound its way to Oklahoma, bringing in tow baggage both real and ideational, tangible and intangible. The Mennonites embarked from Russia with a religious belief system, folkways, and a work ethic advantageous to agriculture. Along with that came more-tangible assets—a proclivity for progressive techniques of soil cultivation and the forethought to introduce advanced strains of seed plants from Russia to the American West. In due time, the benefits of these assets accrued. The initial years of homesteading in Oklahoma put everything to the test. The size and composition of farm yields from the early years through World War I at once revealed the scope of prairie munificence and the genius beneath the one great engine of productivity that eventually would sweep across the American heartland—wheat cropping.

Drought and the challenges of turning the prairie into farmland plagued settlers during the first years. The crops were poor in 1894 and 1895 (Green 1977, 14–15.). The winter of 1894–95 was exceptionally severe (Green 1977, 14–15). Some homesteaders gave up, abandoned their dreams, and moved elsewhere; but eventually the drought broke. By 1897, the wheat crop, blessed by ample rainfall, was plentiful (Johnson 1977, 15). The average yield for the year rose to eighteen bushels per acre, double the 1896 yield (Green 1977, 59). That amount of increase opened markets for Oklahoma wheat and other farm surpluses that in turn made cash and credit more obtainable and homestead life easier to endure. For farmers, the "good times" that brought the century to a close foretold the bounty nature was capable of providing, if not always willing to do so.

All in all, the first twenty years of the twentieth century were, for the most part, years of rapid growth in agriculture. The weather continued to cooperate, and new farming machinery became available. But counter to this trend, greenbugs and grasshoppers attacked fields for a period of time just after statehood. The result was crop loss, and once more some homesteaders, unable to cope, were forced off their land (Wilson 1977). Nevertheless, despite frequent setbacks, production increased, and farm prices overall made uneven but gradual gains. Mennonite communities, too, grew during this period. Several new Mennonite churches sprang up at the turn of the century. Two were Mennonite Brethren congregations—Lahoma, founded in 1901, and Lookout in 1905 (Goertzen 1990). One, affiliated with the General Conference, the Bethanian church, was located at Coy (Haury 1981). In 1906, the last of only three congregations of the (Old) Mennonite Church to be established in Northwest Oklahoma was formed at Newkirk (Erb 1974).

From the late 1890s through the World War I years, Oklahoma farm output increased, the population grew, and farmers experienced modest prosperity. Mennonites were in a better position than most to take advantage of the opportunities. The similarity between the Oklahoma prairie and the Mennonites' farmland on the Russian steppes lent its advantages. Mennonites were said to be "born farmers," entering the world with a plow in one hand and a Bible in the other (Krahn 1949, 12). In reality, the formula relied heavily on persistence, determination, and an understanding of wheat.

As rural life developed in Northwest Oklahoma, production moved from subsistence farming to mixed farming, whereby several types of crops were grown, both for family use and for sale. By the early years of the twentieth century, Northwest Oklahoma farms were producing vegetables and orchard products, dairy and beef cattle, various feed grasses, and a variety of grains. Apple, apricot, peach, and cherry trees took hold in the soil. Gardens offered up cabbage, potatoes, onions, green beans, cucumbers, tomatoes, and other good things to eat. Field crops—wheat, corn, oats, and barley—were found to be especially well suited to the land; yet yields were considerably smaller than contemporary harvests. In those days, wheat that made twenty bushels to the acre was considered a more-than-good crop.

Despite those yields, homesteading slowly turned to center on grain production, and the most prominent among the grains grown in Northwest Oklahoma by Mennonite farmers was wheat. Almost as soon as settlers broke sod in 1893, wheat growing began to nurture and, later, dominate farming as a way of life for Mennonites. Mixed-crop farming, which included raising several types of maize or corn for sale along with wheat, was instituted; nevertheless, in due time, wheat growing was institutionalized as *the* grain for farmers across Northwest Oklahoma. The work of raising wheat shifted with the seasons and involved tending the soil, planting, pasturing cattle on the wheat during its growth, and harvesting the gold-ripe fields.* The agricultural calendar culminated with the grain harvest. The high point

---

*It is a historical precedent and standard farming practice to pasture cattle on sown wheat fields during winter. Cattle (approximately one mature cow per acre) are grazed on this pasture from the time the wheat cover has grown approximately four inches tall, usually in early November, until sometime between February 1 and March 15. The time for removing the cattle from the wheat varies from year to year, depending on the amount of rainfall and the number of days of severe low temperature. Cattle are removed before the wheat begins to "joint," that is, to form heads of grain. Removal of the cattle allows growth of the wheat stems for grain-head formation at the most advantageous time. Wheat that is not pastured is likely to grow tall earlier, making it more susceptible to freezing during the winter months and slower to form heads in the spring.

of the year, full of activity and anticipation, harvest was, and remains, an exciting time. At the turn of the century, harvesting the wheat, as well as oats and other grains, was demanding, both in the number of laborers needed and in the work of those laborers.

Well into the late years of the nineteenth century, grain fields were planted by hand, cut with a reaper or scythe by hand, and bound into bundles by hand. Threshing the wheat was an arduous undertaking. In the years immediately after the run, a few Mennonites in Grant County relied on "threshing stones" that had been brought over from Russia to accomplish the task. These were heavy, notched, cylinder-shaped stones that were pulled by horses back and forth across the stalks of wheat to beat out the grain (Kroeker 1954). The threshing stones were effective but primitive. They were considered quaint even by the few who worked with them in the 1890s. Most of the Mennonite settlers in Oklahoma relied on the threshing machines that had only recently been put to use by the other homesteaders.

Threshing machines separated the wheat grains from the stems and chaff. The machines used a rotary motion, achieved by a series of pulleys and shafts, to tumble and thereby break the stems from the heads of wheat and force the grains from the chaff. Wheat was cut and bundled in the field and transported to the thresher by wagons and teams of horses. Steam engines were introduced to power threshing machines, and later gasoline motors ran the engines to separate the wheat. After threshing, the grain was usually hauled to market at one of the new elevators that sprang up in almost all the small towns that dotted Northwest Oklahoma. The Garber elevator, for example, was built in 1899 (Green 1977, 59). On the farms, the straw that resulted from the threshing process was stacked and used for animal feed and other needs farmers had for it.

Besides the threshing machines, other new or improved farm implements began to appear in Oklahoma. One of the many advances in farming at the turn of the century was the seed drill, which made it possible for farmers to give up scattering seeds by hand. The drill, which came into use during the 1890s, allowed control in the amount of and distance between the seeds planted (Wilson 1977). Another device introduced during this period was the mowing machine. It replaced the hand scythe for cutting in the field. A variety of cultivators also came on the market about this time, and they improved plowing considerably. Self-binders were introduced to cut and tie loose wheat into shocks.

Improvements also extended to other phases of farmwork, including dairy production. Turning the cream separator, for instance, fast became part of the twice-a-day milking routine on virtually every farm. The separating process consisted of processing fresh cow's milk by turning a crank to a series of paddles that divided the cow's milk by removing the heavier cream through a spout. By 1903, the gasoline motor, the most dramatic of the innovations, made its appearance on Northwest Oklahoma farms. By the end of that decade gasoline motors, far more efficient for farming than steam engines, were driving threshers and tractors and transforming the nature of farmwork throughout Oklahoma (Green 1977, 70–73) and across the United States.

Improved implements accounted for only part of the advances in Great Plains agriculture at the turn of the century. Farming practices underwent great change as well. The prairie land was new to cultivation and the topsoil therefore a receptive host to most crops introduced, but successful farming, over the long haul, required knowledge and skill. As farmers, Mennonites practiced highly evolved types of agriculture. They were prominent among the farmers who carefully adhered to the practice of certain types of cultivation, and their accomplishment in these practices was quickly recognized in the yields that accrued from their endeavor. Their farming methods were noted and readily adopted by those outside the Mennonite community.

One cultivation technique used, although it was not practiced exclusively by Mennonites, proved particularly expedient for raising wheat in Oklahoma. The system involved a routine of deep-plowing the stubble remaining in the fields after harvest, then later reworking the topsoil through a number of repeated plowings until a very fine surface consistency was achieved. The Mennonites used this type of cultivation to regularly produce high-yielding crops (Jenkins 1986), and that consequently helped popularize the technique. Although the long-term advantage of the method is now being questioned by environmentalists, this way of working the land before planting and after harvest freed the soil of weeds, supported seed growth, and remains one common practice of tillage across the southwestern wheat-producing states at the end of the twentieth century.

Crop rotation is another farming technique used by Mennonites before it was widely accepted by farmers in general. Most Mennonite farmers were careful not to repeat planting of the same crop in the same soil season after season. Repeated plantings of wheat year after year depleted the soil, often resulting in successively poorer harvests. Corn and other crops often were substituted for wheat on Mennonite farms, while many of their neighbors replanted whatever crop happened to be bringing the highest price at market. This was usually wheat. Mennonites certainly were not the only farmers to engage in crop rotation during the first years of the twentieth century, but most Mennonites used the technique even though crop rotation was far from a universal farming practice at that time. Through the years, the value of the practice has been confirmed, and today crop rotation is a necessary part of effective farmland use.

The single most significant farming innovation credited to the Mennonites is the introduction of Turkey Red seed wheat to America. In their relocation to America, the Mennonites imported some exceptional varieties of seed plants. One in particular was a seed wheat called Turkey Red. The Turkey Red seeds were highly valued by the Mennonites and received priority among the carefully chosen belongings transported by the immigrants to America. Small sacks of this hard red winter wheat and other seeds for the Mennonites' gardens, orchards, and fields were among the few possessions Mennonite travelers were able to bring from Russia to the United States (Stucky 1973, 27–32). The seeds were brought into the country in small quantities, usually only a few pounds per family (Stucky 1973, 27–32). These kernels of grain were especially selected for planting on the new farms. Because they were very small and only a small amount could be transported with families on their way to America, the task of selecting only the very best grains was crucial. Nevertheless, it was often the young children of a family who made the selection. With their keen eyes and small, nimble fingers, it was they who could best grasp, lift, and sort the smooth, round little nuggets. These few precious grains were removed from Russia in trunks and baskets and sometimes sewn into the hems of women's skirts.

No one is exactly certain how the hard red wheat strain from Turkey first arrived in the United States or how much of it was brought into the country. One story holds that young Anna Barkman, only eight years old when her family decided to leave their Crimean home to come to America, was given the task of choosing only the largest, reddest, and most well shaped grains to be brought on the trip. Working daily for a week in her father's grain bin, she discarded the pale, small, soft grains, picking only the very best and packing them into two one-gallon containers. The seed wheat that traveled with Anna and her family to Kansas in 1874 (Wiebe 1974, 107) then became the first of the Turkey Red to be planted in the United States. Other stories date the arrival of Turkey Red to 1873 and credit many families, each bringing on average a bushel of the seed wheat as they made their way to Kansas.

Turkey Red was native to the coasts along the Black Sea and the Sea of Azov (Krahn 1949, 10). It was being grown in the wheat-producing areas of eastern Europe and Asia before 1850 and was traded by Turks, Cossacks, Ukrainians, Greeks, Bulgarians, and Germans (Krahn 1949, 10). Shipments of Turkey Red wheat had reached London markets by the mid-1850s (Krahn 1949, 10). Most likely, Turkey Red did come into the United States from areas in southern Russia during the mid-1870s. Most probably, it was transported to the western plains by many people, both Mennonite and non-Mennonite (Stucky 1973, 27–32). But because its use was widespread and consistent on Mennonite farms, Mennonite people are credited with introducing Turkey Red. Eventually, Turkey Red became one of the first crops planted in the freshly turned topsoil of the Cherokee Outlet. Carried west across the Mediterranean and the Atlantic by ship and by rail through America to the western plains states, the tiny kernels of seed wheat propagated in the virgin fields of the American West and proved ultimately to be a tremendous boon to the austere economy of the pioneers (Hein 1974).

Early pioneers throughout the American West were subsistence farmers. Until the coming of the Mennonite immigrants, most of the wheat planted by homesteaders in the western plains states was spring wheat, planted in spring and harvested in fall, or it was a soft-grain winter wheat, planted in the fall and harvested late the next spring. Neither type was very successful. Spring wheat was suited to the soil, and in some years yields were plentiful, but crop failures were routine. Spring wheat was not hardy. A good stand of wheat often could not endure the extreme range of rainfall amounts and other cruelties of the Great Plains climate. A late freeze could demolish an entire crop. Farmers experimented with soft winter wheat and found that it too was not well suited to plains agriculture. Soft winter wheat needed plenty of moisture and was sensitive to cold winters and climatic changes. In addition, the soft grain heads of this wheat were not disease-resistant. Black rust was only one of several blights that could attack the wheat and destroy entire fields (Stucky 1973, 30).

The lack of one or more dependable cash crops was a major contributor to the low productivity and the precarious economic position of the original homestead farmers in Oklahoma and elsewhere. It was not many years after the arrival of the Russian Mennonites that the planting of hard winter wheat was launched north to south throughout the entire western plains. This strain of wheat formed hard grains at maturity. It was sown in the fall and harvested in late spring or early summer. In only a short time, hard winter wheat came to be the major variety of wheat planted on Oklahoma farms. It could withstand extreme changes in weather. It was a strong, disease-resistant plant that agreed with prairie soil. Turkey Red grew thick and tall and produced abundant harvests. One Mennonite family arriving in

Kansas in the spring of 1874 broke the sod, planted one gallon of the seeds, and the following year harvested three bushels of fine-quality grain (Wiebe 1974, 108). Turkey Red gained attention as a popular variety of wheat. By the year 1904, a Mennonite had walked away from the World's Fair in St. Louis with a gold medal awarded for the outstanding quality of Turkey Red wheat (Wiebe 1974, 105).

The introduction of Turkey Red was perhaps more a happy accident than a planned procedure (Wiebe 1974, 105), but the match of Turkey Red and plains prairie was fortuitous. Milling and marketing the bounty, however, presented challenges. Local mills were not equipped to grind the hard grains of Turkey Red. Some millers rejected it because it was too difficult to process. Refitting the mills required the substitution of steel rollers to replace the stone burrs that formerly had ground wheat into flour (Wiebe 1974, 104–5; Stuckey 1973). To further complicate matters, because of its dark color, some housewives refused to purchase the flour produced (Wiebe 1974, 104). Purchasers initially were appeased when millers mixed some whiter wheat from soft grains with the Turkey Red product. As time passed, consumers grew more accustomed to the darker color and the consistency of the flour made with hard red wheat, in part because Turkey Red produced a strong, glutinous flour with good baking qualities (Wiebe 1974, 105; Krahn 1949, 11). Demand increased both in the United States and abroad (Krahn 1949, 104–5, 12).

Beginning in the 1870s, near the time of the Mennonite immigration from Russia and increasing gradually through the years that followed, hard red winter wheat harvests came to support the infrastructure of the farm belt and spur agricultural and economic development from Canada to Texas. Wheat became the major source of grain income for farmers in Northwest Oklahoma and the foundation for change from subsistence farming to farming for profit in all areas of the American West. Once a sea of grass, by the 1920s the Great Plains had become an ocean of wheat. From September through spring, winter wheat lay a blanket of green pasture across Oklahoma that became, by June, a massive wave of grain. The winter growth was excellent feed for cattle and allowed a profitable mix of livestock and wheat production. Farm life in Northwest Oklahoma began to turn on the axis of wheat culture.

The Russian Mennonites' favored seed grain turned out to be a precise match for the soil composition and climate of the western plains. Wheat production was greatly enhanced by the introduction of effective farming practices, many of them popularized by Mennonite farmers; by the introduction of new farming equipment; and, perhaps most important, by the widespread adoption of hard winter wheat from the Turkey Red strain brought to American by German-speaking Russian Mennonites. Thus Russian Mennonite men and women contributed significantly to the successful melding of wheat and farm livelihood that to this day supports agricultural economics in Northwest Oklahoma.

# David G. Ediger

Two and a half years after their marriage, George Ediger and his wife, Helena, packed up and moved away from Enid, Oklahoma. It was hard to leave his wife's family and her parents, Cornelius and Helena Heinrichs, but they did it. The Edigers relocated because, at the time, George didn't think he could ever get a place of his own in Oklahoma, and he had been öffered work in a mill at Henderson, Nebraska. He had been brought up in a Mennonite community near Henderson, and his parents still lived in the area. In 1912 , not long after they made the move, the Edigers' third child, David, was born. David spent his first years in Nebraska living with his family on a rented farm, riding a paint-colored horse named Dick, and dreaming of being a cowboy.

In the spring of 1992, at age eighty, David Ediger began to talk to his nephew Jerry about those times. All three of David's sons—Louis, Lloyd, and Richard—had, now and then over the years, asked him to write down some of his memories. As David and Jerry worked together, with Jerry transcribing the things David said, David began to remember more and more about his childhood and youth. His story reflects the Mennonite reverence for nature, commitment to agriculture, and life on a working farm in the early decades of the twentieth century. David's recollection of farm life in his growing-up years through the early 1930s begins below, at the time David was six years old and his family made the decision to return to Oklahoma.

During and after World War I, Dad was able to save some money; the price for our wheat and cattle went up quite a bit. He wanted to buy his own farm. Everyone who was a real farmer wanted to own land, and that was very high on Mom and Dad's calendar. They thought renting land was second-rate and temporary. Farmland around Henderson was expensive, and there was no chance that they could afford it.

Mom's folks lived at Enid, and so, of course, she favored moving to Enid. My mom's brother John had bought a farm near Enid and built a three room house on it, but then he had a change of heart about the whole thing and offered to sell the farm and the house to Mom and Dad. About this same time, my mother's brother Cornelius and his wife, Nettie, who was my dad's sister, decided to buy a farm in Oklahoma too; so it worked out good for all of us to leave Nebraska and move down to Oklahoma together.

Before we moved, we held a public auction to sell off what we couldn't take along. All the stuff that remained after the auction was loaded in a boxcar together with Uncle Cornelius and Aunt Nettie's belongings and all of it together was shipped by freight train to Oklahoma. Dad bought a used four-cylinder Buick, and Uncle Cornelius had acquired a new Overland car, so we were all set to make the move.

On the morning we left Nebraska, it started to rain. This called for fastening the side curtains on the cars to keep at least some of the rain out. The first day, we got only as far as Belleville, Kansas, because of the muddy roads. It was dark when we got into town, and, for the first time I can remember, we stayed the night in a hotel. The next morning, it was still raining, so we all boarded a passenger train for Oklahoma, and we left the cars in a garage in Belleville. Later, when the roads were dry, Dad and Uncle Cornelius rode back on the train and brought the cars home to Oklahoma .

When we arrived in Oklahoma, we stayed for several months with Grandpa and Grandma Heinrichs in their two-story house. There was a sandy creek joining their farm on the west side, and not far away was a good-sized bridge. I can remember playing under that bridge, building sand castles, and watching minnows swimming in the clear water. The creek still runs through there today just like it did back then.

Uncle Jake Heinrichs wasn't married yet, and he was still living at home when we moved in with Grandpa and Grandma. I was completely fascinated by his full-sized cattle pony and his .22 rifle. Unfortunately, both of them were off limits to a six-year-old kid like me.

After a few months, we finally moved to our new farm. The house had two bedrooms and one kitchen-family room. It had an outside concrete cellar for storing food and an outhouse. After five years, Uncle Abe built us a second story with bedrooms for us kids. The barn had room for four horses, and we used a piano shipping crate to store feed and oats for the horses. Hay was stacked outside, close to the barn. Eventually Abe helped Dad build a granary, a chicken house, and a machine shed. When I was twelve, the barn was enlarged to hold eight horses, and later on an area was added with stanchions for milking ten cows. Until then, we milked outside every morning and night, rain or shine, winter and summer.

When we moved to Oklahoma, my dad was very conscious of water, and he was very critical of the water on our farm. In Nebraska, we had deep wells with good, soft water, but the main well on our farm in Oklahoma was salty. We had a windmill on

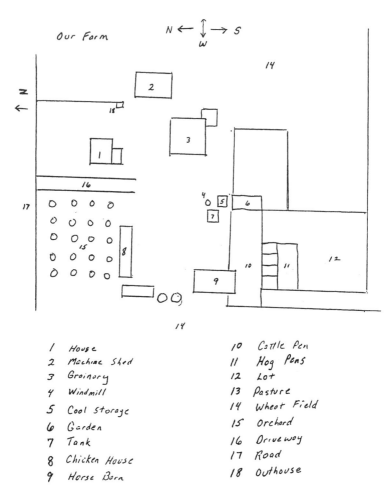

Our Farm

N ← ↕ → S
        W

| | | | |
|---|---|---|---|
| 1 | House | 10 | Cattle Pen |
| 2 | Machine Shed | 11 | Hog Pens |
| 3 | Grainary | 12 | Lot |
| 4 | Windmill | 13 | Pasture |
| 5 | Cool Storage | 14 | Wheat Field |
| 6 | Garden | 15 | Orchard |
| 7 | Tank | 16 | Driveway |
| 8 | Chicken House | 17 | Road |
| 9 | Horse Barn | 18 | Outhouse |

David Ediger drew this layout of his childhood home, including barn and other outbuildings, for a memory book he and his nephew put together.

the well, and the windmill ran all the time. The cattle could drink the water, but it didn't taste good for us to drink, so we had another well by the house. It was a shallow well, and I could pump all the water out of it in about ten minutes of pumping. The well would refill, and it tasted good, so we got by with it. A lot of people in our area had cisterns [to catch rainwater because it was so hard to get a good well]. As soon as Dad had time in the winter, he dug a pond and built a dam in the pasture. That's where I learned to swim.

Altogether, Dad bought 240 acres, with 200 acres of that in cultivation. The farmland wasn't very good land, never was and still isn't, but that's what my dad could afford, and so we had to make the best of it. Not long after, Dad had a chance to rent the Smith quarter across the road west. We also rented the Else place a quarter-mile east. All of these farms were pretty poor, too many alkali spots. We had 300 acres of wheat out, but we really weren't big wheat farmers. We didn't have fertilizer, so twenty bushels an acre was the best we could expect. It helped a lot that we didn't have many expenses: no fertilizer cost; no fuel cost, until we started using the tractors; and no repair bills. We did all that work ourselves.

We got up every morning about 5:00 a.m. to start chores. Dad took care of the horses. He would whistle them up from the pasture and feed them. Each horse had an oats box, and he brushed all the horses while we were milking. Most of the time, it was still pretty dark then, so we would have to use a lantern for a while.

The horses came right up when Dad called them because they knew they would be fed, and sometimes the cows would come up too. Dad usually wanted us to let the cows out at night so they would graze in the pasture while it was cool. I had a pony, and if we needed to run the cows in I liked getting the saddle on and riding out to round them up. We kids all milked; Mom even helped us with that, until we got almost done with the milking, and then she would go in and start breakfast. Mom was good at milking, and she liked to do it. We didn't have to tie the cows or anything—they would just stand in the lot and eat hay while we milked. We had one-legged stools. I carried the milk bucket in one hand, and in the other I carried the stool. I would hold the bucket between my knees and start milking. If you didn't know any better, it didn't seem like a bad job. We had fifteen to twenty milk cows. They were pretty fresh [able to give milk], except for the three months before they were going to calve. When the cow calved, we took the calf off her and started milking her again. The cows milked good, and we had good, big calves to sell as yearlings. We would have about fifty to sell every spring. They were pretty good sized—about five hundred pounds.

Every morning, after we finished milking, we would separate the milk and then feed the calves. We turned our De Levalle cream separator by hand. It had twenty little disks, which you put together and tightened up with a wrench. It was heavy when it was all together. When you cranked it, all the disks would spin inside the separator. The tank and strainer on top would hold two or three buckets of milk. It had to be cranked pretty fast, and it would hum when it was running up to speed. Someone had to keep cranking it for twenty or thirty minutes to run all the milk through. The cream came out one spout into a small bucket, and the skim milk came out the other spout into a big bucket. When we were done, we would rinse it with cold water, then take it apart and clean all the parts with boiling hot water; then it was ready for evening milking and doing everything all over again.

Usually, while my brother Corny was finishing his job cranking the milk through the separator, I would start feeding the calves with the skim milk. I liked that job. We always had a bunch of feeder calves, all over the yard and in the pasture. Dad always sowed wheat early to have wheat pasture, and when the calves were weaned from the skim milk we fed them, they were ready to go on wheat pasture.

We had our own calves plus some Dad would buy for one dollar apiece from other dairymen who didn't want to mess with raising them. The dairies would call Dad when a calf was born, and he would go and bring it home. When we got the calves, we had to teach them to drink out of a bucket. First, you let them suck on your finger, and then you pull them down into the milk. They'd be drinking on their own after about a week. We fed them whole milk for the first month. When they were older, each calf would drink about a gallon. Some cows milked enough to feed three calves, and we usually had enough calves to drink all our milk. If we did have some left over, we would mix it with grain and feed the hogs the slop.

Dad knew about hog feeding; he had done a lot of that in Nebraska. Up there, hogs were fed corn, but in Oklahoma we fed them ground kafer corn which we raised. We usually didn't fatten hogs to market fat [the desired weight for butchering]; we just raised the sows and babies and sold them to others who fed them out.

All the time I was growing up, that's the way we had chores to do, year-round, every morning and evening. By seven o'clock in the morning, we were through with chores and were inside eating breakfast. After all that work, we were ready to eat big. Breakfast was fried eggs, fried potatoes, and oatmeal. When I came in and was washed up, my job was to stir the oatmeal, a whole big kettle full. I had to stay with it so it wouldn't set on at the bottom [of the pan]. Everything we ate was all nourishing stuff that we grew on the farm: real butter we churned ourselves; fresh eggs from our chickens; and milk just thirty minutes from the cow and still warm. It was whole milk and had 4 or 5 percent fat, but we worked that off pretty quickly.

When I started doing fieldwork, I was only about eight years old. My brother Corny and I would do the plowing. We plowed with horses. Corny was thirteen; so he could look out for me and see that the harnesses were set right and all that. We had a Case tractor, but we used it to run the thresher. You had to buy fuel for a tractor, and we already had horses. They could eat oats.

We had riding moldboard plows, pulled by four horses. Each plow had two twelve-inch moldboards. We didn't moldboard-plow all our ground each year because it was slow going and we couldn't get it all done before the ground dried out. After the ground was too dried out, we plowed the rest of it with disk plows. [Moldboarding, disking, and other types of tillage were differentiated by the type of plow blade used to accomplish the task. Moldboard and disk blades were used to break through wheat stubble that remained in the field after harvest. The blades turned the topsoil, leaving it in large clumps.]

We always had good horses and good harnesses. For field-work, we hooked them up four horses abreast. The only time we ever had them two in front, two behind them, was for pulling the wagon down the road when it was muddy. Other-wise, two horses could pull the wagon. For plowing with the moldboard plow, the two horses on the right side would be your best team. They were the older, stronger horses, and they knew how to turn corners. The other two horses would be your younger, less-experienced horses. When you were pulling the disk or the drills, you would have your good team in the middle, and the other two horses on either side of them. We tried to plow five or six inches deep, but that pulled pretty hard on some of our ground. We had a handle on each side of the plow and could adjust either side deeper as needed. You could almost never make a whole round without adjusting the plow some. It would just pull too hard in some places.

For us, our main team of horses was our pride and joy. The pair had to be matched up for height and strength, and that was the art of it. At any farm sale, the horses always sold first. I think working with the horses was one of the best things about farming back then. For fieldwork, the double-tree hitches could be adjusted so the lad plowing could have control proportionate to the horses' strength and size. When we were plowing with the moldboard or disk plow, the front right horse would know to stay in the furrow [made by the previous round with the plow], the other horses would be out of the furrow. The main-team horses knew how to turn corners—they had to go past the plowed part, and then they would come around short. That left only a small corner unplowed; we would come back with the disk later to clean that up. We did a good job. We could almost finish a twenty-acre patch in one day; then we could start a new field the next day.

We walked the horses back to be home at noon. They took deep drinks of cold water from the tank, and then we put them in the barn. We fed them oats and forked them some hay in the manger. Corny and I would eat dinner and relax while the horses were resting. By 1:30, we were ready to walk the horses back to the field and hook them up. The horses were my friends. I'd rub their noses when they were resting and talk to them. They were like any pet. They liked to please you, if they were treated right. I always got attached to the horses I worked with. We always had dogs too. They liked to follow along behind while we plowed, and then they could catch a rabbit. [The activity of plowing would disturb rabbits, forcing them to run from the fields. This, in turn, gave the dogs opportunity for a chase.] That was their fun.

After we had plowed or disked all our ground, we would wait for a rain and then begin harrowing. [This type of tilling broke the clumps of earth created by moldboarding and disking into smaller particles of soil.] We used a spike-tooth harrow. We kids were small enough that we could have put a board on the harrow and [ridden] on it [that is, let themselves be pulled around by the horses similar to riding on a wagon], but Dad thought we might fall off and get our foot stuck, and so I walked behind it.

It didn't really work the ground down very much, but it was all we had then.

We started sowing wheat about the first of September so we could get wheat pasture. We always sowed with horses. When you sowed with horses and the drill, you didn't just go flying across the field; you had to sit on the back and make sure the tubes [which scattered the seed from the drill] were all open and everything was working right. That was Dad's job. He always wanted to do the sowing himself. He knew just how he wanted it done, and he was very particular. I would be harrowing or spring-toothing [another form of fine-tilling, designated by the type of plow used] ahead of the drills with the other horses. Our first drill was an Emerson. It was cheap. I guess that's why we had it. A few years later, we moved up to a Van Brunt. It was the best kind of drill. They were bought out by John Deere. It was a single-disk drill with fluted feet like John Deere drills still have now. You could sow twenty acres on a long day with good horses. Once Dad sowed 120 acres in one week, and that was a lot. We bragged on that for a long time.

Fieldwork was different then, and so was work in the house. Cooking for a family was an all-day job. We ate a lot of German food—lots of dumplings and homemade noodles. When someone got sick, you would cook up a big batch of chicken noodle soup, and that would fix them up.

It seems like we had a lot of good seasonings then that we don't pay as much attention to now. Herbs and dill—all those things were raised in the garden and then dried. They stayed good all winter. We always had a big garden—potatoes, tomatoes, onions, beans, peas, cucumbers. Sometimes we planted peas with the wheat drill on the edge of the wheat field where the wheat was thin. We had lots of peas then.

I remember when they came out with the pressure cooker for canning— before that we used hot water and boiled the jars. The pressure cooker was a big help. The ladies pressure-cooked all summer long to have fruits and vegetables ready for winter. All this food was kept in the cellar. From one end of the cellar to the other, there would be shelves full of Ball fruit jars, half gallons and quarts. We used big jars, not the little pint ones.

Once a week, we churned cream to make butter. We had a churn which held seven or ten gallons of cream. You cranked for thirty minutes or so, until the cream would turn to butter. We had a mold that was big enough to make six pounds. It made pretty butter blocks too. We had a mold once with a pattern on it. When the butter was pushed out, it had a picture of a cow on the top. I remember that mold from the time I was very young.

The color of the butter was determined by how much green stuff the cows got. If they were on wheat pasture, the butter got dark yellow. Dad always saw to it that the cows had enough green stuff so the butter would have a good color. If you had the cows on too much wheat pasture, it made the butter taste kind of green too, so we had to regulate that. Sometimes we would take the cows off the wheat for a couple of hours before we shut them in at night.

We didn't need to buy much from the grocery store—sugar, flour. People who bought coffee usually just bought the coffee beans and roasted them and ground them themselves. The few groceries we did need we traded for butter we had churned or eggs we had raised ourselves. We ate as good or better than we do now because the food was all good stuff we had raised ourselves. Of course, we needed a lot of energy because we burned a lot of calories working.

Mom would never let Dad say grace until she had bread on the table. Bread is the staff of life, and we were thanking God for the bread, so it was important to have bread there when you were praying. I guess the thinking was that if you didn't have anything else to eat, if you had bread you were still all right, and we should be fully thankful for it. Of course, the bread on the table was pretty obvious because it was a loaf about eight inches by twelve inches long. When mom would slice the bread, she didn't cut it on the table, she always stood up and held it in her arm and cut it across. I don't know why she did it that way. My dad knew how she felt about thanking God for the bread, and he fully agreed with her about it. If everyone got in too big a hurry or if she had forgotten the bread, she would say, "Vacht a bate" ("Wait a minute"), and she would go get the bread; then we all stood up and gave thanks to God.

During the wintertime we had catch-up jobs to do. One job I didn't care for was cleaning out the chickenhouse. We fixed fence, and it seemed like we had a lot of fences because our fields were smaller. We always had a lot of hogs and baby pigs to take care of.

Another job in winter was cutting firewood. Often, we would cut trees from a creek someone wanted to clear out. One year, a tornado went through east of us and knocked down a bunch of trees. We cut the wood and hauled it all home.

Dad spent most all of his time in the winter working the machinery over. To him there was no excuse for not having all your machinery worked over and in A-1 shape for summer. We didn't take anything to the dealer to get it worked on. We did it all ourselves, even major engine repairs. If we had to overhaul an engine, we did that at home, and Dad liked to do it.

At first, people didn't know how to fix an internal combustion engine. In Kansas City, there was a Sweeney's School of Mechanics. You could go there and learn the basics of engine repair. Pete Cornelson attended Sweeney's and learned about engines, and Dad hired him to come and overhaul our engines. Dad learned a lot from Pete.

On the car, the crankshaft bearings always needed adjustment. They had shims, and every so often if you were going to take a trip or something, you adjusted the bearings. After they were tightened, it was hard to start the engine by hand, and you had to pull it with a team of horses. All our tires were hard. They had sixty to eighty pounds of air in them. Sixty pounds was normal for a car, and when you pumped sixty pounds by hand you had a pretty good workout.

In the evenings in the winter, I did homework and studied my Sunday school lesson. We played a lot of checkers and the like. We got good at checkers. We had all kinds of table games that we played too. We didn't have many different magazines to read, but we worked through the Ward's and Sears catalogues thoroughly—the wish books. I read a lot of Western story magazines. My folks weren't too thrilled about that. I bought the Western stories used at the pawn shop for fifteen cents apiece.

We wrote letters to relatives. Mom especially wrote a lot of letters to her brothers and sisters and Dad's brothers and sisters. That would be about fifteen families to keep in touch with. Then we kids would write to our cousins in Nebraska too. "Dear cousin, We are all fine here. Hope you are the same." Anyway, it gave us something to do.

The holiday celebrations, especially Christmas dinner, were something that all the grandchildren looked forward to. We loved getting the brown paper sacks Grandmother made for us kids, filled with Christmas candies, dried fruits, home-baked cookies, and peppermint candy. The big dried prunes in our sacks along with raisins were the same kind we used in Pluma Mus or with sweet gravy; we called it Manschel.

When I was a kid, the adults never played games or anything when they got together. Playing card games was too much like what the world did. We just sang hymns and songs, and someone would pray and lead in devotions. When the ladies of the church had a bridal or baby shower, they would all sit in a circle. They would go around and each one would quote a Bible verse, and that was the entertainment. It was pretty low-key stuff.

Everybody in our family but Mom played instruments. We did a lot of playing and practicing in the wintertime. After

supper, my mom would say, "I'll do the dishes; you go and play."
So we would. I learned to play the violin, banjo, ukulele, and
later on I learned the Hawaiian steel guitar. You could play
melodies with that. We played church songs. We had a string
band of a dozen or so neighbors. Some of the church deacons
played in it. We practiced once a week in the winter, and we
played at church conferences.

In the winter, the cattle were on wheat pasture, and they ate
straw from the straw stacks. [During wheat threshing, the
residual straw and chaff were blown out through a spout on the
threshing machine, thereby creating a large straw stack.] We had
some big stacks, twenty-five feet high and eighty feet long. We
tried to put the stacks about one-eighth mile from the barn.
[Farmers were careful to have the threshing machine set up to
run near where they wished to have the straw stack located.]
We usually had six or eight teams and wagons to help us. The
more wagons you had, the bigger you could make your stacks
of straw that blew out of the thresher. If we had enough teams,
we could make big stacks, and that big straw stack was what you
wanted for the cattle in the winter.

We would pitch the hay, and Mom always did the stacking on
top until I got old enough. If the stacks were flat, they would
shed water, and the middle would stay good. The cattle would
eat into them and make caves, fifteen feet deep. We kids weren't
supposed to, but we would play in these caves when the cattle
weren't in there.

The stacks held up good after they had settled. I trapped
skunks on the sides of the stacks because they would hang
around those warm places. Sometimes we had some straw left
over, and, since it didn't keep good in the summer, we would
take the hayrack and load up the stack bottoms by hand and
scatter it on the fields where we were going to plant feed. We
hardly ever burned a stack bottom, but some people did, and,
once they were lit, the stack bottoms would burn for a week.

In the winter, we loaded hay with pitchforks onto the hay wagon and then hauled it to the cattle and pitched some off. Sometimes, if we had them shut up in the yard, we fed them there. Most all the farms had haystacks around, but we didn't put up too much hay because, as I mentioned, we made straw stacks when we threshed.

Harvest was certainly the busiest time of year. Lots of extra help would move into the community, and everyone would get after it. The way we harvested and threshed took a lot of help. We used binders [a machine that cut and tied shocks of wheat] and separators [threshers] while I was growing up. At first, we pulled our binder with horses, but then we hooked it up so we could pull it with our tractor.

We started cutting and binding our wheat about two weeks before it was ripe, when the straw still had some green in it. We cut our oats first and knocked it out. We had a seven-foot McCormick Deering. It had a mechanical knotter. When my dad was a kid, they tied the bundles together with wheat straw wound into a cord. He showed me how he used to do it. You could adjust the binder to make the bundles the size you wanted them. The mechanical knotter would come around and tie the bundle with binder twine.

Dad ran the binder, and he always made good bundles. Dad was always very particular that the bundle be tied right in the middle. Then it would be balanced. The bundles needed to be good because they had to be handled three times [in making shocks, in lifting them for transporting, and in off-loading for threshing]. When we threshed someplace and had bad bundles to work with, Dad would say it looked like they had a ten-year-old kid running the binder.

With good bundles, it was easy to make good shocks. The binder had a bundle carrier on the side that held six bundles. You didn't have to stop to drop them off; you just tripped a lever with your foot, and the bundles would drop off. On the next round through the field, you would drop them at the same place; so you ended up with long rows of bundles. The wheat heads were all on the top of the bundle, and you would lean two bundles together and then stand ten more bundles around them until you had a round shock.

The shockers, usually us kids, went down the rows of dropped bundles making a shock every couple of swaths. If there were a lot of us kids, we tried to keep up with the bundles as they came off the binder. It was fun for us kids to try and keep up that way; then we could say we had just pulled off the field with the binder and it was all shocked.

When the shocks were ripe [dry enough for threshing], we would get the separator [thresher] set up and start hauling in bundles. Each team of two horses pulled a hayrack, and we pitched the bundles on that. The horse teams were trained to move along the shock rows while you walked beside and pitched the bundles on, saying, "Whoa" to stop and "Giddap" to go. Usually, we had a field pitcher, an extra man, to help load the wagons in the field by placing bundles on top, so the guy with the team could make a taller load, but sometimes we did it with just one guy on a wagon.

By the time that I was old enough to remember, tractors had already replaced steam engines. The steam engines were very powerful, but they were harder to keep running and not at all practical for fieldwork. The tractors ran the threshers with a belt like the steam engines had done before. [The operation was set up by pulling the threshing machine into position, once a farmer decided where he wanted his straw stack, and maneuvering it into exact alignment with the tractor that would provide its power. Any deviation from the proper axis would throw off the long, wide leather belt connecting the separator-pulley to the engine's clutch-pulley. It was necessary to ease the tractor backward to obtain the correct belt tension, then the machine could be started and the bundles fed into it (Green 1977, 71–72).

At the threshing site, we had one hayrack pulled up on each side of the separator, so one guy had to pitch his bundles over the belt. You had to place the bundles just right into the feeder house. Dad was particular that each bundle was lengthwise and ran head-first into the cylinder; otherwise, the heads would thresh hard. It made a big difference. When the wagons were loaded in the field, all the bundles were placed with the heads toward the inside. Then they would be lined up and ready to go into the thresher.

Dad and Uncle Abe owned a threshing machine and tractor. They threshed for the neighbors while Corny and I did the plowing at home. In 1928, we bought a 1527 John Deere, and we used it on the threshing machine for several years. It burned kerosene and had steel wheels. We used it for heavy fieldwork too, but we still used horses for all the harrowing and sowing.

When we boys got older, Dad bought Abe out, and then Corny ran the separator, and I ran the tractor. Most of the farmers in the area had their threshing done by a big commercial outfit [custom crews of as many as twenty or more men who traveled from farm to farm during harvest season (Green 1977, 71–72)]. [The owner of the equipment] was someone who would move in, not a farmer from here. He would provide all the hayracks for hauling bundles and all the guys to run the machinery. My dad and Abe charged about half as much to thresh because we had the farmers provide some of the labor and machinery. Each farmer we worked for would usually furnish a rack and team and a pitcher [additional person to help].

It was my job to keep track of how much help each farmer had provided during the threshing; when the season was over, we would even it all out. Dad usually had only two extra guys hired, plus my cousin. Dad would get her to stay with us and help cook for the threshing crews. Of course, some of the bigger farmers in the area also owned their own separator and enough wheat of their own to keep it busy.

The basic design of the separator was like the conventional machines [designed to operate wheat combines] today. In the front was the feeder house and it pulled the bundles into the machine. The separator man would stand on top of the feeder and watch the bundles feed in. The feeder wouldn't start turning until the cylinder was up to speed; it had a weighted clutch on it.

The feeder had knives on it that would turn and cut the twine as it pulled the wheat bundles into the cylinder. The guy on the tractor would watch, too; you couldn't just dump the wheat in there. The thresher had a cylinder. Those cylinder teeth knocked the straw into small pieces.

From the cylinder, the wheat ran through a beater to beat it loose from the head. A grain pan underneath the whole thing caught the grain. It had a corrugated bottom to shake the grain to the back. After the beater, the straw walker would move the straw out the back and shake out any remaining grain. It had a fan underneath to blow the chaff out and also a return elevator to rethresh any unthreshed heads. The straw all moved back to the blower and blew up the tube and onto the straw stack. You could lengthen or shorten the tube, and it had a nozzle at the end with a rope to shoot the straw just where you wanted it. If you knew what you were doing, you could make good stacks. My dad was particular about the stack, and he could see from where he was running the tractor what the stack looked like.

Dad always ran the tractor until I was old enough to do it. You always had to have someone on the tractor watching everything, ready to disengage the clutch. We called him the engineer, and that was always my dad. Then that was my job. I did it for many summers. I would drive the tractor down the road, pulling the separator. When I got to the field, we would find out where they wanted the straw stack. When the separator was in place, we would unhook the separator and bring the tractor around so that it faced the separator. They would put the belt on, and I would back the tractor into the belt. When the belt was still slack, the pulley would start to turn, and I could see when it was lined up; then I got it tight enough so that it was off the ground. It weighed 150 pounds, so it didn't slip.

Once the threshing got started, my main job was to watch everything, with my hand on the clutch. If somebody slipped and threw a pitchfork into the feeder house, I had to be right on the clutch and stop the separator before anything got into the cylinder. A good engine man had his eye right on the feeder house, ready to shut everything down if horses got spooked or the blower belt came off. The whole separator could plug up tight with straw if you weren't watching.

Before I was big enough to run the tractor, my job was to take the dump rake and clean up after we had some of the shocks picked up. There would be some loose stuff left from shocks that had broken and such, and I would rake along the shock row and dump what I got in piles. They would pick that up and thresh it too. I did a lot of after-raking around where we had threshed. We hurried at harvest time, but we took time to do all those extra things and get all we could.

On the separator, the grain went up an elevator and ran into a little bin that held a half-bushel. You could adjust it with a set screw to get an accurate half-bushel weight. It would trip and dump out wheat whenever it filled up. Then the wheat ran down a chute into one of two or three waiting grain wagons. When we were starting at a new farm, they would have me measure it with a half-bushel bucket when it came out. The farmer always wanted it to be completely full, because he paid by the bushel. We had to check it when we changed to a different field or variety of wheat, since some wheat is heavier. Dad was always generous to have a good half-bushel, because the farmers would get a better deal that way. I remember we charged ten cents a bushel for threshing the first year we started.

The half-bushel bin had a mechanical tally that turned numbers, and it would run up to one thousand. Lots of times, we would put nine hundred bushels a day through it. We would have two or three fifty-bushel grain wagons backed up next to the separator. The little bin had a spout, and so when it dumped you could run the grain to any one of the wagons. Sometimes we used a trough that would put the grain to the front of the wagon, but mostly it would dump the grain on the back, and I had to shovel it to the front.

For our own crop, we filled up our granary at home and hauled the rest to the Kremlin [Oklahoma] grain elevator. The wagons didn't have any dumping mechanism. We shoveled the wheat off the wagon into the granary. The wagons were designed so one guy could shovel from the front and one from the back. Before I was old enough to run the tractor, I hauled wheat while the threshing was going on. I could make one trip to Kremlin in the morning and another one in the afternoon. Usually we had at least one wagon on the road to Kremlin and maybe another one going to the bin at the farmstead; so it took quite a bit of arranging to manage all that. That was the exciting part. It was the busiest time of the year, harvest time.

I remember the first combine [this machine combined the multistep harvest into a single set of processes performed in the wheat field] I ever saw. It was in the field next to our school. Henry Kroeker had got one. He was a big farmer. It was pulled by horses, but pretty soon after that they put a tractor on it. It didn't have a wheat bin on it; [instead,] the horses walked alongside of it and pulled the wagon, and the wheat ran continuously from the combine out into the wagon.

The best yield we ever made was twenty-one bushels to the acre, but some farmers who had better farms could make thirty on a good year. Of course, we didn't use any fertilizer then, except for manure sometimes, and our varieties [of wheat] had not been bred up to a have a longer head and other good characteristics that wheat has now, but even though our yields were fifteen to twenty bushels [per acre], the straw was like thirty- to forty-bushel wheat is now. We usually sowed a bushel and half per acre. Tractor-pulled combines [which cut and threshed the wheat in the field] came into use in about 1933.

# PART TWO

# *Confrontation*

## THE GREAT WAR, 1914–18

Autumn drifts gently into Northwest Oklahoma. The mercury slides slowly downward during September, bringing some relief from the blistering August heat. The eighty-plus September temperatures feel mild in comparison. The first vibrant blades of wheat grow their way through the red Oklahoma dirt and make their stand during these last hot weeks of summer. Greener than grass, in no time at all they are about as thick and tall as most suburban lawns. Pastures pale from the relentless summer sun are upstaged by the vibrant green of newly sown wheat fields.

The colors of fall show themselves delicately and slowly. Thick native meadows that remain intact still make cover for quail, pheasants, wild turkey, and deer. The sun-yellowed buffalo grass, bluestem, mesquite, purplish ironweed, and clover lie down low. Gradually a gold hue begins to run down tree branches and up creekbed bushes. Sunflowers bloom on late into October. Plum thickets take on a lovely ruby tint, and hedge apples glisten among brittle leaves. The gullies and draws shine with the auburn of elm, red cedar, and tawny cottonwood.

Fall lingers in Oklahoma, procrastinating into November and occasionally managing to hang on until early December. When it goes, it's nearly always swept away by a cold, wild wind from the west and north that roars down out of the Rockies, rolls over the panhandle, and tears through the level grass and wheat of Northwest Oklahoma, picking up speed as it goes. It sweeps the trees clean, scatters leaves everywhere, and downs any false hope for a temperate winter. The winter wind pierces heavy clothing and illusions. It is frigid and persistent and tough to cope with. But Oklahoma wheat, tenacious and resilient, holds verdant despite winter's most severe conditions.

When World War I blew through, it exploded the sleepy frontier life of Mennonites in Oklahoma into the twentieth century. It rocked the very foundation of Mennonitism awake to home-front as well as battlefront hostilities. Reaction from the general public to anti-German propaganda shook the separate social existence of the Mennonites to its core. Moreover, lack of support from any official government policy in recognizing the status of pacifists left Mennonite men with no alternative to military service.

These threats that jeopardized the very existence of the Mennonite ethic—nonresistance to violence and maintenance of an isolated society—are the subject of part two. The era of the First World War is locked in Mennonite memories as a period of siege. The attacks are framed as dangerously hostile, unwarranted assaults on individuals and groups because of their religious beliefs, attacks that were accompanied by coerced conformity to the dominant majority. Despite the extreme stress under which Mennonites lived during the war years, the individual accounts center not so much on hardships as on family, friends, work, school, and church—the details of everyday life. The events leading to and surrounding World War I are covered in chapter 6. Here the court-martial of Pvt. Henry Becker, who was sentenced to life in Leavenworth prison, reveals the price paid for religious principle.

# The Meaning of Freedom

A number of the men in our community who took a position for peace
found themselves in prison.
        —*Wilford Ulrich*

In the years that followed statehood, the first power-driven machinery—tractors, trucks, and other equipment—began to make farm life less strenuous. Still, it could be said that life on Oklahoma farms did not become easier with these power-driven implements so much as it simply became more bearable. With years of perseverance and favorable weather, farm yields continued by spurts to get better. Consumer goods that farmers needed were more easily obtained. High-quality leather shoes and "specialty" items were frequently in stock at the local general stores, but cash to purchase the goods remained scarce. Oranges and bananas were considered luxuries. Flour sacks still provided material for many women's wear. Job opportunities outside farming remained limited, and farm income, though improving, remained low (Todd and Curti 1961).

The fate of the early Mennonite churches mirrored the uncertain ups and downs of prairie life. At statehood in 1907, there were as many as thirty-seven Mennonite congregations meeting in the Cherokee Outlet (Erb 1974). Most were associated with the General Conference or with the Mennonite Brethren. Many of the first group of churches, those established prior to 1900, continue to this day. A few, however, did not remain viable. The Medford Mennonite Brethren church disbanded in 1910 (Goertzen 1990). Both the Zion General Conference church at Lucien (Haury 1981) and the Mennonite Brethren church at Lookout dissolved in 1912 (Goertzen 1990). The (Old) Mennonite Church had found enough followers to start up a congregation at Newkirk, but dwindled in number and dispersed in 1906. The church closed its doors sometime around 1910 (Erb 1974). For the most part, though, the years after statehood were years of growth for Mennonite congregations. Across Northwest Oklahoma, the churches increased in membership and stability. What defined Mennonitism during these years, however, was not the church life of the group but the verities of modern, worldwide warfare, which spread across the ocean and reached deep into the very heart of Oklahoma.

During the years prior to 1914, Mennonites as a group had come to be looked upon by society outside their community as just one among many elements that made up the population of Northwest Oklahoma. There was a certain ambiguity to their identity. Although they dressed plainly, their plain dress was not particularly distinctive because the financial position of most of the general population dictated similar dress. Their thrift and devotion to simplicity resulted in an austere mode of living, yet their austerity was not particularly distinctive since many around them lived in near-poverty. On the whole, their farming endeavors were similar to those of their non-Mennonite neighbors, and their children more often than not attended the same schools. They did not stand out as an exclusive, radical religious sect. They were noticeable simply because they spoke German, associated with their own kind, and avoided politics. They were viewed by the outside community and their own kind as well not so much as a group that withdrew from society as a group that moved parallel to it.

The Mennonites considered themselves 100 percent Americans. They worked hard, paid taxes, stayed out of trouble, and exercised their First Amendment right to freedom of religion. They identified with the American "creed." The First Amendment guarantee of freedom of religion had played a large part in their decision to make America their home (Rippley 1976). They had come to America on the promise of that freedom. Opposition to war, to capital punishment, and to the taking of human life in any form were fundamental tenets of the Mennonite faith. One of the primary reasons the Mennonites had emigrated from Russia was to maintain their doctrine of nonresistance (Smith 1927, 1957).

As a group, Mennonites understood the promise of religious freedom to mean that no one would be forced to do what went against one's own conscience. The United States government never directly granted a request from emissaries of the Russian Mennonites to exempt the immigrants from military service (Smith 1927); nevertheless, the guarantee of freedom of religion under the First Amendment and the assurances of politicians and businessmen interested in promoting settlement in the West indicated to the Mennonites that they would not be obligated to participate in future wars (Haury 1981). Mennonites came to America, moved west, and eventually settled in Oklahoma, confident that their particular idea of religious freedom and its caveat, pacifism, were guaranteed. Not confronted by war, the issue was largely ignored during the first twenty years of Mennonite life in Oklahoma (Haury 1981).

In this atmosphere, Mennonite loyalty to their adopted country was taken for granted by Mennonites and by those in the larger society. Through the process of living alongside their "English" neighbors, Mennonites over the years became familiar with the American way of doing things and with local customs. Alternatively, Mennonite economic advances through hard work, thrift, prompt retirement of debt, and sound farming practices were admired by the community at large. While the Mennonites did stand apart from society, they and the larger society were both comfortable with this pattern of marginality.

When war began in Europe in 1914, however, the United States was flooded with anti-German propaganda, and the Mennonites were suddenly cut off from mainstream America. The propaganda, exported primarily from Great Britain, was effective not only against Germany; it also turned public opinion away from German culture and German Americans (Sowell 1981). Early on, there were Americans who supported Germany's cause in the war, some of them of German heritage, but as the war in Europe continued, fewer and fewer expressed a favorable attitude toward the Central Powers (Rippley 1976).

Nevertheless, the rancor spread. Anti-German feelings in the United States mounted as events appeared to be leading America ever closer to involvement in the war. Even President Wilson spoke disparagingly of "hyphenated Americans" (Sowell 1981). This was understood to mean "German-Americans," whose loyalty was supposedly as divided as their label (Sowell 1981). The anti-German sentiment that was aimed at presenting Germany as an aggressor and at turning American opinion against the German nation roused a powerful backlash against German Americans. Public opinion galvanized against them as the nation was caught up in a rising war spirit.

While the American nation was on its way to war, the German-speaking Mennonites in Oklahoma remained neutral in their thinking. They rejected all war. They had no sympathy with Germany's war policies (Coon 1988), but they, like many other Americans of German descent antipathetic to the German war cause, were snared by anti-German hysteria.

When Mennonites came to America, their theology of religious freedom implied to them the freedom to establish autonomous communities impervious to governmental control or sanction from the outside world. Life in rural Oklahoma had necessitated some adaptation of Mennonite traditions and customs. Over the years, economics, public schooling, interchange with non-Mennonite neighbors, and other circumstances within and outside Mennonite society resulted in a certain amount of Mennonite acculturation. Cradled in the pioneering spirit of rugged individualism prevalent in the early days of western settlement, it was easy for Mennonites in Northwest Oklahoma to exist apart from but alongside the social milieu. The vast majority of Mennonites found no conflict between the practice of their religion and their loyalty to America (Juhnke 1975). Pacifism as a tenet of their belief system was therefore constitutionally sanctioned, or so they thought. They were astounded to learn that others did not hold the same opinion (Huxman 1993, 283).

On the whole, Mennonites were shocked that their interpretation of the First Amendment was not an interpretation acceptable to the majority of Americans living in Oklahoma. Most of the general population did not perceive religious freedom from the same point of view as the Mennonites. For the majority of Americans, religious freedom was aligned with individual freedom—the freedom of an individual to worship how, when, and where he or she pleased. From this point of view, there was little or no relationship between worship and fighting for one's country. This difference in perspective, together with anti-German propaganda and rising war sentiment, worked to place the Mennonites at an extreme disadvantage. In the years preceding America's entry into the war and continuing throughout World War I, Mennonites were made objects of shame and abuse. They were easy targets for fear and anger in an America that raged against the German empire.

But Mennonites were not the only ones to suffer ridicule, coercion, and violence. As a group, German-speaking persons and those with German-sounding names were treated like outcasts (Coon 1988). German language instruction was dropped from the curriculum of public schools, and the names of towns throughout Oklahoma were changed. Korn became Corn; Kiel became Loyal; and Bismarck became Wright (Coon 1988). In Major County, where six (the largest number of) Mennonite churches were located, notices were posted on buildings that read, "God almighty understands the American language. Address him only in that tongue" (Rohrs 1981).

The German language press was particularly hard-hit by the discrimination. Between 1885 and World War I, there were at least sixteen German language newspapers published in Oklahoma. These papers carried local news from German settlements in Oklahoma and

Kansas, news from Germany, information about farming and agriculture, and local advertising (Rohrs 1981). Only two of these papers
remained in existence after the war. The others were closed by threats
and/or loss of circulation and advertising. The last survivor continued
to be printed in Enid until 1935 (Rohrs 1981).

Largely because the Mennonites from Russia and Europe spoke
German and because they did not favor America's entering into any
war, they became prime targets of physical violence and harassment.
A Mennonite was taken from his home and painted yellow. Mennonite
communities were vandalized, and their personal property destroyed.
There was at least one tar-and-feathering (Coon 1988; Rohrs 1981).
And these activities did not lessen with America's entry into the war
in 1917.

Some of the discrimination against Mennonites and other German-
speaking people was an outgrowth of civilian councils of defense. Set
up nationwide, the councils were intended to generate support for
the war effort through armed forces recruitment and fund raising
(Rohrs 1981). Some of the councils in Oklahoma, however, turned
their activities toward building what they termed "patriotic attitudes,"
which, in reality, bordered on the extralegal (Coon 1988). Instead of
curtailing such activities, the Oklahoma state council expanded the
scope of its mission.

Across the state, German language use continued to be a focal point
of contention. In May 1918, the twenty-five county councils in Oklahoma were directed to forbid the use of German in any public
meeting, including religious services (Rohrs 1981). Just as insidious
were the disparaging remarks and other informal sanctions that circulated through the general population and were to some degree
successful in stifling use of the German language.

The public was on edge, and it was difficult for those of German
heritage to predict just what might set off controversy. For example,
simply hearing a language the majority of Oklahomans could not
understand being transmitted over the state's recently installed telephone systems sent shock waves through the general population. Tele-

phone exchanges transmitted in German over rural party lines became an immediate concern for public safety. In Grant County, a civilian council of defense instructed the telephone company officials to prohibit the use of German in telephone conversations (Rohrs 1981).

It was during this time that publicity drives promoted the purchase of U.S. war bonds. Highly publicized, the bond sales were supported by broad segments of the general public as a sign of patriotism; they were seen to be a validation of the American cause. Liberty Bonds were advertised widely, and large numbers of purchases were interpreted as widespread community support for the war effort. With all segments of the population being encouraged to buy, Mennonites began to feel subtle and not-so-subtle pressure to contribute as a show of national allegiance. At best, most Mennonites resented the pressure placed on them to buy bonds. At worst, the bonds represented an onerous extortion, a literal buyout of religious conviction. Some Mennonites purchased the bonds. Others did not, because to those Mennonites the bonds represented an investment in military armament.

The separate paths that once ensured peaceful coexistence between Mennonites and the dominant society had crossed. If resentment seethed in the Mennonite population, fear was by far the strongest emotion. In practically all communities, Mennonites experienced the intimidation of insinuations whispered or insults shouted. Fear kept Mennonites at home. Hoping to stay out of harm's way, they avoided going into town to shop or conduct farm-related business. They relied on their churches for emotional support and for personal contact. The churches served as a refuge for like believers, but at the same time to the outside world they stood as symbols of resistance.

Mennonite churches became focal points, the markers of the tension between the group and larger society. In the eastern part of the state one Sunday afternoon in 1918, the Eden church, part of the General Conference, was burned to the ground. After that, the congregation held their services in a member's barn until it too was burned (McKee, Coon, and Kroeker 1988). The persecution became

intense enough to drive a few Mennonites out of Oklahoma. Some
of them found refuge in Kansas; others fled to Canada.

At the outset of the war, Mennonite men, like all other American
men of draft age, faced induction into the military. The Selective
Service Act of 1917 provided for exemption from combat, but it did
not define noncombatant service (Juhnke 1989). The definition of what
exactly did constitute noncombatant service was of particular concern
to Mennonites, since about half of all conscientious objectors during
World War I were young Mennonite men (Hartzler 1922). If Mennonite men were drafted away from farming, which was considered
vital to the war effort, what would their status be in the military?

No complete records detail the exact disposition of Mennonite
men in Northwest Oklahoma eligible for the draft during World War
I. A few may have been exempted from service, some may have served
in the military as noncombatants, and others may have served in the
regular army. Overall, Mennonites sought exemption but found local
draft boards in Oklahoma to be unsympathetic to conscientious objectors (Coon 1988).

Nationwide, Mennonite men were frequently inducted directly into
military camps (Hostetler 1983). Some of the resisters were furloughed
to farm programs, but in Northwest Oklahoma many Mennonite men
who were of draft age were inducted into the military. There the
conscience of the conscientious objector met the iron will of the U. S.
Army. A pattern of behavior emerged among Mennonite inductees—
they generally refused to wear military uniforms or to participate in
training (Hostetler 1983). This behavior, of course, flew in the face of
army discipline. At Camp Travis, in San Antonio, Texas, at least forty-
one conscientious objectors, many from the southwestern states, were
found guilty at court-martial, handcuffed, and sent by train to Fort
Leavenworth, Kansas (Coon 1988), to serve out their time. The original life sentences they were handed were reduced to twenty-five years
at about the time they entered prison.

When the war ended in Europe on November 11, 1918, the
announcement was greeted with great joy across all of Oklahoma

(Gibson 1984). The joy for Mennonite congregations, however, was tempered with concern, for as late as March 1919, 135 conscientious objectors still remained imprisoned at Fort Leavenworth, some of them Oklahomans. Of those court-martialed at Camp Travis, five had died during their imprisonment.* Among those remaining were six men from Northwest Oklahoma (Juhnke 1989, 236). Five of them— Henry J. Becker, Simon Unruh, Jake Jantz, Joe Jantz, and Pete Unruh—were of the New Hopedale church in Meno. The sixth, Albert C. Voth, was from the Mennonite church in Goltry. It was April 1919 before the first of these men were released from prison and given dishonorable discharges from the army.

From that point on there was no going back. The reality of World War I—the draft, the anti-German activity, the fear, the lingering male-volence—all of it demanded change in the Mennonite way of life. The pressures brought to bear proved too much for some congregations. A Mennonite Brethren congregation at Coy, established in 1912, lasted only short three years (Goertzen 1990). The Bethanian General Confer-ence Mennonite church, also at Coy, dissolved a year later (Haury 1981). The Lahoma Mennonite Brethren church struggled on until 1923 (Goertzen 1990). Fostering new congregations also proved difficult during the immediate postwar years. One church was launched in 1918. It was the first and only congregation of Krimmer Mennonite Brethren in Northwest Oklahoma and was set up in Medford, where a group of General Conference Mennonites had had a church since 1897. The Krimmer group, too, was short-lived. It failed in 1923 (Goertzen 1990).

Direct pressure from outside brought on during the war was followed by a restructuring of thinking within the group after the war.

---

*John Klaassen, the son of the Reverend Michael Klaassen of Cordell, died of the influenza in 1918 while serving his sentence at Leavenworth. The body was shipped home in uniform. His father removed the American flag draped over the casket and put civilian clothes on his son before he performed the burial service. This act aroused such furor among the non-German community in Cordell that Pastor Klaassen, fearing for his life, left that same day for Canada (Sprunger 1986). Later, about half his church membership followed (Kroeker 1989).

Part of the initial reaction of Mennonites to the wartime events was triggered by the group's collective memory. They had suffered for their stand on peace in Switzerland, in Germany, in West Prussia, and in Russia. They hadn't expected it in America. Regardless of the suffering, the Mennonites emerged from World War I strengthened as a religious community, and largely because of the experiences of the war, Mennonites across the United States felt an inner compunction to serve the war-needy. When released by the government, some Mennonite men joined a relief unit in France under Quaker auspices (Hostetler 1983). This humanitarian effort marked the beginning of combined large-scale, voluntary benevolent programs among the Mennonite churches to give relief to war victims, victims of natural disasters, and other unfortunate people (Juhnke 1975).

The war, in many ways, prompted a transformation in the practice of Mennonitism. English replaced German in church services. Most Oklahoma churches made the switch to English just before or during World War I (Rohrs 1981), although some returned to using German in services after the war ended. The few German schools associated with the churches were closed about that time. For a while some churches offered two services, one in German and one in English. Other churches conducted services in German but added some parts in English. It was not until the 1950s that Mennonite churches ceased using the German language in worship services altogether (Haury 1981).

Initially, there was much debate in the churches over the use of the English language in worship services, but after the use of English became the norm, most Mennonites began to consciously advance the viewpoint that the German language was not as important to the meaning of their faith as was following their religious convictions (Haury 1981). Mennonites reconceptualized their religion, and its relationship to their citizenship, as a response to pressures outside the group. The conditions of post– World War I life forced Mennonites to drastically revise their conception of themselves as a religious body and the relationship of their culture to American society.

What the Mennonites did not give up during World War I was their practice of nonresistance. They offered no retaliation for the pain they suffered, demanded no payback for unpunished acts of violence toward them or economic losses incurred, voiced no public recrimination, uttered no acrimony outside the group, sought no counterspin of positive publicity. They suffered in silence, and they obeyed the draft law. They also held to their principles and stood firm in a quiet, unyielding, nonagressive peace position against the purchase of war bonds and participation in military service. Through this, the Mennonite belief system remained intact. Their cause, however, went unnoticed outside Oklahoma. There was no official organization among peace churches nationwide, and the general public showed little interest in supporting pacifism. Conscientious objectors were not ever mentioned in books that chronicled the history of the era (Barone 1990).

# Henry J. Becker

Henry Becker was born in 1894 in Kansas and moved to Ringwood, Oklahoma, when he was seven. Henry was one of eleven children. His father had come from the "old country." The Becker family spoke Low German in their home and read German newspapers. Henry learned his catechism in church and did not believe in military service, but he said the church never held special meetings or gave any special instructions about the World War or the draft. Henry's father was concerned over the fighting in Europe and refused to buy war bonds, but Henry never considered moving to Canada as other Mennonites did, or refusing to register. At the time of his induction into the army, Henry Becker was twenty-three years old, a baptized Mennonite with a sweetheart named Ruie May. Henry said he figured on taking his the way it came.

His account as a World War I draftee was edited from a taped inter-view conducted on November 28, 1969.* It also was built on inter-views with his daughter, Phyllis Jantzen.

We had one of the worst [county draft board records for refusing military exemptions to Mennonites]. This county is known to be tough. The boys know if they get an exemption of some kind they've got to work for it or they won't get it. I was in the first draft they ever had, and I guess there were about sixty-five of us from Major County. From our church, there were four more besides me.

[In September of 1917, Henry Becker joined the other first-round draftees in Fairview, Oklahoma, where they boarded a train and were sent to Camp Travis near San Antonio, Texas.]

I was there nine months, and, of course, after we got court-martialed, I spent nine months at Leavenworth. When we got there, we learned there were other COs [conscientious objec-tors] there. I guess, maybe [we learned this] purposely. There were two hundred of us [assigned] all over the camp; we weren't in one bunch at all. I had one of the boys [another CO] with me. They just happened to put us in the same company. It was the 134th Artillery. [The army] still pulled their cannons around with horses at that time. They had trucks, but the cannons were pulled mostly with small mules.

We had certificates showing that we were Mennonites and that we were supposed to have noncombatant work. But the captain paid no attention to that. He wasn't rough or anything like that. He told us to go ahead, just like the rest [of the soldiers], and when he got different orders, why, he would give them to us. No, no [there was no opportunity to declare a con-

---

*A complete transcription of Henry Becker's words is part of the Schowalter Oral History collection of Bethel College.

scientious objector stand at that point]. We had to ask for permission to talk to the captain, and we presented certificates to show what we objected to. That's when he told us to [do whatever] everybody else [did].

The first thing they did when we got [to the camp] was to issue uniforms. You could either destroy your clothes or send them home. That's kind of interesting, because when [it got to the point] where we were court-martialed, they court-martialed us on the grounds of disobedience of orders: We refused to wear the uniform. But we had worn the uniform. [At the trial, the defense attorney for the COs argued that the blue fatigues issued and worn by all soldiers, including the COs, were a uniform or the equivalent. Some COs charged were known to have worn the khaki uniforms issued. Becker's daughter had several photographs of her father in uniform.] I had my uniform for nine months.

I was in the artillery, and the first thing we had to do was learn to ride horses because the army pulled the cannons with horses and mules, mostly mules. We had to hitch the cart together and pull it. I didn't have to learn to ride, because I had been riding horses ever since I was a little kid. But a lot of boys didn't [know how]. They came out of towns, and they couldn't even stay on a horse. I kind of enjoyed it, but I always knew what I was training for—to be able to ride a horse pulling around a cannon; that was the purpose of it.

We just went along that way for quite a long while. And they said they were watching all of us boys drill. We all had the chance to become officers, they said. If a fellow were good enough, why, he could even become a commissioned officer. When we had been there, oh, I'd say maybe two or three months, they picked me and my buddy [the other CO assigned with Becker] to attend officer training school. I learned more about the army then. I knew what they were doing. We protested; we wanted out of the officer training school. We told them we didn't believe in war, and we didn't want to train to be officers. The officers told us, "In here it doesn't make any difference what you want to be; it's what we make out of you." Then two, three officers came every night, and we had our books [about the army], and they'd explain the whole thing to us, and I still remember what turned me against it. [An officer] said, "War is nothing but wholesale murder, and we have been appointed to do the job." Another thing I still remember. He said, "Hate like hell." That's just the way he put it. "You're no good as long as you love your enemy; you can't make a good soldier." That turned me against it more than anything else, but by then we knew what it was all about.

We got out of that officer training school in two weeks. We got orders transferring us to depot brigade. There were not only COs there, there were other soldiers too. We worked just like the rest of them, and we were under the same command. And where we worked, [it was ] where they issued all the clothes for the soldiers—the new ones and also those who were getting ready to go overseas. [Those] I was drafted with—they were the first bunch to go—and that turned me against it more than anything. They would issue each boy a rifle when he left, and so we had to carry those rifles in. We had to unload them, and then we were supposed to issue them a rifle—each one of them. I was to give him the rifle, and he could go on and do the dirty work while I stayed back. And this is the way [things finally happened].

As long as we did what they told us, we didn't have much trouble. When we started objecting, we ran into some trouble. It finally come to a head when they were pushing us to work in all the kitchens on Sunday. We took our turn working in the kitchens like all the rest of [the soldiers] in the company that we were attached to. So they got the idea, I think mostly to break up [our Mennonite] Sunday service—[the army] held services in the YMCA and places like that—but not too many soldiers attended. Well, they ordered us to work in different kitchens all over the camp. They excused the regular soldiers when they were supposed to be on duty, and we would do all the kitchen work all day [every] Sunday. We protested, and that kind of got things started. We hadn't exactly turned down the work, but they told us, "The Bible says if you don't work, you don't eat." So we didn't work, and we didn't eat. We didn't get any food on Sundays. We didn't object to that; we didn't say nothing about it. On the third Sunday, they called us to headquarters, and they lined us all up and talked to us first, then one took over and he gave us a cussing. Nobody knows how hard he could swear and how loud. [Henry laughs.] Then they let us go back to the companies where we were attached. We all went back to work, the work we [had been doing] before, on Monday morning.

About that time I kind of dropped out of the picture—I got sick. I went to the infirmary, and they wouldn't take me. They said I wasn't sick, [that instead] I was playing sick. I had to go back to the company. When I couldn't take it no longer, some other boys took me [to the infirmary again]. I passed out. I guess I rolled on the floor. Then they took me to the base hospital. They discovered I had pneumonia and the mumps at one shot, and it was thirty days before I got out [of the hospital]. While I was gone, they transferred the other boys.

[After being released], I was kind of running loose for a week. When I got out of the hospital, I hadn't had a shave or a haircut, and the first time I looked in the looking glass, I hardly knew who I was. Nobody paid attention to me. I'd go ahead and eat when the rest of the soldiers did. But I didn't get orders to go out to work. When I found out where [the other COs] were [in camp], I just packed up my blanket and stuff, and I just walked out there. Nothing happened. The [military authorities] didn't bother me. I just went out there. I became the company barber. I cut all the boys' hair. We weren't doing anything. They didn't assign us work.

We were forty-five [COs] but dwindled down to forty-one when we finally got court-martialed. I'd say thirty-five were Mennonites. We were mostly General Conference. Four were Mennonite Brethren. There were three Church of Christ; one was Catholic. One was a Jehovah's Witness, but he left us. I don't know what happened to him.

Like I said, when I was ordered [earlier] to unload rifles, then I knew the next order was that I'd have to give out those rifles with an eighteen-inch bayonet on the end. Give them to the same boys that I was drafted with, right out of this county. They were there; I even visited some of them. I'd have to issue a rifle to boys I got drafted with, and then [I would be] staying here. That just didn't appeal to me.

We had no experience and didn't know what to do, and just gradually [our role grew] on us while we were in camp. I don't think we made a mistake. It kind of grew on us. Some of the churches thought we made a mistake; [they thought ] we were too radical. [Our church members got] worried about it, and my home preacher came out to visit us. He wanted to tell us we were going too far and that we were causing trouble. He argued with us, and we didn't appreciate that. We [hadn't had any advice] before. [But] after we had made our decisions, then they wanted to advise us that we doing wrong. We didn't want [the minister] to come back. We had already gone too far. We couldn't back out anyway. Oh, I guess we could have, but it would have made us look pretty cheap. So I think we made a pretty good decision.

It went on quite a little while that we were in camp [living this way]. Then we were called up, one at a time, and they read the charges against us. Of course, they were false right then, because the charges were disobedience of orders: We refused to put on the uniform. [However,] we had the fatigues, blue denim clothes on. That's all we ever wore when we worked. [Proceedings of the court-martial indicate each individual in the group

refused an order to wear the khaki uniforms when new uniforms were issued.] They told us we were charged with disobedience of orders and to hire a lawyer. We told them we wouldn't
do that. We told them that whatever they did to us would be all
right. They said they couldn't hold a court-martial without a
lawyer— they'd have to appoint one for us. We told them that
was all right too. Then they wanted to know whether we'd be
satisfied if they'd appoint one of our boys to represent the whole
bunch instead of trying each one of us separately. They wanted
to appoint Harry L. Charles. He didn't happen to be a Mennonite. He was a Quaker from the Friends Church. Well, that
suited us just fine, because he was quite a bit smarter that the
rest of us. He did a very good job.

I received pay while I was in the army part of the time and
then when we quit [working], we didn't take no pay. They
wanted to give it to us, but we didn't take it.

One thing I left out that I should have told before is that when
we were in the detention camp, they came and got one of the
boys, Earnest Lamb. He was from the Church of Christ; he
wasn't a Mennonite. They put Earnest on a rough cobblestone
sidewalk and gave him about a half sack full of rocks to carry
on his back, and then they walked him as long as he could walk
without any food or water. They'd let us go up there and see him
and talk to him, but he had to keep on walking. He wouldn't
give up, though. He was pretty tough. He didn't even get very
unhappy; he laughed about it. But he finally got so he couldn't
walk anymore. His knees just gave out on him. Then they built
him a cage about twelve or fifteen feet high. They still didn't
feed him, though. They didn't even give him drinking water.
Well, of course, all this didn't come from headquarters. It was
all put up by the officers we had. I think they wanted us to see
how rough they could get.

So this Harry L. Charles, the same person who [later] represented us [at the court-martial], he asked me to accompany him,

because we were pretty good chums. He told me what he wanted to do, and he wanted to know if I would go along. [Becker agreed.] He wrote out a telegram and we found a little money. In his telegram, Harry told about this Earnest Lamb, that he was being starved to death. Then Harry found a Negro soldier. The soldier was just standing out there in the rain. And we went out there, and Harry talked to this Negro soldier and gave him the telegram and let him read it and gave him some money and asked him to send it because we couldn't go to the telegram office. And he helped us, the Negro soldier; he sent that telegram to the headquarters of the Friends Church.

The very next day orders came from Washington, D.C., to get that man out of there and feed him. So that aroused [our officers] pretty much. Later we got notice that they were trying to find out who did it, how it leaked out. Well, Harry L. Charles and I were the only ones who knew about it, and we didn't say. We wouldn't speak up. We just kept quiet. That made them pretty mad, but they took Earnest down, and they fed him and brought him back to camp. [Henry laughs.] He was pretty rough-looking by that time.

I think they did this to Earnest to make an example out of him. Generally they picked on one of the Mennonites. I don't know whether they thought that Earnest was just sliding along with the Mennonites or maybe they thought his church wouldn't back him. Most generally, [all] the churches did back the boys, though.

Another thing I forgot that I should tell is that they came for another person. They came and got Albert Voth [Voth's account is also recorded in the Schowalter Oral History Collection at Bethel College], but he had a little better luck. He was pretty well educated too. They wanted to starve him into doing what they asked him to do. They just put him in one room up there. A soldier knew about it, and [the soldier] felt sorry [for Voth]. He'd slip around on the back side and bring him water every day. He slipped him some apples and stuff. They didn't know [Voth] was getting any food, but he did. That's the way he kept going.

[The court-martial was held June 7, 1918. The charges centered on the refusal of the men to wear the army uniform. Harry Charles, twenty-six years old, was the only defendant questioned and the only witness for the defense. Charles appeared before the court dressed in an army uniform, while the other defendants wore blue fatigues. The following questions and responses have been edited from Charles's testimony.]

QUESTION:   Are you an American citizen?

ANSWER:   Yes, sir.

QUESTION:   You have been enjoying the liberties guaranteed by the American government?

ANSWER:   I have, sir.

QUESTION:   What obligation do you feel that you are under now to protect those guarantees?

ANSWER:   Sir, I feel that I am under obligation to serve my country in ways in which I conscientiously can.

QUESTION:   Serve it how?

ANSWER:   In ways which I conscientiously can.

QUESTION:   You have enjoyed its protection, have you not?

ANSWER:   Yes, sir.

QUESTION:   Now it is threatened to be overthrown, or to be destroyed, and the masses with it; what obligation do you feel, what moral obligation do you feel you have for the benefits you have enjoyed?

ANSWER:   As I stated before, I feel that I should perform such constructive work or part that I can.

QUESTION:   These liberties are being assailed by a force that will destroy them unless you destroy that force.

ANSWER:   I base it solely on religious ground. I fully realize the political significance of the situation and also the obligation.

QUESTION:   I will ask you if that Society of Friends was not organized by Germans or a society of Germans?

ANSWER:   No, sir, it is purely an English organization.

QUESTION:   Most of these forty-one men are of German descent—these forty-one accused—are they not?

ANSWER:   To the best of my knowledge they are.

QUESTION:   You are willing to testify to this court that no two of them ever got together there and discussed whether or not they should wear the uniform?

ANSWER:   I am willing to testify that no two of them ever got together and made any decision about what they would do about it.

QUESTION:   How about discussions? Did they ever have discussions about what they should do?

ANSWER:   No, sir.

QUESTION:   How do you know that?

ANSWER:   So far as I know, I should have said, sir.

QUESTION:   The reason you decided to wear the uniform was the result of an individual decision on your part to do so?

ANSWER:   Absolutely.

QUESTION:   Nobody coerced you into doing so?

ANSWER:   No, sir. I decided to do it for the reason I stated, that I did not wish to directly disobey an order, and at the same time make known the reason I do not like to wear it.

QUESTION:   Do you know whether or not a soldier in time of war is permitted to wear any other clothing than soldiers' uniform?

ANSWER:   I think they are not, sir.

QUESTION:   And that uniform which these men are wearing is legalized as a part of our uniform?

ANSWER:   I don't know, but I understand it is to be used while on certain duty.

QUESTION:   If soldiers could wear nothing except the uniform, this must be a part of the prescribed uniform?

ANSWER:    That might be, sir.

QUESTION:    And they are, therefore, wearing clothing issued for use in the military service?

ANSWER:    Sir, . . . If a man wears the blue clothing in civilian life he would not be arrested as a soldier, but if caught wearing khaki he is arrested.

QUESTION:    They are civilians in disguise, then?

ANSWER:    Yes, sir, civilians in disguise.

QUESTION:    You stated you did not wish to directly disobey an order. Have you ever or would you directly disobey an order?

ANSWER:    Sir, if it came to a question of absolute right and wrong in my conscience, I would, in regard to conscientious objection.

QUESTION:    What do you mean by right and wrong?

ANSWER:    I say, sir, if I see it as a conscientious objector. To make it clear, if I were ordered to shoulder a gun I should be forced to disobey the order.

QUESTION:    Suppose it comes to a showdown of your life or the other fellow's. Then what do you feel would be your duty?

ANSWER:    Sir, they will have to take my life.

QUESTION:    You would give up before you would fight?

ANSWER:    I would, sir.

QUESTION:    Would you be willing to help a soldier who had been wounded?

ANSWER:    Certainly, sir.

QUESTION:    Then would you [be], or do you know whether or not these conscientious objectors would be, willing to go into an ambulance company and go out on that no-man's-land and pick up wounded soldiers without having a firearm? Would they be willing to do that?

ANSWER:    I think they would not do that.

QUESTION:    They would not be willing to pick up a wounded soldier and help him?

ANSWER:   They might if they were civilians but not as a part of the army service.

QUESTION:   If the army is the government then, it is simply an objection to being a member of the government?

ANSWER:   No, but being a member of the army.

QUESTION:   Well, the army is the government. Do you object, then, to being identified with the government?

ANSWER:   I had never interpreted the army as being a part of the government (*United States* v. *Butz et al.* 1918).

[In other testimony Charles affirmed that he would refuse an order to kill another human, and he testified that he objected to wearing the uniform because it placed him in a false position. The trial lasted one day. The defendants were found guilty. The original sentence was hard labor for life but was soon lessened to twenty-five years.]

After we were court-martialed, they let us go back to camp. Everything was quiet over there. And all at once here came [a detachment] on horseback, a bunch of them. And they just gave us so many minutes to pack up [to be taken away]. That was the roughest experience we had. They'd ride right close with their horses; they pushed the boys [on foot] right along. I could take it all right. It was awful hot when we went. The horses would be trampling right close to our heels. There were two or three [COs], who just couldn't make it. They gave out and the army brought an ambulance along then and let them ride. The rest of us went on [walking] to the stockade. We were prisoners then.

We were in the stockade about a week. In the morning, we'd be on the east side in the shade, and then in the afternoon we'd move over on the west side and be in the shade. At night, we'd just sleep on the ground. We were given two blankets to sleep with. It was pretty tough. We didn't object.

Then one night, just before dark, they sent a bunch of soldiers to take us to the train. They lined us all up, two and two, and snapped handcuffs on us. About that time, it started thundering and lightning and getting dark. We had just the worst rain that San Antonio ever had, I guess. It rained and thundered and lightninged something terrible, and we would keep on a-goin'. The soldiers had to go right with us. One soldier walked right alongside of me. He said, "You see what your religion did to me?"

We kept on walking to where the railroad cars were, and they loaded us all in. We just poured water out of our clothes. All the clothes we had were what we had on. The only thing else we had that they didn't take away from us were our Bibles. They never take your Bible away from you.

They unloaded us in Kansas City, and then they took us out and give us a little exercise. We rode about thirty-six hours, I guess. And we didn't get any sleep, because of having handcuffs on. I got zero sleep. The cuffs start cutting you; they wake you up. You can't sleep.

[After reaching the prison], they marched us all inside Leavenworth and took the handcuffs off. The first lecture we got was by the prison chaplain. Told us what the rules and regulations were. First he said, "I don't know why you boys are here," he said, "that's none of my business. I don't ask anybody why he came here." And then he said, "I feel sorry for boys that made a mistake and get sent here, but anybody who won't take part in this most holy war," he said, "I have no sympathy with." Now, he gave himself away, because he mentioned that.

Well, they just put us in prison and locked us up. [They] assigned us to different kinds of jobs, and we finally wound up in the garden detail, and we ran the dairies. When the flu epidemic hit, they had a hospital inside the prison. That soon filled up. [The epidemic was most intense in North America in the fall of 1918. More than 668,000 died from the flu or complications stemming from it during the years 1918 and 1919 (Crosby 1976).] [The prison hospital was] all loaded down with boys with the flu—that's what I got. [The prison officials would] just give you plenty of blankets and open the window. It was pretty cold, but they gave a lot of fresh air. They had one doctor coming around once a day with an order to give you quinine salts— that's all you got. The flu was rough in those days. [The sick] would get up to go [to the bathroom] and at times, when they [would] have to wait, they'd just pass out on the floor. [When that happened to someone], we'd just get up, pick him up, and put him in his bed and crawl in too. A lot of [the prisoners] came out of it, but a lot of them didn't. [The hospital] didn't have enough help. When [men died], they rolled them in blankets and laid them out along the side of the hospital, outside of the hospital, those that were dead. Then they'd get them ready and ship them home. And our boys, five of our boys from Camp Travis, out of the forty-one [sent to prison], five of them died. We didn't object to the [medical] treatment we got at all. Lots of them made it, and lots of them didn't.

Well, we were over there [in Leavenworth prison]. We behaved. We didn't intend to run off. One Sunday [after the] noon meal, they called us together, all of us who were conscientious objectors. We didn't know what they had in mind. We were supposed to report in the rotunda, they called it. When we got there, they said they were going to take us out to the dairy and try us out to see if we could milk. Well, that suited us all right. It was about a mile out to where the dairy was. They had about two hundred cows. They had a lot of them. I think maybe there were thirty or thirty-five of us. We had to run three dairy barns. They couldn't very well run a dairy, because most of the other prisoners couldn't milk a cow, and they didn't care, you know. Everyone of us could milk except two of us. They took all the other boys off that they had working out there. We were under guard. They'd always take us out under guard. We'd have to go out three times a day to milk. They fed them cows a lot, and they were all Holsteins.

So pretty soon they decided that we weren't going to get away, and they gave us all a star parole. When you were star-paroled, they printed your number across both of your [pant] legs and across your [shirt] back and with a star above it. And if you had a star, they gave you a pass, and all you had to do was show your pass to the guard, and they'd open the gates [to fenced areas outside the prison walls] for you and let you go through. But we still had to go [in and out of those gates] every eight hours. There was one big feed bin over [in the dairy area] that they wasn't using any more for feed, and we decided if we'd make double bunks in there, we could all stay there so that we wouldn't have to walk back and forth all the time. We would be right in among the dairy barns there. We went to headquarters and told them what we'd like to do. And about the next day we got the orders so that we could move out. We moved into that feed bin, all of us, and they'd bring our meals out there—three times a day in one little old wagon; they still used a horse to pull it.

The dairy barns were nice, clean, and warm. And we just jumped out of bed and ran a little way, and we'd be in a diary barn. Each one of us had six cows. And each one would take care of his own cows; we fed them grain and milk. But we didn't have to clean the barns, because the ones that did the milking weren't supposed to do that. The barn was always as clean as this [room] right here because they had plenty of help. There were about fifty cows in one barn, and everybody would stand at the door, and when his cow came along—the cows were numbered too, like we were—all went by number. When your cow would come along, you'd just grab a horn. We had one guy there, he came from the Amish. He was a clown. He'd always get a hold of their tails. He was always cutting up. That's the way we passed our time out there. We were getting along all right.

Just before we got to go home, they turned it over to us and let us run it. They'd just come and look once in awhile. We were there all by ourselves, because they told us we knew more about a dairy than they did. They came around once and me and several of the boys were sitting on a log and they asked us whether we played baseball. We said when we had a chance, but we didn't have much of a chance in there. "Well," [one of them] said, "let's see what I can do." The next day he came back out there with a whole baseball outfit: bases and bats and balls and gloves and everything. He just gave it to us. So we made us a baseball diamond.

But I hadn't got much of a start on that when my discharge come along. After we was there, oh, maybe seven or eight months, they sent the board of inquiry out, and Secretary of War Baker was there too. He was just among us like another person and talked to us. He didn't say anything to abuse us, not a word. They had roll call, and everybody had to answer. Pretty soon, they called [the name of one of the men who] was dead, and then one of the boys said he died. And the [person who was calling the roll] called one again, and we told him, "He died." Pretty soon he stopped and looked up and he said, "How many of you fellows died, anyway?" We told him five of them did.

They reviewed us, and asked different questions, and anybody could answer who wanted to. They asked us how we were treated, and everybody said we were treated all right. We had no objections, and they found out there wasn't any hatred or anything going on, and they just stopped the sentence right there. They reviewed the whole thing. They decided they couldn't legally keep us there. They shouldn't have sent us there in the first place.

We were supposed to be in there for twenty-five years. We didn't object to anything. We just took what they gave us, and we got treated fairly well. The food wasn't too good, but there was plenty of it. We got out of all the cussing and swearing you get in [an army] camp and other places like that. If you behaved in there, you didn't have any trouble. We were supposed to be sentenced to hard labor, but when you were raised on a farm, like I was and most of the boys were, that wasn't hard labor to us. It didn't amount to very much. Oh, it kept us busy, fooling with cows three times a day.

I was one of the first ones to get [released and] sent out, practically the first one. I guess maybe they did it alphabetically, and my name being Becker. . . . I didn't know that I was going to get sent out. I was called to go to the tailor shop and be measured for a suit. We knew what that meant. [I went with] three other boys, who weren't all COs. The [prison officials would] buy you a ticket to wherever you wanted to go. They'd give you a little money to eat on. They'd give you back the money you had when you came in and your watch. Then they'd let you go out a free man.

So that's about the end of [my story]. I could talk for two days, I guess, and not tell the whole story. I never objected to the draft. Young men ought to be drafted, but they should have some constructive work to do. I kind of lost confidence in [the church] because we were given no instructions on what we were supposed to do, and then they started objecting to what we had done. [Overall] I still think we've got the best church going. My confidence in America was strengthened after they decided they'd give the conscientious objectors a pretty good break, and I think a lot of it was because we did take the stand we did.

Becker was released from prison and given a dishonorable discharge in April 1919. He returned to farming in Meno and lived out his life there. He married his childhood sweetheart, Ruie May, fathered three daughters and a son, and attended the New Hopedale church in Meno. Ironically, the only problem he had over his war record came from his own Mennonite church brothers. Primarily, it was the congregational leaders of his New Hopedale church who could not understand why he and the others had taken the stand they did. When Becker decided to run for the local school board, his greatest opposition came from other Mennonites who declared him ineligible because of his prison record. "If the English folks objected to it," said Becker, "I would resign, but . . . since you guys are Mennonites, . . . I won't." Becker won the election and subsequent elections. In all, he served on the local school board twenty-three years.

Henry Becker wrote this poem to Ruie May before she became his wife. No matter what life brought to Becker, he was never entirely separated from his prison experience, as the poem below reflects.

### My Dream

If she would only come back to stay,
my darling sweetheart Ruie May,

And take me in her loving arms,
And love me with her sweetest charms,

And promise to love but me and only me,
With love so true as true can be,

And promise that she would be true,
As long as life would permit her to,

And promise me to be my loving wife,
To live with me through all her life,

And seal her promises with a kiss,
Oh! my darling sweetheart little miss.

Oh! then I would be the happiest boy,
That ever lived, and sing and shout for joy.

Just because she had promised me
So honest and so true to be.

Then me and her would go out all alone.
Along the quietest country road we'd slowly roam,

And look at the planets, moon, and silvery stars.
We would forget all about the prison bars.

We'd sit down beneath some shady tree,
Where not even the moon and stars could see,

And there I would take her upon my knee,
Just to tell her that I would be

Just as honest and as true,
As she to me had promised too.

I would lay my head upon her breast,
To listen to her heart, that's beating fast.

I would ask her to be at perfect ease,
For my love should last 'til her heart would cease.

And there in my arms I'd clasp her tight,
And hold her there through all the night.

Just because I love her so,
That I could not afford to let her go.

And from her lip a kiss I'll steal,
Just to make the covenant seal.

And I know that it would be sweet,
For my sweetheart is hard to beat.

Oh! she is my sweetheart, little turtledove.
She is the one, I so dearly love.

If she would only come back to stay,
My darling sweetheart Ruie May.

***

If I knew that this would make you mad,
It would make me so very, very sad.
But since I know that you can take a joke,
And laugh at it till you almost choke,
So, I will send it along for you to read,
To prove to you that I am a friend indeed.
But if you don't believe I mean what I say,
Just come back to me and forever stay.

—Henry

*Born in Frantzhal, South Russia, on May 6, 1841, Elder Johann (John) Ratzlaff was among the first leaders of the Meno congregation. He died in Meno on November 10, 1914. (From the author's collection)*

Adam and Sarah (Schroeder) Ratzlaff and their family. Sarah died from complications related to the birth of her ninth child. Left to right, Dan, Bill, Adam, Otto, Clara, Harrison, Anne, Edd, Sarah, and Marie. (From the author's collection)

*The Adam Ratzlaff family pose before their home, located north and west of Orienta. Surrounded by seventeen children, Adam and his second wife, Bena Frantz Ratzlaff are shown seated near the center of the group. (From the author's collection)*

*Cornelius C. and Helena Heinrichs are shown here dressed for winter travel. Cornelius, also known as C. C., is holding his Bible. (From the author's collection)*

*Seven children of Cornelius C. and Helena Heinrichs pose with their parents. (From the author's collection)*

Men stack hay on the George Ediger farm. George Ediger was the father of David Ediger, who wrote about growing up on this farm. (From the author's collection)

*Farmers Dave Penner and John Penner and a third man line up their teams for plowing. (From the author's collection)*

*Ediger family members gather outside David Ediger's boyhood home. (From the author's collection)*

*Dave Ediger and his brothers pose together in their "dress-up" clothes. Brothers Cornelius, John (who later married Helen Siemens), Dan, and David are the sons of George Ediger and grandsons of Cornelius C. and Helena Heinrichs. (From the author's collection)*

George Ediger sits on the tractor in the foreground while others run the thresher and build the straw stack shown in the background. (From the author's collection)

*Henry J. Becker was photographed in 1917 in his World War I army uniform. Later the charges for which Becker was found guilty and sent to Leavenworth prison included refusal to wear a uniform. (From the author's collection)*

*Helen Siemens Ediger and her brother John (left), about the time they and their parents escaped Russia and made their way to the United States. (From the author's collection)*

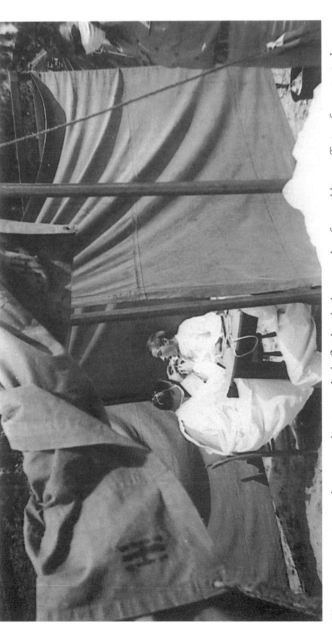

Wearing a protective mask, a researcher inserts body fluids, which were taken from soldiers suffering from atypical pneumonia, into the nose and mouth of a Mennonite medical volunteer. Special enclosures set up in an isolated area were used for exposing the volunteers to the disease. (From the author's collection)

*On the deck of the SS* Park Victory *Harry Martens is outfitted in a life jacket and ready for departure. (From the author's collection)*

*The first home of newlyweds Ruby and Walter Regier was in Meno, where Walter taught at the Oklahoma Bible Academy. (From the author's collection)*

Only prairie surrounded the first building of the Meno Preparatory School, founded in 1911. The school became the Oklahoma Bible Academy in 1917. (From the author's collection)

*Students gather outside the second building erected for the Meno school.*

*Oklahoma Bible Academy students went out to Enid and other towns during the 1940s to teach children's classes using a "flannelgraph," a flannel-covered board that provided a stage and served as a magnet for flannel-backed cutout figures of people, animals, and objects. Storytellers, like those above, evoked action and scene changes by adding and removing the flannel figures as the story progressed. (From the author's collection)*

*Some cooking was done in the basement of the OBA dormitory that housed students who lived too far away to commute daily to the school at Meno. (From the author's collection)*

*A brick structure for classes and worship was added to the growing Oklahoma Bible Academy campus in 1935. The school's initials appear over a main entrance. (From the author's collection)*

*The first church building at Meno was erected north of the cemetery on land given by Elder Ratzlaff. The building was dedicated on March 6, 1897. (From the author's collection)*

A second church building was constructed for the growing congregation in Meno in 1914. Men who attended a church conference gather before the new building. (From the author's collection)

*Attendees at a Mennonites of North America meeting held in 1914 in Meno gather before services begin. In addition to large tents set up to accommodate the crowd, the Meno Preparatory School building (in the background) and a temporary wood building (on the far right) were pressed into service, the latter for cooking and eating purposes. (From the author's collection.)*

*Members gather outside the Zoar church at Goltry. (From the author's collection)*

The Mennonite Brethren church located north of Enid was built with two entrances. This was a common practice in Mennonite church construction. One entrance was to be used exclusively by men, the other by women. Until midcentury seating at worship services was usually sex-segregated. (From the author's collection)

# PART THREE

# *Transition*

## AFTER WORLD WAR I TO THE 1990s

Spring is the most bountiful time of year in Northwest Oklahoma. Early rains deliver bright redbud, pale plum, and other trees full leafy blown along rich river bottoms. The rivers are brought alive by slim running creeks that cut steep paths down through topsoil, then into red clay. Eventually, the runoff makes its way to the shallow low banks of the North Canadian and Cimarron, where wide sandy bottoms separate thin, meandering threads of cool water.

On the great expanse of softly rolling terrain stretching above the river bottoms, the native soil flourishes rich in controlled, refined, well-tended splendor. Though they still bloom white and blue with wildflowers, the pastures are fenced now. The alfalfa smells sweet. And on land that will grow the wheat, flat green fields, which during winter pasture cattle, stretch for acres and acres. Once the cattle are removed, the grasslike carpet of wheat, fed by spring rainfall, shoots up several feet tall almost overnight, then slowly turns from green to golden amber, ripe waves of grain. Sometime in June or, on rare occasions, as late as July, when the moisture content of the heads tests just right, the perfectly ripened wheat begins to pour out of the fields, bushel upon bushel, out of the combines and into the trucks, into the cylindrical on-farm metal storage bins or down to the grain elevator and then into the larger trucks, off to the huge elevators in Enid, into the waiting railroad cars bound for flour mills or Gulf Coast export, bushel upon bushel, hundreds upon thousands of bushels of wheat, glistening brown, dusty, the refined gold of the farmer's life.

That's in a good year. Nothing, neither advanced farming methods nor the most resilient of seed, can completely shield the crop from too much rain at the wrong time, not enough rain at the right time, a severe late freeze, hail, or most dreaded of all—a tornado. If spring is the most bountiful time in Northwest Oklahoma, it is also a season that cannot be taken for granted.

Part Three addresses the forces that have shaped and continue to shape the modern Mennonite identity. Despite the many changes brought on largely by events and pressures outside the group, outside Oklahoma, and outside the United States during the second half of the twentieth century, group continuity has been regenerated. Industrialization and the transformation of agriculture brought on by the depression of the 1930s and dust bowl days, followed by a boom in farm product demand during the World War II years, forced a reorganization of Mennonites' relationship to their work. The bombing of Pearl Harbor and America's entry into the Second World War again drew attention to the Mennonites' stand on the peace issue and reopened old wounds of prejudice and discrimination toward German ethnics and pacifists.

In the 1950s and 1960s relaxation of Mennonite mores and the demands of a national economy led to a more open, acculturated Mennonite society. Yet Mennonite identity remains intact. A reorientation in the way individuals perceive and communicate their Mennonite identity has taken place. What has changed are not the basic themes of Mennonitism but how the themes are viewed. Nonresistence is now discussed as "the peace initiative," but this is less a change in theology than a change in the way the theological message of nonresistance is presented. The Mennonites' message of pacifism and rejection of all violence—nonresistance—now is defined as an individual responsibility also directed into many types of efforts to relieve human suffering. The peace initiative includes help for victims of natural disasters as well as victims of war. Further, the visible barriers that Mennonites erected in the past to protect the group's religious ethnicity have been greatly altered. The Mennonite lifestyle has renewed itself as a calling to preserve the separate life by existing "in" the world without being "of" the world—that is, not adopting "worldly" values and behavior. Individual Mennonites' stories of daily life provide reinforcement for the changed interpretation of what is God's work, their own work as livelihood, and their worship in church. The structuring of these collective-memory frames, never static, is an ongoing process, and one that continues to nurture the Mennonite identity.

Chapter 7, which begins the final section, deals with the Great Depression and the swings between economic gain and loss throughout the life of one Mennonite woman. World War II and the maturation of the Mennonite peace stand are discussed in chapter 8, which includes the narrative of two conscientious objectors. Chapter 9 reflects on the values of Mennonite education and conveys the impressions of both a teacher and a student. Chapter 10 looks into the religious community of Mennonites in the postindustrialized era and the experiences of a couple whose church-centered lives bridge the gap between ethnic origin and religious community. Chapter 11 brings the story to a close.

# CHAPTER 7

# Dust, Bust, and on to the Next War

It was rough. We didn't have money.
At least Mom made a big garden, at
least we had something to eat.
—*Emerson Unruh*

During the World War I years, Mennonites set themselves apart from the general population in Northwest Oklahoma, and the general population in turn set them apart. Mennonites actively supported this separateness by avoiding contacts with those outside their own group.

It was the visible elements of German culture that attracted prejudice against Mennonites (Rohrs 1981). From World War I onward, the German language and Old World tradition and customs became liabilities. As a result, Mennonites began to assimilate more rapidly into the larger society. The most dramatic changes in Mennonite society occurred when the German language was phased out of services. Moreover, forces outside Oklahoma continued to bear more directly on Mennonite life. Roosevelt's New Deal, following years of drought and a nationwide depression, changed the structure of farm life, if not the economic viability of most farm families. And through these years, Oklahoma Mennonites were compelled to turn their attention outside the United States, as concern mounted for fellow worshipers who remained in Russia and a second world conflict loomed on the horizon.

Despite the hard times during World War I, Mennonitism as a belief system continued to sustain itself in Oklahoma. There was even growth, although slow and slight, in the number of Mennonite churches established in Northwest Oklahoma during the 1920s and 1930s. In Major County, a Mennonite Brethren church formed in the town of Ringwood in 1920 (Goertzen 1990). The Saron church in Orienta grew larger, and members built a new brick church in 1929 (Orienta 1958, 1). Aside from the reclusive Holdeman Mennonites, churches of the General Conference and the Mennonite Brethren churches remained the two viable subgroups. But the membership base of these churches underwent substantial change in Northwest Oklahoma.

The loose organizational structure of the churches, a deliberate outgrowth of the Mennonite theology of the ministry of the laity had fostered independence in congregations. Theoretically, each congregation was unique, operated by a priesthood of believers. Leadership came from the congregation. When the churches were able, each called its own ministers. Each church conducted its own business and set its own rules under the auspices of the separate Mennonite subgroups, which were essentially, in this part of Oklahoma, either the General Conference Mennonite Church or Mennonite Brethren. By this time congregations of the (Old) Mennonite Church and the Krimmer Mennonites in Northwest Oklahoma were expiring.* (Goertzen 1990). In practice, church life did vary from congregation to congregation, but in regard to the social life of the churches, similarities among congregations and between the branches of the church outweighed the differences. During the post–World War I years, the Mennonite faith began to take on the characteristics of American Protestantism (Engbrecht 1985).

Major changes profoundly affected the church during the 1920s and 1930s. In particular, church activities increased and a pattern of

---

*After mid-century the central organization of the Krimmer Mennonites officially merged with the Mennonite Brethren (Plett 1985, 326).

church life that closely followed the organization of other Protestant denominations began to emerge. The Mennonite Central Committee, a relief agency that included American Mennonite groups in its membership, was founded (Smith 1957). Youth groups and vacation Bible schools were organized. Ladies' aid societies grew. Sunday morning services became shorter and Sunday evening and Wednesday services were introduced. The Vorsänger gave way to a song leader who led the congregation from English hymnals, held neatly in racks attached to the backs of pews and available for each member. The itinerant preacher gradually was replaced by a pastor who devoted full time to his church and was paid for his place in the pulpit. Attendance, which had dwindled before the war and had lost ground with the closing of some churches, began to slowly surge upward. In the mid-1920s, this increase in attendance was brought about partly because the youth of the church were attracted and held by all the new endeavors (Hostetler 1986; Epp 1977) and partly because of an increase in the farm community population. Growing numbers of believers in the Enid area called for an official Mennonite Brethren church in the city of Enid. This relieved members of the hardship of traveling north a few miles beyond the city limits to worship with the rural church group at North Enid. In 1935, Grace, a General Conference affiliate, also was formed in the city of Enid. In 1937, part of the Grace membership broke away to establish another General Conference church in Enid. They called their new church Bethel (Kuschel 1989).

As America's politics moved away from foreign alliances and national sentiment turned toward isolationism in the 1920s, the missionary movement caught hold among Mennonites. Opposite to the trend in American policy to withdraw from international affairs, Mennonites became interested in worldwide expansion. The mission field of endeavor had been established by Mennonite groups as early as the 1880s (Haury 1981, 160–61). By the turn of the century, the movement attracted increased attention from the major Mennonite groups. Additional missionaries were dispatched to Africa, the Far

East, and other parts of the world (Hostetler 1986). Before 1930 American Mennonites had founded a total of sixteen programs serving Native Americans and foreign missions (Kauffman 1931). Organizing new Mennonite churches in America's cities was also considered mission work. A brother of the Enid Mennonite Brethren church, A. A. Smith, was selected the first city missionary of the General Conference. He served in Minneapolis and in Lodi, California (Fiftieth Anniversary of the First Mennonite Brethren Church 1947).

The practices that separated the Mennonites from society became less noticeable, both inside and outside the churches. The somber weddings that in the past had included a lengthy sermon became more conventional, with more elaborate ceremony. Candles were permitted for decoration, and bridesmaids attended the bride. The weddings were still quite solemn, however. Kissing by the bride and groom at the close of the ceremony was considered highly distasteful. Marriage of Mennonites to those outside the faith increased during the 1920s and 1930s, but it was still uncommon.

Nonconformity remained a major tenet of the church. As the differences between Mennonites and the larger community began to disappear on the whole, the differences that did remain became significant boundaries between the church and those "of the world." Prescribed moral behavior served as the major barrier between the Mennonites and other Oklahomans. Attitudes toward alcohol serve to illustrate the Mennonite position on social nonconformity. Even though drinking alcoholic beverages was strictly against the Mennonite ethic, membership in groups such as the Women's Christian Temperance Union was discouraged (Haury 1981). As harmful as drinking might be to individuals and families, joining any organized public, political effort promoting prohibition was not considered appropriate for Mennonites (Haury 1981). Tradition called for maintaining a church community unaffiliated with social and political activism. The national experiment with prohibition had little effect on and caused little change in the habits of the Mennonite community.

Alcohol consumption, smoking, and dancing continued to be banned, as was card playing and most paid public amusement. Whether or not to allow the children to participate in public-school-sponsored sports events was a topic of heated debate within the church. The competitive nature of athletics and the "brief" uniforms girls wore in play were equally problematic. (At the time girls' uniforms were usually loose-fitting tops and full-skirted culotte pants.) As for other types of physical recreation, relief from the blazing Oklahoma sun during the hot summer months via "mixed bathing," i.e., men, women, and children swimming together at public parks, was definitely not approved.

The Mennonite men and women did make some adaptation to the changing clothing styles of the era. As women across the country followed the trend to shorter skirts, the Mennonite women raised theirs too, but only to heights somewhat shorter than the pre–World War I fashion of six inches above the ankle. Mennonite women were not seen in bright colors or sleeveless blouses until the 1930s and 1940s. Neither were they permitted to wear makeup or to sport any of the new bobbed or permed hairdos until years after most other women did.

Historically, the Russian Mennonites had readily accepted any new inventions that advanced their farming enterprise. In contrast to the more conservative Anabaptist groups, the Amish, and some Old Order Mennonites, who still live today without benefit of electricity, automobiles, or telephones, the General Conference Mennonite Church and Mennonite Brethren in Northwest Oklahoma followed the example of their Russian forebears. They were among the first to make use of power-driven machinery and other labor-saving devices Americans acquired in the 1920s and 1930s. Shortly after introduction in the marketplace, electric lighting, automobiles, harvesters, tractors, and other modern conveniences could be found in Mennonite homes or in their barns.

Talking on the telephone, via the newly installed rural party lines, however, was a different matter—a far more controversial one. The telephone offered opportunity for idle talk. But it also networked Mennonite farmers to the feed store, gain elevator, and machine shop and Mennonite families to the pharmacy and nearest doctor. Eventually talking on the telephone was deemed permissible in most Mennonite households, but conservative Mennonites in Northwest Oklahoma such as the Holdeman continued much longer to ban in-home use of telephones.*

By the 1920s radio waves crisscrossed the lonely grasslands, but listening to the new receiver sets and driving into town to see "picture shows" were strictly prohibited. These were considered "worldly" and categorized with dancing and other activities thought to be harmful or to lead to association with persons of "low" character. Listening to the radio became a more acceptable practice to the Mennonites as the years rolled on partly because, like the telephone, it broke down isolation in the sparsely populated rural areas and partly because it was a source of news and important information, particularly weather reports, which were of vital interest to the Mennonite farmers.

The large numbers of horses that were taken off farms by the army in World War I were never replaced by farmers after the war. Manufacturers who had geared up production of trucks during the war found farmers a prime outlet for their products after the war (Hurt 1991, 3). The early tractors were used primarily for plowing or running stationary equipment such as the thresher, but improvements fostered by the International Harvester, John Deere, Allis-Chalmers, and Massey-Harris companies during the 1920s improved the efficiency of the machines. The power lift, which enabled the farmer to raise and lower plows and disks automatically; the rubber tire, which replaced iron- and steel-rimmed versions; and the three-point hitch, which used a hydraulic system to hold plows at a preset depth, saved the farmer time and effort (Hurt 1991, 20).

---

*For a discussion of how Old Order Mennonites and Amish people adapted to the use of the telephone, see Umble (1996).

By the mid-1920s tractors were pulling combines across wheat fields. The early combines were a combination of two machines: the header, which cut the stalks, and the thresher, which removed the heads. Some combines carried grain tanks, but the earlier versions required a wagon or truck to be driven alongside to catch the wheat after it was harvested. The straw was returned to the ground by combining and most Oklahoma farmers let it lie there, since it was not thick enough to prevent subsequent plowing and it had low value as livestock feed. While the combines saved labor, one man was still needed to ride the combine, one to drive the tractor, one or more to haul the harvested wheat to a storage bin or grain elevator, and someone, usually the farmer's wife, to cook for the crew. Farmers with less than 100 acres of wheat to harvest most often found that it did not pay to own a combine. A good deal of the cutting therefore was done by custom cutters, who provided a combine and extra labor for a fee.

Increased production and increased demand for wheat forced a progressive shift from mixed-crop farming to specialization in wheat and its affiliated farm product, cattle, but these changes were not rapid and did not automatically result in a higher farm income. For most of the nation, the 1920s was a decade of rising expectations and general prosperity and the 1930s a decade of great economic depression. For most of the people of Northwest Oklahoma, including those who were Mennonites, both decades were years of hardship. Throughout the country, farmers did not enjoy the benefits that Americans in general shared during the golden years of the 1920s. Although farm prices and production increased, land values across the United States rose more than threefold (Todd and Curti 1961). Specialized, cash-crop farming and increased use of machinery required more acreage and less manual labor to generate the same standard of living. Unlike the early homesteads, which ran first on self-sustenance and later on mixed-crop production, many of the post–World War I farms began gradually to depend more on wheat as a cash crop. Moreover, most of the economically successful farms were larger than the 160-

acre plots the settlers had claimed a generation earlier. Farm prices fell and the price farmers paid for goods rose during the decade (Todd and Curti 1961). Unstable markets in the United States and worldwide helped cause farm prices to continue to fluctuate downward and farm surpluses to build. The 1929 stock market crash, bank failures, and below-average rainfall exacerbated the problem.

Academics who have reviewed the patterns of wind erosion, rainfall (or lack of it), and farm population shifts disagree as to whether only the panhandle part of Oklahoma was officially part of the great midwestern dust bowl of the 1930s or whether other Northwest Oklahoma counties meet the "dust-bowl standard" (Lambert 1983, 66–84). Mennonites who remember farm life during the Great Depression have no doubt that they were a part of that dust bowl. It is true that the areas most frequented by the worst dust storms did not include Northwest Oklahoma. Still and all, too many lives were altered as too many days passed when rain-starved, plow-churned topsoil was propelled upward, pushed eastward, and converted to fierce, wind-driven dust particles that seeped through closed doors and windows, pelted people as they scurried from shelter to shelter, and drifted like snowbanks along fencerows and next to buildings. The cause of the dust storms, which occasionally still frequent Northwest Oklahoma, has been credited to a combination of the area's cyclic pattern of several years of plentiful rain followed by extended drought, the cultivation of marginally productive grassland, and the practice of deep-plowing then fine-tilling the grain fields.

The drought, dust storms, and depression of the early 1930s created cases of extreme poverty. Farm foreclosures rose. The rate of farm population decline increased. The governor of the state, "Alfalfa Bill" Murray, insisted on emergency relief measures and allotted half-acre plots between the state capitol and executive mansion for hungry people to plant vegetables (Morgan and Morgan 1977, 126).

As the depression deepened, Mennonite people did not actively seek political solutions to the problems that faced them personally and collectively. Yet they didn't refuse the New Deal solutions passed by the Roosevelt administration either. Designed to help the small, family farmer, the New Deal legislation in effect drastically reshaped—actually reinvented—the way all farmers did business. In one fell swoop, the legislation moved running a farm from a local and nature-dominated enterprise to one where nature and the farmer interfaced with federal administrative agencies. In setting price supports for farm products, the Agriculture Adjustment Acts of 1933 and 1937 overturned the traditional structure of American farming. The Farm Credit Act shored up the farm loan system. These pieces of legislation set farm policy for the next fifty years (Rasmussen and Baker 1986, 201). Farm policy implementation, however, was susceptible to vacillating national economic and political trends. While the intent of the FDR-era legislation may have been to help the modest, mixed-crop, and subsistence farmers, the result was to set up a system that benefited most another type of farmer. The farm credit legislation secured the financial cushion, and the parity price supports, which eventually covered many farm products, cemented the foundation of farm profit with what could be grown best for cash in Northwest Oklahoma—wheat.

Other New Deal farm programs—federal crop insurance and rural electrification programs—were of great benefit to farmers across the country during the depression years and after. Especially helpful to Northwest Oklahoma farming were the soil conservation programs. Northwest Oklahomans also benefited along with the rest of the nation from the impact of Social Security legislation, which provided for the elderly, and the Civilian Conservation Corps and the Works Progress Administration, which put people without jobs to work. No amount of economic pump priming or social engineering, however, could, in the end, create rainfall or enrich unarable soil or expand a 160-acre homestead to provide for all a farmer's grown sons or shake the country completely loose from the depression. The times remained tough.

Some Mennonite churches suffered from the depressed economic times and shifts in population. The Lahoma and Ringwood Mennonite Brethren churches dissolved during the 1920s, as did the Krimmer group at Medford. Friedensau at Perry folded in 1935 (Haury 1981). Churches had to be boarded up and schools had to be consolidated. Frontier settlements of school, church, general store, and post office that blossomed after the run fast withered away if they were not close to a railroad stop or one of the highways that motorized transportation had brought into being. These latter towns, the commerce-based and county seat towns such as Enid and Fairview, and others like Meno grew during the 1920s and 1930s into viable community centers. Their lumber yards and hardware stores, drug and dry-goods stores, feed and seed stores, machine shops, and gas stations supplied the farmers' now more diversified needs. Grocery stores, because they stocked canned goods and often bought the farmers' produce for resale to townspeople, also succeeded during the Great Depression. The small towns offered middling prosperity to the depression-locked rural countryside. It was not enough, however, to prevent further decline in individual farms or sizable numbers of people from drifting out of Northwest Oklahoma.

When mortgages were foreclosed and farmers defaulted on loans, many left Oklahoma for opportunities elsewhere. Large farm families started to become a liability rather than an asset. Young people were forced out of farming and into seeking employment in Northwest Oklahoma towns and in urban areas such as Wichita, Oklahoma City, Tulsa, and Dallas. Some Mennonites of the area and their families were among the many who sought a better life away from the Oklahoma farm. An estimated 350,000 people migrated from Oklahoma, Arkansas, and Texas between 1935 and 1940 (Norton et al. 1993, 780). It was often tenant farmers and sharecroppers who made up the greatest portion of the poor-white farm population displaced across much of the South during the Great Depression. There were landless individuals who rented farmland in Northwest Oklahoma, but most of that area's land was not conducive to the growth of cotton and other crops that utilized tenant labor. Thus, many of those who were forced off their farms in Northwest Oklahoma were the farm owners themselves.

California became a popular destination for those leaving Oklahoma, and Mennonites found their way to the Golden State along with many others. Once in California, Oklahoma Mennonites sought work as fruit and vegetable farmers or in the nut groves or in California industry. In 1920 there were approximately ninety thousand Mennonites in the United States (Epp 1962, 53), and nearly twelve thousand of them were located in California (Marzlof 1992, 4). Several Mennonite churches served the growing California community and Mennonite institutions of higher education were located in the state (Hostetler 1983). Some Mennonites who fled the dust bowl remained in California; others later returned to Oklahoma. A degree of individual migration back and forth between the West Coast and Oklahoma continues to this day, and Mennonites are proportionally represented among the total number of Oklahomans who relocate. Overall, most migration from Northwest Oklahoma during the 1920s and 1930s was not from the farm to California, but from the farm to a nearby town or city.

Not every family in Northwest Oklahoma suffered during the depression. A few escaped economic hardship. Some Mennonite farmers were able to make ends meet by growing most of what their families needed. Others ran fairly successful cash-crop production operations, and some, as royalty owners, became rich from the oil boom that mushroomed around Garber, in Kay County, and in other oil fields during the early 1920s. Many were not so fortunate. For the most part, the decades between the World War I and World War II were not years of prosperity. They marked, instead, the beginning of several economic and social trends in Northwest Oklahoma that have continued to accelerate over the years, including fluctuating farm prices, increasing farm production, increasing farm size, increasing farm debt, and decreasing farm population. These trends have led to a great deal of economic insecurity for farmers that continues to the present.

Inadequate farm income, the growth of trade and nonfarm industry, wider associations outside the church, and a veiled but recalcitrant undertow of residual public censure shaped the Northwest Oklahoma Mennonites' struggle to cope with World War I and its aftermath. Contact with Mennonites who remained in Russia was difficult. The counterparts of the Oklahoma Mennonites in Russia faced similar, but far more dire circumstances. Beginning in 1914 with the outbreak of the war, combat, revolution, economic chaos, hunger, contagious disease, and the sheer compounding of misery plummeted all of Russia into turmoil. Furthermore, Russia's part in the war against Germany caused Germans of Russian descent to become victims of a growing nationwide hate campaign. In Russia, use of the German language was prohibited in public assembly and in the press, and German property holders were compelled by government to sell their holdings (Toews 1967, 23). More than twelve thousand Mennonites were inducted in the Russian army; six thousand of them went to battlefield ambulance corps and hospitals (Epp 1962, 28).

Despite the Russian Mennonites' contributions to their country, virtually every Mennonite became an object of suspicion following the revolution of 1917, when the treaty of Brest Litovsk ended Russia's participation in World War I and brought German occupation troops into the Ukraine. With the Russian role in World War I finished, the arrival of German occupation troops in 1918 did provide Ukrainian Mennonites a semblance of security from the marauding bands of anarchists and robbers who terrorized inhabitants with plunder, rape, and murder. Eventually, the withdrawal of the German army from Russia, accompanied by a major outbreak of typhoid, left the Ukrainian Mennonites even more vulnerable and dead center in the path of the opposing Red and White armies.

As the armies of the civil war ravaged back and forth time after time across the once fertile and productive Mennonite farmlands, the two oldest settlements, Chortiza and Molotschna—from which the families of many Oklahoma Mennonites had emigrated—were hit hard. In just a few calamitous years, virtually all farmland was laid waste amid unbearable human suffering. From 1914 to 1921 more than 2,250, or 2 percent of the total Mennonite population, died of starvation, disease, exposure, or eruptions of violence (Toews 1967, 47). Mennonite values were strained to their limit. At one point, a small band of Mennonites took up arms and fought the marauding bandits and the organized forces (Toews 1967, 34). But relocation, the traditional Mennonite solution to oppressive political circumstances, appeared to be a more viable alternative for most Mennonites. Efforts to organize large-scale emigration out of Russia began as early as 1919 (Toews 1967, 50).

Some Mennonites simply took flight. Without plans, place of refuge, or any future in sight, they fled south to Black Sea harbors (Toews 1967, 80). Some had funds, but many were destitute. They set out alone or in small family groups, carrying what they could of what little they had left. One path of escape led through to Batum in Turkey,* an onerous waystation, where the damp climate contributed to outbreaks of typhoid and malaria and where poor housing and inadequate food for the émigrés earned it the title, "that place of death" (Toews 1967, 80). American and European Mennonites began to learn of the situation in Russia through letters from relatives and articles in Mennonite-sponsored newspapers. The Mennonite faithful in Oklahoma and elsewhere began to donate money, food, and clothing, but the donations often failed to reach their destination. Attempts to arrange emigration for large numbers of these people also proved exceedingly difficult (Toews 1967).

Mass migration of the Russian Mennonites required finding a country that would provide agricultural opportunities and welcome an idiosyncratic cultural group of substantial size. In the United States, strict immigration laws upheld by a strong, post–World War I, anti-immigrant sentiment kept out any large-scale group relocation. Unstable worldwide economic conditions worked to discourage other nations from opening their doors to the resettlement of Mennonites

---

*Batumi is a seaport on the Black Sea in the region called Georgia, formerly a part of the USSR, near the Turkish frontier. The city was ceded by Turkey to Russia in 1878. Prior to 1936, the city was known as Batum.

as well. Finally, in 1922, Mennonites in Canada, many of whom had been part of the first wave of Russian immigration during the 1870s and 1880s, persuaded their government to accept others now desperately in need of a new homeland (Epp 1962, 139). Then it fell to the Canadian Mennonites to finance the mass emigration. Emissaries were sent to Kansas and Oklahoma to generate support, but they met with very little success, in part because their request involved the purchase of shares in a Canadian corporation as the way to finance the relocation. The U.S. Mennonites balked at the plan (Epp 1962, 133–34). The Oklahoma Mennonites wanted a more simple method and more direct control. Eventually, financing was generated for around twenty thousand Russian Mennonites to relocate to Canada between the years 1922 and 1929 (Toews 1967, 196). Many more wished to emigrate but were not able to get through the red tape to be placed on the Canadian quota lists. Smaller groups of Mennonites were accepted by Mexico (Toews 1967, 156–67), Paraguay, and Brazil (Toews 1967, 258).

Inside Soviet Russia, the maturing Communist administration acted against almost everything linked with Mennonitism, for the church was associated with ethnic enclaves, religious activity, and private ownership of land—all major targets of dissolution under the first five-year plan of the Communists, inaugurated in 1928. Nevertheless, Mennonites fell into the category of skilled farmworkers who were needed en masse to build the new Communist economy. In 1929 more than fourteen hundred churches and Christian organizations in the USSR were closed (Epp 1962, 230). Ministers were exiled. Sunday became a workday. Mennonite men were subject to removal and forced labor. The majority were shipped off to work in the northern European forest areas. Most banished Mennonite families were sent to the Ural Mountains or to the Far East or to work in gold mines in Siberia. An estimated thirteen thousand Mennonites were exiled (Epp 1962, 265). The exchange of letters between Oklahoma families and Russian relatives became even more difficult.

Individual and single-family movement with or without government permission resurfaced as viable means of exit (Epp 1962,

242–62). The few Russian Mennonites who did find their way into the United States and to Oklahoma usually were those who made it to Batum, or other eastern European ports, and eventually got direct financial assistance either in the form of donations from individuals and single churches in the United States or in the form of sponsorship, whereby U.S. Mennonites underwrote the relocation expenses of individuals and families on the basis of their agreement to repay or work off the debt once they arrived in the United States (Toews 1962, 80).

By 1935, Soviet collectivism governed farm production; most church buildings had been converted to clubhouses, stables, or other uses (Epp 1962, 267); and the Russian Mennonite population was in extreme poverty. Only one possible escape route remained open, east across Asia, across the Yenisei River, then south, over the Amu River, and into China. More than thirteen hundred Mennonites had passed into China this way (Epp 1962, 240–41; Toews 1967, 199). Under Stalin, communication of Mennonites with the outside world began to shut down completely, although ninety thousand to a hundred thousand Mennonites still remained in the Soviet Russia (Toews 1967, 262). Some Mennonites became active functionaries of the Soviet regime. Most suffered tragically. It is not known exactly how many Russian Mennonites made their way to Oklahoma during the 1920s, but those who succeeded did not find an easy existence awaiting them.

## Helen Siemens Ediger

Helen Ediger is a women with tender eyes who wears a well-washed shirtwaist and sensible shoes. The Rock of Gibraltar wrapped in a housedress. Helen Ediger has the look of a classic Oklahoma farmwoman. She's a woman who, in her prime, probably cooked for an army of harvest hands in the morning, drove a truck for them in the afternoon, fed them supper, washed their dirty clothes at night, and

then did it all again the next day. In combining this work and mother-
hood, the jobs just merged as they ran round the clock. The women
who led this kind of life didn't give out—and they didn't give in.
Helen Ediger weathered the storm in coming to America, weathered
childhood in the Great Depression of the 1930s, weathered farm life
in agricultural economies small and big, weathered the demise of the
family farm. Her experiences mark several turning points in the
Mennonite definition of righteous labor, pious living, and close
community. We spoke on two occasions, and Helen later mailed me
additions to her story.

I was born October 14, 1919, in the Crimea in southern Russia.
I was a little past three years old when I came with my parents
and brother to America. In Russia it was a dangerous time; the
country was torn in a civil war. The Red Army, or the Bolshe-
viks, won, and the borders were closed. Conditions became
worse, especially for Christians, and the bountiful country
became a place of starvation and death. My parents decided it
was best to leave.

My parents were John K. and Helen Paukratz Siemens. In
Russia my father was first a schoolteacher and later went to a
Bible school [seminary]. After graduation, he was ordained as a
minister of the Mennonite Brethren Church. I know that my
parents were fairly well-fixed financially. My mother owned
land. Now that area where my parents once lived is a resort
area, but the revolution made their life very difficult.

When the Communists took over, they shipped our people
out of there to Siberia or other places. During this trouble, our
family—my parents, brother, and I—escaped under the cover
of night. I think my folks left Russia illegally. They heard rumors
that some people had managed to escape and had embarked for
America. Preparations were made secretly, and soon two groups
managed, with much difficulty, to board a ship at the Black Sea
that took them east.

My parents' first destination then was Batum, Turkey. My parents had money when they left Russia, but they were relieved of it. The people in Turkey, well, they just took it, robbed my parents as they came ashore at Batum. So there they were—stranded and without funds. From February to September they narrowly escaped death from starvation and poor living conditions. They really were what is known as "displaced persons." I don't know the details of what happened next, though quite a number of children died before they got to America. In the group of 277 people, in all 69 died before we left Batum. Finally we were able to sail to Constantinople with financial aid from the United States.

From there, in some way some people from Nebraska learned about our existence and sent money for my folks to come over to America. [The Nebraskan Mennonites probably learned about us] through the Mennonite papers. There were many people in many countries who were helping the Russian Mennonites during the Russian revolution. They did it as a good deed to help some of the displaced persons who were trying to get out. Word was passed to the churches who in turn asked the members to help these refugee people.

In December, we received visas and money from a farm family in Nebraska, for the twenty-three-day trip on the French ship *Canada* that carried us to America. The money sent to my parents paid for our tickets, third class. Third-class passage meant no food was provided aboard the ship, and we were almost totally without money to prepare for the trip. My parents just took crackers and cheese and some food like that when we went on board. On the trip over, my mother was a very brave lady. She showed her courage after the ship was underway. We had so little to eat, and one day she saw where the crew was throwing food overboard [from the first-class tables]. There was so much food being thrown away, and we were hungry. She went to the chef and said, "There are so many people down here [in third class] who sure could make use of that food. Why do you throw it away?" After that, when he had a big bowl of something he would come to the top of the stairs with it, but he wouldn't give it to just anyone. He would give the extra food only to my mother. So, for the remainder of the voyage, my family and some of the others in third class got a little of the ship's food that way. At the end of the voyage, we came to shore through Ellis Island and took the train all the way across the country to Henderson, Nebraska, where we were welcomed into the P. P. Buller farm family on January 6, 1923. I remember that long train ride. I remember being so tired on that long, long train ride. I'm sure I was tired from all the rest of it, too.

When we arrived in Henderson, we realized that those who had sent the money hadn't understood that we were a family. They had seen [on documents] the names Helen and John and Helen and John, but they didn't know the second Helen and John were my brother and I. Our benefactors just didn't understand that we were children. They thought that we were two different couples—adults. They had expected two couples to work for them [to help repay the cost of the trip]. However, what was sent to them was a family, my father, mother, brother, and me. Here we were, however, and here we stayed. By August my parents' work finished paying off the debt. After the debt was paid, my dad taught a Bible school in Henderson and did evangelistic work. We must have been there over two and a half years. Then we went to North Dakota where Dad was a preacher and evangelist.

When we lived in North Dakota, my dad served a Mennonite Brethren Russian church and preached in the Russian language. My father served four churches. In the fall of 1925, we moved to McClusky, North Dakota. Here Dad served eight churches in the area. It wasn't unusual for him to preach three times a day on Sunday, sometimes in German, other times in Russian or

English. He alternated the Sundays he spent at each church. The churches would try to have weddings and other special events on the Sundays when he was there. But funerals, those came when they did. That was an extra trip. By this time, the depression was so bad that nobody could pay for the services of a preacher. The members would bring in a half quarter [that is, half of a quarter side of beef] or something else off their farms as a contribution to my father's upkeep, but by then there were five children in our family. It was difficult, and Dad's voice was giving out from all the speaking.

The depression hit North Dakota before it hit further south, so my parents moved to Madrid, Nebraska, and Dad got a job working for a Mr. Fleming at the John Deere agency as a "parts" man. Dad also drove a school bus and took some speaking engagements. Then it really got bad around Madrid. People simply weren't able to pay the bills. One day, Mr. Fleming just told my dad he couldn't pay [his] salary anymore. Mr. Fleming was so sorry about it. He felt horrible about it, but he had a big family, and his own boys needed to work for him so that they could get by.

When that happened, my dad decided he wanted to move to Chicago, and my mother said, "With all these children?" There were six by then, and she said that no way was she going to move to Chicago. So we moved to a farm near Madrid where Dad helped the owner of the farm for about three years. It was rough, but soon we had pigs and chickens and some cows to milk. With Mom's big garden, milk and eggs, and delicious homemade bread, we ate well. I don't know how my parents raised us on what little income they had all those years.

In all the places we lived, we always went to a Mennonite Brethren church. When we moved to the Enid area, we went to the country [North Enid] church. By this time there were seven children in the family—three boys and four girls. In Enid, my dad taught Bible school and did evangelistic work, which

kept him away from home a lot. Then Mom and Dad moved to
Fairview [Oklahoma], and Dad served a church there. From
there they went on to serve several other churches and eventually moved to Hillsboro, Kansas. Dad worked in the creamery
there for quite a while. Then, when they were almost retirement
age, they took over the nursing home in Buhler, Kansas. They
retired in Hillsboro, Kansas, and they both died there. Altogether, Dad and Mom lived in Oklahoma for fifty years.

Our upbringing was strict. We were to obey our parents, and
no smoking, drinking, dancing, playing cards, or going to the
movies was allowed. Reading the Bible and having prayers was a
daily thing. We were encouraged to read the Bible and other good
books on our own. We all had to promise when we joined the
church we wouldn't curl our hair. My seventh-grade and eighth-
grade years were at a public school out in the country. There, at
that school, almost all the children were German kids. My
Sunday school was always in German. My folks taught High
German to us at home too, so we would learn it, but, really, my
mother would have benefited very much if we had talked English
to her. My folks were insistent that we learn German, but, you
know, if you don't keep it up, you lose it. Still, I know I would
get along all right if I went to Germany today.

     After eighth grade, it was just impossible for us to get high
schooling. We were so far from town, out on the farm. One day,
though, a man came to my dad. He told Dad that there were
people [from the church] who would pay the tuition if I wanted
to go to Corn Bible Academy [a Mennonite boarding school in
Corn, Oklahoma]. I wanted to go. When I was at Corn Academy
there were some girls there who had their hair cut and had
permanents, but most of us had long hair. It didn't bother me
to keep my hair long. It's strange to me now, though, that my
younger sisters did cut their hair and had permanents, but I
didn't until much later. I didn't have my hair cut until after I was

married. All in all, I studied for two years at the Corn Academy. In the meantime, the folks moved near Enid, and I had my senior year at home at Kremlin High. All of us children went to some Bible academy or school. My brothers and two younger sisters went to Tabor College, a Mennonite Brethren College in Hillsboro, Kansas.

Financially it was easier for our family in the Enid area because we older children were able to get jobs. We gave almost all the money we earned to help out at home. I did housework for awhile and then worked in a small grocery store for over two years until I was married. You see we [my age group] weren't just out on the farm by ourselves, like the older generation were. Most of us had some kind of city jobs where we worked with people other than Mennonites. I began to see John G. Ediger and was married to him two years after graduation. John had gone to a church school. In the early days, in many places there were Bible schools for children. I know John went to a little Bible school right on the churchyard. He graduated from a two-year Bible course. John never did get through high school, but a high school diploma was hard to get at the time.

After John and I were married December 15, 1940, we moved to a rented place on a farm where we had a house, other farm buildings, and pasture where John had some cows. My parents gave us a Jersey cow, a sow, a dozen chickens, and a rooster. John's parents gave us a team of horses and a dozen chickens, and they butchered a pig for us. John and I had the usual farm life together. We farmed big eventually, but not at first. It was hard to get a start in farming; we needed so many things. The first few years, John helped his dad with his farming in return for the use of his father's machinery when his dad's farming was done. We decided we needed our own machinery, [and] we were able to borrow some money to get a start.

Later we had to move to another place. We rented two quarters [a half section] of land with a house and buildings on it. At first we sold our eggs and cream in town. During the war, with so many young men in service, milk was needed badly. So we built a milk house and bought milking machines and a milk cooler. At first we had to use a compressor to run the milkers and cooler because we couldn't get electricity. The Gold Spot Dairy picked up the milk. Later we bought a farm north of Breckenridge when our daughter Judith Ann was eight months old. We lived there for fourteen years. Our son Gerald was born while we lived there; he was six years younger than Judy. We gradually were able to rent more land, so we had to buy more and bigger machinery. By now we had closed our small dairy and raised beef cattle and brought in steers to utilize the wheat pasture.

The children attended school at Garber. As they grew older and began to take part in more school activities, the bad roads became quite a problem. Many days when the weather was bad, the bus could not come out as far as our place. Also, the farms we rented were scattered, and John had to be able to get out so that he could take care of the cattle on our rented farms. We needed to do something! So we sold the farm, bought some grassland in the Lucien area, and bought a house in Enid. This didn't really solve all our problems either. John needed a place to work on machinery and park the cattle trucks.

So after five and one-half years in town, we bought the three acres of land near Enid and built it up. First we built a large metal shed, a shop. Later we built a nice home. There were grain bins and there was a place for the hired men's mobile home. This place served our needs well. John and I lived there until he died of cancer in October 1984. When he died, we were still in full-time farming. We had bought some farms in 1980 and had traded in our Lucien land on them. We were farming big when the bottom fell out [of the economy] for farmers. I just couldn't handle it on my own, not with the kind of things that were going on. The price of land and farm products dropped so drastically.

I lived in our home there two years longer until I settled the estate. I sold, and I sold, and I sold, and I sold. I had trouble selling the farms. But I had to sell the farms to finish paying for them and take care of some other farm debts. After the farms were sold, I still had the house and the acreage left, but I decided it was too much for me to keep up. So I sold it all and bought a smaller place in Enid, where I now live.

I think one of the biggest changes in the church came when we welcomed outsiders into the church, that and when we went over from the German to the English. We grew up and were married amongst our people. Since we have gone over to the English [language in church], we have other people who don't have our kind of names in church. Mennonites used to feel kind of like the children of Israel—stay with your own kind—don't get mixed up with other people. The change from German language to the English language was gradual. It was hard for the older people who had always had German services. But many of the younger people no longer understood the High German spoken in the Sunday school classes and services. I know the first time I read a magazine in German, it was almost sacrilegious to me because all the German I had ever used was always related to the Bible and church. But even now, every so often, someone [in church] will tune up a German song, and we'll sing.

One other thing that has changed in the church is that they did away with lay ministers. You know, you really can't progress and grow using only lay ministers. Lay ministers didn't even get paid. Now that people [the clergy] are being educated, they require more [financial support from congregations]. Today we have three or four people in the church who are paid: the minister, the assistant minister, the secretary, and perhaps the choir director. Another change—the biggest change, I think, in the church—is that, when we grew up, there was a more negative approach. Now the change is to a more positive approach to Christianity; that is a big improvement. They [church leaders] don't go into detail so much about "don't do this, don't do that." Today the message is "love your neighbor." It's more on the positive. In the past, it was, almost like, if we did all the things, we'd get to heaven. That's really not what Christianity is all about. There's been lots of changes. Accepting the change? Actually, these days, the people who've had trouble accepting the new ways, well, they have just about died out.

Over the years, we've had very little contact with those left behind in Russia. My family had some relatives who also came across to America at the same time we did. I remember, many years later, at their fiftieth wedding anniversary, the two of them sold their wedding rings and sent the money to the starving people still in Russia. [Later] another relative went to Russia with a tour group. While traveling, he met an aunt we still have over there. From that contact, she began to write and still writes to us, and she is almost ninety. She writes beautiful letters; even at her age, the script is just beautiful. While our American relative was in Russia, he told our Russian family that someone here [from our family] had sent some money to help. And they told him that one of my [Russian] aunts had to spend a long time in jail because some Americans had sent over some money. I don't know if it was the money from the wedding rings or not. Now days, it is a lot better [in Russia] than it was. Our Russian aunt who writes us says things are well. She says, "We're going to have plenty to eat this winter." She's in Siberia.

Although we had much to be thankful for over the years, we had our hard times and much illness too. Early on, John had a ruptured appendix and gangrene had set in. Later he had to have back surgery, which limited his work. Two times I had to spend several months in bed. During all this, we had our church to lean on. We were active in the church, singing in the choir, teaching Sunday school, ushering, greeting people, taking part in the missionary service. We served on the food festival committee for many years. After John's death and settling of the estate, I had to have cancer surgery and radiation. I am a survivor for ten years, but I don't have much energy.

Our children are on their own. Gerald and his wife, Cathy, are attorneys in Fort Wayne, Indiana. When Gerald started college, he told us, "I'm not a farmer." It didn't come as a surprise. When my husband first met Cathy, John just loved her. We both just loved her dearly. Judy and her husband gave us a granddaughter, our only grandchild. Judy attended Tabor [a Mennonite college in Kansas] for one year and later worked as a psychiatric nurse in Little Rock, Arkansas, for many years. Now she is in Fayetteville, enrolled in the University of Arkansas, hoping to get her Ph.D. in psychology. Our granddaughter, Roxanne, is in college in San Diego, California, near her father.

Through it all I have had my strength from my faith in God's love, the sacrificial death of his son, and the comfort of the Holy Spirit. We also enjoyed many friends and were able to host many people in our home—ministers, missionaries, the young people who visited our church, our children's friends, and our many relatives. I have slowed down and don't do so much anymore, but I have many happy memories.

# CHAPTER 8

# *Men of Conscience*

It seems to me pathetic, the public's
willingness to believe the worst.
———*Art Johnson*

During the 1930s, the rise of Hitler and Nazism in Germany and events leading to America's entry into World War II once again brought pressure to bear on Mennonites living in Northwest Oklahoma. But this time the situation was somewhat different. The immediate consequences of this second of global onslaughts included (1) a growing demand for grain and beef that increased farm production and income, (2) another wave of fierce anti-German and anti-Mennonite prejudice in Oklahoma, and (3) the military draft.

In the aftermath of the First World War, most Americans, and certainly most Mennonites, wanted nothing more than to shore up broken internal relationships and to shove the war into the past. It was fear of entangling foreign affiliations that influenced public opinion nationwide. Many Americans in the 1920s and 1930s considered themselves isolationists, who believed the best policy for the country was to remove itself from Europe's political squabbles and from military alliances and interventions (Norton et al. 1993). The stage was set for the United States to turn its back on the League of Nations and the league's ill-fated attempts to achieve world peace. But the nature of current and future events would prove that this dream—of a nation totally withdrawn from international problems—was totally impossible.

An American peace movement driven by activist groups that advocated arbitration and other strategies to resolve international disputes was also a part of the postwar political scene (Norton et al. 1993). The movement, however, never really got off the ground and did not receive widespread mainstream political support. By the outbreak of war in Europe in 1939 the American pacifism movement had almost completely dissolved (Eller 1991).

For farmers, with depression-era problems, the economy at last bottomed out in the late 1930s. The New Deal legislation that encouraged soil conservation, provided for the aged and poor, created jobs, and set the price of farm products based on agricultural prices during the period of 1910 to 1914 began to bring farm income up. By 1939, this legislated system of "parity" assured farmers at least 72 percent of their 1914 purchasing power (Perrett 1973). Whether price supports and the other New Deal policies actually improved the standard of living for farm families in Northwest Oklahoma is debatable; nonetheless, by 1940 parity made farm prices not all that bad.

As hostilities increased abroad, events in Europe began to shape the nation's farm, as well as its foreign, policy. Even as the farm economy inched upward from the depths of the depression, grain surpluses still existed. In 1941, the United States had a carryover of 400 million bushels of wheat from the previous harvest (Isern 1952, 29). Yet both production and prices were on the move forward. Short-term Washington strategies were based on a need for increased crop yield and beef cattle to meet the obligations of a recently passed Lend-Lease Act, which was designed initially to provide Great Britain with military equipment (Norton et al. 1993, 809). Production goals were set in Washington and incentives offered for meeting or exceeding them (Perrett 1973, 405). Idle acreage went back into cultivation, but this time with greater care taken to build and maintain fertile soil.

There were fewer farmers in the late 1930s to meet this challenge. The dust bowl and the depression had pulled population off family farms. The 1940 census showed Oklahoma's population decline from the 1930 figure was so great that the loss of a seat in the U.S. House of Representatives was warranted. Moreover, as war loomed ever nearer on the horizon, industrial expansion picked up across the country. Partly because its mild climate permitted ground and air training most of the year, Oklahoma became the center of intensive military buildup (Gibson 1984, 161). Facilities at Tinker Field near Oklahoma City kept the Army Air Corps in B-17s, B-24s, and B-29s. In Northwest Oklahoma, the Enid base trained U.S. pilots, and at Ponca City, a training facility was used for schooling British and Canadian pilots. Oklahoma ranked eighteenth among the states in war contracts and facilities (Morgan and Morgan 1977, 135).

All this activity drew farm labor out of Northwest Oklahoma. Some headed north to the Wichita aircraft plants. Others were attracted to jobs around the military bases in Enid and Oklahoma City. Also, in the nearby cities other, nonmilitary manufacturing jobs offered high wages and steady work (Nash 1979, 139). Finding harvest hands became difficult, even though the pay increased substantially as America moved closer to war. Oklahoma was not California or Texas. Farm owners couldn't use migrant families to bring in the crops. Wheat harvest required strong adolescent boys and men. Despite the demand, available manpower for seasonal harvest work began to dry up; city jobs offered year-round security plus good money.

The post–World War I political climate brought changes in the Mennonite churches as well. Through the years 1925 to 1940, a movement to articulate the Mennonite peace theology developed. Mennonites had been totally unprepared for the treatment they received (Haury 1981) from the larger society during the World War I era. But the hard lesson was learned, and the Mennonite churches were not unprepared for the next world war. A crucial difference between World War I and World War II troubles in relation to the churches' peace stand rested, not in any change in basic beliefs, but in the response of Mennonites to the pressure that was again brought to bear. A good many churches and their leaders were involved in shaping a statement of the Mennonite position regarding peace (Toews 1986). The roots of the idea integrated elements of an alternative service plan that grew out of the problems encountered in World War I, the privately organized voluntary work camps that served Europe and the United States during the interwar period, and the Civilian Conservation Corps program (Sibley and Jacob 1952, 112).

Once developed, the strategy was put into action by the Mennonite Central Committee, the general association of the major Mennonite groups. Documents were prepared, the assistance of other pacifist groups enlisted, and political lobbying undertaken in Washington to promote the interests of young men from the "historic peace churches." Churches identified as historic peace churches included Mennonite groups, the Friends (Quakers), and the Church of the Brethren. The united, political effort—which included organizing, seeking support from constituent groups and sympathetic allies, political negotiation, and compromise—marked a decided change from Mennonites' past beliefs about participation in public affairs. During congressional hearings on how best to achieve prewar military preparedness, among many groups and individuals who testified in support of recognizing freedom of conscience were spokespersons associated with the Women's International League for Peace and Freedom, the National Council for the Prevention of War, the Disciples of Christ, the Methodist Commission on World Peace, and the Federal Council of the Churches of Christ in America (Sibley and Jacob 1952, 46–47). Even though they were beginners, the historic peace churches' activities produced results (Huxman 1993). The Selective Training and Service Act of 1940 included a provision for conscientious objectors—The Civilian Public Service. By and large, the system set up by this law continued to exist for more than thirty years.

Civilian Public Service (CPS) represented a compromise acceptable to those who believed in peaceful nonresistance and to those who demanded that all men of draft age serve their country during war. CO status was not limited to members of the historic peace churches but was offered to any who by reason of religious training and belief claimed the status. An appeals system to adjudicate disputes regarding the assignment of status was set up. Those identified as COs were offered noncombatant service in the regular military or, alternatively, in the Civilian Public Service. Certified COs were to participate in "work of national importance," for which they were to receive no pay and their dependent families no benefits. Later changes in the law extended the length of a Civilian Public Service draftee's commitment to six months beyond the duration of the war.

Inclusion of provisions for COs in the Selective Service Act was considered a major accomplishment by the historic peace churches. The act protected Mennonite men from the kind of treatment received during World War I, but the implementation of the CO provisions created a new relationship between the nonresistance movement and federal government. During the World War II years, the conflict over conscientious objection was converted from an issue between church and state—between Mennonites as a group and the dominant society—as it had been during World War I, to an issue between the individual Mennonite and the dominant society. In other words, the issue was focused on the tension between a man's justification of himself as worthy of CO status and his local draft board's opinion of him.

Before the start of the Second World War the Mennonites found themselves at odds with the general public over the interpretation of the Selective Service Act. Again, the practice of pacifism, in the minds of most Americans, was not held to be a religious value protected by the Constitution. But some significant differences existed between the Mennonites' circumstances in the two wars. These differences lay both in the expression of prejudice toward Mennonites by the general public and in the amount of discrimination dealt the group. Prejudice and discrimination were both less overt during the years leading up to the war and, later, during the war itself.

On the whole, among the general population Mennonites no longer carried the overt stigma of a German faction or the image of a religious cult, withdrawn from society. There had been a considerable degree of acculturation and assimilation of Mennonites into mainstream society during the two decades after the armistice in 1918, and Mennonites were no longer thought of as foreigners (Coon 1988). Few questioned the patriotism of German Americans in the late 1930s (Sowell 1981). The vast majority of German Americans did not identify with Nazi Germany nor was there the political support for German nationalism such as existed in America before World War I. In this regard, Mennonite sentiment was recognized as similar to the judgments of the larger community. What developed as pre–World War II anti-German sentiment among Oklahomans and the nation overall was directed outside the country, toward Hitler as an individual and the German nation.

There was little fear of German Americans as a group (Rippley 1976). In fact, visible signs of German ethnicity within Mennonitism were practically nonexistent (Rohrs 1981). Everyday use of the German language and almost all symbols of German heritage had practically disappeared in Oklahoma, eradicated by the assault on German culture during the World War I years. Nevertheless, just as they had done in World War I, Mennonites generally refused to purchase war bonds, and this refusal stood as symbolic proof to the community at large that Mennonites were not interested in contributing to the American cause. Once again Mennonites were viewed as disloyal by the established society. But it was the refusal of Mennonites to fight that attracted most of the negative public attention. Instead of fearing Mennonites as Germans and a threat to national security, as had been the case in World War I, the American public during World War II thought of Mennonites as cowards (Coon 1988). Mennonites who did not serve in the military were stereotyped as selfish, weak shirkers whose interest in protecting themselves outweighed their responsibility to fight for their country. Taunts and vandalism and ridicule were used against them. Some anti-German slurs were hurled. Frequently Mennonite families arose to find yellow paint had been splashed on their barns and houses during the night (Kroeker 1994, 94). In one incident overzealous war activists broke into a church in Enid. American flags were rarely found in Mennonite churches at this time because of the religious dictum forbidding participation in any form of politics, yet one Sunday morning members of the Enid congregation entered their church to find an American flag placed in the center of their sanctuary. They understood its message. Rather than remove the flag they left it where it had been placed, as a reminder of the relationship between church and state and of the conflict between patriotic duty and religious conscience. In the 1990s, the American flag was still displayed in that church. Even though it had been moved to a corner, it remained visible near the front of the sanctuary.

In other incidents prior to and during World War II, eggs were thrown at Mennonite churches, and in one Oklahoma town a brick was thrown through the office window of a Mennonite attorney who represented young Mennonite men before their draft boards. The same attorney also had his office stormed by an angry mob who protested his work with conscientious objectors (Coon 1988). In late 1942, the Oklahoma American Legion passed a resolution calling for the repeal of the conscientious objector provisions in the 1940 Selective Service Act. The resolution was introduced in Congress by Sen. Elmer Thomas, a Democrat from Lawton, but the effort dissolved from lack of support and no other states took similar action (Kroeker 1994, 95).

Once the Selective Service Act took effect, more than 16 million young men appeared at precinct election boards across the country to register (Flynn 1993, 21). The law required the registration of all men between the ages of twenty-one and thirty-five. The age range was later extended to cover men from eighteen to forty-five. A lottery determined which registrants would appear before local civilian draft boards; the boards in turn determined which of those men would be selected to fill each state's quota. The quotas guaranteed the soldiers would come proportionally from each state. The local boards were expected to exercise good judgment in selecting only those men whose induction would not adversely affect the economy. Group deferments were forbidden, but local draft boards were allowed to defer, when appropriate, individual men such as those employed in "vital" industries, students, physicians, and farmworkers. Religious ministers and those studying for the clergy were exempted from service, but they were required to register (Flynn 1993, 19).

The language of the law was also interpreted to mean that single men were called before married men and married men before married men who were fathers. Deferments were made in hardship cases; these were mostly given when the draftee established that other family members were dependent on him for financial support. A 1-A classification identified those immediately available for service and 4-F was assigned to those unfit to serve. To screen inductees, two physicals were required: one at the local level and one at the time of induction. By the end of the war in 1945, 49 million men had registered for the draft, and 10 million had been inducted. With the addition of volunteers, the eventual size of the armed forces was 12 million.

To plains-states farmers, the initial effect of the war buildup—and later, of the war itself—on wheat farming was slight. Depression-era surpluses and a sluggish farm economy prevailed. "We already have more wheat than we know what to do with," U.S. Secretary of Agriculture Claude R. Wickard acknowledged in April of 1942, as he spoke to a meeting of wheat farmers in Enid. Yet the secretary urged the farmers to grow more wheat as a patriotic duty. Even with carryover wheat still in storage, Wickard told farmers to raise and store as much wheat as possible in on-farm storage tanks or granaries and put their faith in government (Isern 1982). Meanwhile, in the summer of 1942 the total draft pool of men eighteen to thirty-seven was 22 million. Of this total 1.5 million were deferred as farmers (Flynn 1993, 63). In the fall of 1942 about half of Oklahomans still farmed (Morgan and Morgan 1977, 133); however, farm-labor shortages remained on the climb and were beginning to cause an uproar in Congress. Senator Tydings of Maryland suggested all farmers should be deferred as long as they remained working in agriculture.

The demand for increased farm production intensified. By 1943, U.S. grain reserves were depleted because of the growth in consumption and a light harvest. As the war continued, federal commodity programs were used to encourage production rather than discourage it, as had been the intent and the case during the depression years. In 1944, farmers were asked to seed 11 million more acres than in 1943, a nearly 10 percent increase (Isern 1952, 31). Meat and other foods were rationed.

By July 1944, local draft boards were responding to the need for farmers on the home front. Some 17 percent of all male farmworkers aged eighteen to thirty-five enjoyed job deferments while only 9 percent of nonfarm workers in the same age group received deferments. Three times as many males under age twenty-six got deferred for farming as for nonfarming jobs (Flynn 1993, 65), but throughout the war draft boards remained reluctant to defer a young, single farmer over a married man who was not a farmer, or a nonfarmer with dependents. Only late in the war did it become easier to draft men from war-related industry jobs than to draft a farmer (Flynn 1993, 68). A survey found more than 70 percent of the public agreed that young men should be kept on the farms (Flynn 1993, 68). The immediate postwar need for wheat and beef was projected to be tremendous. In addition, the Roosevelt administration had made promises to countries in western Europe to supply them with grain during reconstruction after the war.

So, with a severe farm-labor shortage, a government demanding ever-increasing farm yields, a draft that provided deferment for farmwork as essential to the war effort, and a trend in draft boards nationwide to defer farmers, retrospective logic dictates that Mennonite men would have little difficulty dealing with their local draft boards. That, however, was not the case in the collective memory of Mennonites in Northwest Oklahoma. While a national lottery identified those to be drafted, local boards had control over deferments, which were decided on individual merit (Flynn 1993, 13). The idea behind the draft was to create a "fair," or egalitarian, system of selection. The draft was managed by the Selective Service, which, as the name implies, selected from the pool of eligible men only those with certain qualifications to serve their country. Placing the selection of the actual draftees in the hands of local draft boards was part of the national politics of fairness. Local draft boards, with knowledge of their communities, were considered by the Roosevelt administration to be the most politically desirable and expedient public arbiters of young men's lives. Members were appointed and generally were businessmen and others well known in the community.

In Oklahoma, the administration was through county draft boards. Overall, these citizen draft boards were accepted by the general public as equitable entities for passing judgment on who should go and who should stay, and their decisions were backed by the federal government. In a review of national statistics, Flynn (1993) found that at one point in 1943 one out of every six indications went to appeal and in more than 69 percent of the cases the decisions of the local boards were upheld (Flynn 1993, 60). Actions of the local boards, however, were "hardly bureaucratic routine" (Flynn 1993, 59). The boards were inconsistent in applying the standards of the Selective Service legislation (Flynn 1993, 30). In Northwest Oklahoma, for instance, there were precious few farmwork deferments for Mennonite men, and it was said that the most "extreme and best-corroborated examples of gross discrimination against conscientious objectors in connection with occupational deferments occurred in Oklahoma" (Sibley and Jacob 1952, 64).

According to Selective Service procedures, each registrant was required to fill out a questionnaire covering personal information. On this form a man could claim CO status. In Washita County, just south of the Cherokee Outlet, the board for many months gave virtually every person who registered as a conscientious objector the status of nonessential farm laborer, despite the fact that the individuals involved were in most instances clearly entitled to occupational deferment and included men who were married and married men with dependents (Sibley and Jacob 1952, 64). In a recent interview, one man who was called up estimated that during World War II not only he but more than forty-five other men from his Northwest Oklahoma Mennonite church of about two hundred members did not receive farm deferments and were inducted. Those figures would indicate that essentially no Mennonite of draft age was deferred.

County draft boards throughout Oklahoma were reluctant to honor requests for CO classification (Kroeker 1994, 91). In theory, the provision in Selective Service legislation that COs need not be members of peace churches appeared to broaden the scope of the draft legislation. In practice, instead of merely establishing membership in the church, when a Mennonite man was called in the draft he had to *prove* his sincerity and *prove* that his belief was associated with religious training and faith (Flynn 1993, 45). If a man made use of the CO option in registering for the draft, then he was required to fill out a second, longer questionnaire that asked more-detailed questions about his religious beliefs. Then a man could be called before his board for questioning. Typical questions included, Do you owe any obligation to your country? Why should other men fight for you? What are your political affiliations? What is your social philosophy? What would you do if your sister (wife or mother) were raped? (Sibley and Jacob 1952, 62). Sincerity, demonstrated in part by a CO applicant's response, was deemed more important than official church membership (Flynn 1993, 46).

Boards, often composed of war veterans with little training in theology and little sympathy for pacifists, had difficulty applying the qualifying standards. The local boards made decisions not entirely on the basis of the personal history of the candidate. Rejection of the request for CO status was certainly not out of the question. Once the local board approved the CO status, draftees were given two choices: noncombatant service within the regular armed forces or civilian alternative service. Nationwide, local boards' decisions were generally upheld by substantial percentages, but in most cases regarding CO status that went to appeal from Oklahoma, the appeal board overturned the negative rulings of the Oklahoma draft boards (Kroeker 1994, 91). The largest number of CO classification appeals in any county in the United States originated in the Major County seat of Fairview, Oklahoma (Kroeker 1994, 91).

The Selective Service legislation required that all those who were inducted perform some service to the nation, regardless of religious convictions (Flynn 1993, 47). Overall, the age-old Mennonite association of agrarian occupations and nonresistance still held, and most Mennonite COs selected the Civilian Public Service as an alternative (Bush 1993). Statistics show that 6,116 pacifists refused both noncombatant and Civilian Public Service and were imprisoned for violating the Selective Service Act; 4,441 of those were Jehovah's Witnesses. No statistics are available regarding the number of Mennonite men nationwide or in Oklahoma who served prison terms during the war, but statistics do show that 310 of those jailed were members of "small" religious groups, which presumably would include Mennonites (Kohn 1986, 47). No reports of Mennonite men in Northwest Oklahoma who went to prison could be located.

The passage of the Selective Service Act fostered a new phase of peace church cooperation (Keim and Stoltzfus 1988, 104). Key questions had to be answered. How would the Civilian Public Service program be organized? Who would be in charge? How would it be financed? President Roosevelt, who originally thought that the COs should be kept away from the public, so as not to attract attention, and be drilled by army officers (Keim and Stoltzfus 1988, 111), soon washed his hands of the problem and delegated it to the Selective Service. The plan eventually worked out by the peace churches and the Selective Service was a hybrid system. In order to gain control over the treatment of the COs to be assigned to the camps, the coalition agreed to fund the operations. The Civilian Public Service was under the auspices of federal regulation but was organized and administered by the pacifist groups themselves (Smith 1957, 813). The

Mennonite Central Committee supported the idea. One church leader offered that Mennonites would gladly pay their share of the bill, even if every Mennonite farmer had to mortgage his farm (Keim and Stoltzfus 1988, 113). It turned out that the churches underwrote the costs of supplies, including food, and paid the staff. Individual COs were responsible for their own personal needs, such as clothing and spending money. By the war's end, the cost to the churches to support the CPS camps was 3 million dollars. If the U. S. government had paid for work accomplished at the CPS camps at the same rate it paid for the army, the cost would have been more than 18 million dollars (Sibley and Jacob 1952, 124).

The camps were under civilian direction, which was the goal of the churches, but the actual work performed in the camps was under military direction. There were various kinds of camps, including agriculture, forestry, and construction. Complaints arose about the CPS men working without pay, and complaints arose about what some termed the "menial" tasks at some of the camps, which had been intended to provide work of "national importance." Furthermore, the fact that most of the camps were in remote areas did keep the CO agenda isolated from the public (Anderson 1994).

As the war progressed, CO activities broadened. Some Mennonite men were assigned the hazardous job of fighting forest fires. Others were assigned to do public health work. After the United States entered World War II, more nonresisters were assigned to work in mental hospitals. Of the fifty-one mental hospital units, Mennonites administered twenty-five (Hershberger 1951, 59; Smith 1957, 814). Some COs volunteered to serve as human guinea pigs in medical experiments and were infected with such diseases as typhus, influenza, malaria, hepatitis, and polio (National Service Board for Religious Objectors; Kroeker 1994, 90). Amendments to the Selective Service Act made it impossible for CPS assignees to engage in relief service outside the continental United States. Near the war's end, however, when the United Nations Relief and Rehabilitation Administration (UNRRA) was set up to relieve the human suffering that resulted from the destruction of World War II, men who were drafted into the CPS were allowed to volunteer their help (Silbey and Jacobs 1952, 228). The UNRRA shipped livestock to devastated areas, distributed food to millions of needy persons, and helped revive agriculture and rebuild industries.

In total, most of the COs from Oklahoma worked in state mental hospitals or on conservation projects (Kroeker 1994, 90). At the end of the war, CPS veterans received none of educational benefits provided by the government to those who served their country in the military. Out of the 11,996 persons nationwide who served in the Civilian Public Service during World War II, a total of 4,665 were Mennonites (Smith 1957), by far the largest number of any denomination.

Not all Mennonites who were drafted chose to go into the Civilian Public Service as conscientious objectors. Although federal legislation provided for the Civilian Public Service to accommodate the religious beliefs of Mennonites at the outset of World War II, nationwide about half of all Mennonite men eligible for the draft still chose to enter the military (Smith 1957). Many served as medical corpsmen or in other capacities as noncombatants. It is possible that a few entered into regular service as combatants, although there is no documentation of this. Cleavage between General Conference Mennonites and Mennonite Brethren widened on the issue, with Mennonite Brethren for the most part more willing to serve in the military as noncombatants and those of the General Conference more willing to hold themselves out as conscientious objectors. But the line between the groups on the issue was not clearly drawn. Respect for personal choice in the matter was agreed upon by both groups.

It seems clear that a substantial number of Mennonites no longer supported the doctrine of absolute refusal of all forms of government service during war. The assimilation of Oklahoma Mennonites into the general population can be observed most notably in this respect. Even though no statistics detail the exact disposition of Mennonite men through the Northwest Oklahoma draft boards during the World War II years, the *Daily Oklahoman*, the state's largest newspaper, reported in 1942 that in Washita County, in the west-central part of the state, only about 15 percent of Mennonite men who registered for the draft signified they were conscientious objectors. Other reports for the same area show that about 42 percent of General Conference men went into Civilian Public Service (Coon 1988).

In all of Oklahoma there were 1,511 COs on the rosters of local draft boards. In comparison with the rest of the nation, Oklahoma ranked eleventh among the states in numbers of CO registrants (Kroeker 1994, 92). The Oklahoma CO registrants represented 0.27 percent of the total number of men in the state who registered for the World War II draft (Kroeker 1994, 92). Of all the men registered for the draft nationwide, only a tiny minority—less than 0.20 percent—sought conscientious objector status, and the ratio of Oklahomans seeking the status was less than 1 percent higher than that of the nation at large (Kohn 1986, 46; Sibley and Jacobs 1952, 84). Yet Oklahoma draft boards were far less willing to grant the status than were draft boards in other states, and among the most stringent of all Oklahoma draft boards were those in Northwest Oklahoma.

During the World War II era, Mennonites expected trouble, and latent conflicts between them and their neighbors did surface. Unhealed wounds from the previous war were reopened, but the actual violence directed toward the group was less and the prejudice was more covert than during the First World War. That was little consolation. Selective Service legislation notwithstanding, the peace position went unsupported. Precious few deferments were bestowed on Mennonite farm laborers. Conscientious objectors worked without pay, and few Americans recognized that, in service to their country, COs were reshaping the nation's mental hospitals, giving themselves over to medical experiments, and undertaking other work that risked their own safety.

The director of the Selective Service said he was convinced that the boys from the peace churches were in good faith unwilling to contribute to the taking of another life but were honestly willing to give up their own lives to help others (Kroeker 1994, 92). In North-west Oklahoma, however, that recognition was not forthcoming. Instead, never, with the exception of the First World War, had so much public censure been directed toward so small a group.

## Leonard Schmidt and Harry Martens

Leonard Schmidt and Harry Martens are veterans of the World War II Civilian Public Service camps. In the 1990s, both continue in church service and continue to be active in the occupation that they gave up only briefly during the war years. After the war, each went back to what he knew. Leonard started with six or seven cows and a bunch of chickens on a place his bride's father let them farm almost fifty years ago. With spreading wheat fields to the back, his home now sits on the edge of Meno, a once vigorous but now shrinking small town named for Menno Simons, a sixteenth-century church founder. Harry lives some distance away at Fairview. He runs a beef cattle operation and raises wheat and alfalfa with his oldest son. Harry's son and his family have their house on the 160 acres homesteaded by Harry's father in 1893. That particular piece of property, claimed in the Cherokee Outlet run, has been passed down from father to son through three generations of Martens and has remained in the family now for more than 100 years.

Harry kept a diary and later put his memories of World War II down in two essays. He titled one "Mule Skinners' Memoirs: The True Story of 'Ocean-going Cowboys' in the Post-W. W. II Mediterranean." The other he called "Guniea Pig Experiment: June-August 1945." Leonard gave his account of the war years at the New Hopedale church one weekday morning when several members got together for the purpose of sharing their personal stories. What follows combines part of the interview taken at the group meeting in Meno; a second, personal interview with Leonard; a one-hour telephone interview with Harry; and excerpts from Harry's essays.

# *Leonard Schmidt*

It would have been easier to go into the army. I mean as far as public opinion is concerned. But I thought of the time that might come—a time when I would have to face somebody, maybe a guy from a church in a different country, a person who was a Christian and was in the army, and I would have to pick up a gun and shoot him, shoot my own brother. [Silence, and a long pause.] It's all according to everybody's conviction, you know. I know people that I consider to be Christian people, and I respect their beliefs. Some people just went into the army, and they went out on missions for noncombatants, and I respect their position. If that's what they believe, then that's what they should do.

The local draft board had the final say about whether you got to be CO or not—whether you went to camp or whether you went to the army. When you were drafted, you either went to camp or you joined the army, one of the two. [A farm-worker deferment for Mennonite men was extremely rare.] I was from Goltry, and I received a letter to appear before the draft board at Cherokee [in Alfalfa County]. I applied for a CO position, and I was never questioned on it. Now, the draft board might have gone back to my community to check to see what I was like and how I lived, but I never heard about it. I never had one bit of trouble with my draft board. As far as I know, I was the only Mennonite drafted out of Goltry and out of Alfalfa County. Nobody else in our church at Goltry went besides me.

When I went to [Civilian Public Service] camp, I rode a train for two days and a half just to get from Oklahoma to Hill City, South Dakota. That's how the trains ran during the war. The train picked up several other COs down south at Corn and Cordell and Clinton [Oklahoma]. When they got to Fairview, they picked up several more besides me, and from there we went into Kansas, and there we picked up a lot of kids. There were right at 100 of us [COs] on that train. We just showed up and got on the train. There was no supervision or army personnel on the train.

When I left home, I was wearing summer clothes. When I arrived in South Dakota, it was real cold, and there was snow on the ground, and it was sixteen miles from the train station to the camp. The camp directors met us at the train station with government trucks. They [put] us in the back of a truck, and we rode that way to camp. Our camp was at the site of a Civilian Conservation Corps camp that had just been closed. It was reopened as a new CO camp, and we were the first to arrive. In addition to the 100 who came on my train, there were 33 people who came from Pennsylvania. [The total capacity of the South Dakota camp] was 150. We went there to build a monstrous dam to supply water for Rapid City. The dam was going to be used for water for the city and irrigation of sugar beets and other crops. It had just barely been started by the CCC before the war began.

We met some opposition from the townspeople and in the camp when we first got there. The atmosphere against us was very hostile. People would call us "conchees." They would say it behind our backs, but it was meant to be heard. It even got down to the point that people were calling us "yellow bellies." All in all though, we didn't have the opposition that our people had in World War I. In the camp, they tried us out, too. Our bosses tried us out every way they could. We had government foremen. They reported to the Bureau of Reclamation. Most of them were military men or had been military men. We had some bosses who had sons in the army. The first thing, they took us out to work in the early-morning winter when it felt like forty to eighty degrees below zero, just to see whether we would go. Nobody from a peace church refused to go. Then the government men saw that we really believed, and we were conscientious in what we were doing. When they saw that everybody went out and did the work, well, then they brought us in until afternoon. After that, they began to wait until afternoon to take us out, when it felt like it was only thirty below zero outside. One way or another, we always worked eight hours a day on the project.

But there were those in camp who wouldn't work. Some of those boys, including some ol' boys out of New York City, had a little bit of a rough time, you know. There were always a few sour grapes. My idea was that some of these people were just dodging the draft, and, when they got to camp, well, they didn't want to work either. You could figure that if it was cold, real cold, they would be sick. It never failed. We couldn't get them up; they just stayed in bed. One morning, one of these guys wouldn't get out of bed, and some of the guys who were still around because they had just finished work on another shift took him outside, carried him out bed and all. He just laid there in the cold and still wouldn't get up. That kind of guy had a "little" rough going with the government foremen. You know, it didn't take the foremen long to figure out who was not doing the work. It didn't take them long to figure that out. Now, those guys got a hard time from these government foremen. They really got the law laid down to them. And their not working caused the rest of the fellows to have a black eye among the public.

I had no complaint about the government foremen. The camp director [who was appointed by a coalition of pacifist denominations] directed everything that went on in camp, but when we got in the trucks and went to the project to work, we were always under government supervision. I developed a lot of respect for those government men who had sons in the army. If you did your job and lived up to what you believed, you got along just fine. Pretty soon they found out that we were working for nothing. [Conscientious objectors did not receive wages.] The churches and our parents helped us get through camp. We paid our own way. We furnished our own clothing. The Mennonite Central Committee provided food. When we got there, the CCC camp had just closed, but there were still a lot of clothes there that the government had furnished the CCC, and they turned them over to us—heavy coats and overshoes. Boy, we got a lot of wear out of those things. Oh, yes, they were good clothes.

They heated everything with wood, you know. They had what they called a "night fire." It got so cold there at night that every night, every two hours, someone would come through all those barracks, to fill the stoves so that we would have wood to burn through the night.

The government supervisor lived in camp with us and ate at the same table with us. His wife and the family were living there, and, of course, our camp director lived there. We had a business director; he and his wife were there. The business director did all of the buying for the camp—the food and so on. We were on meat rationing during the war, like everyone else. For a time, it was impossible to get meat. We ate liver for days. I never knew they made liver in so many different ways. Liver, liver, we had liver for dinner, we had liver for supper, every day and every day. But they finally got other food for us. We had plenty to eat after the initial entry there, but so many people came in at one time that they simply couldn't supply us. We also had powdered milk and cold-storage eggs. We were as far off as 150 to 200 feet from the mess hall. In the morning, when I'd go out for breakfast, if the wind was right, I knew whether I was having cold-storage eggs or not. You could smell them that far.

There were about 150 of us in that camp, and we never had any big friction among us. There were about 40 guys to a barracks. Forty people in one building, bed on bed, bed on bed—when you can have 40 guys in one barracks and not have a squabble every day, which we managed, that was an accomplishment in itself, I thought. We got along real good. We learned to live together. I never knew of a fistfight. We lived together for three years and did not have any incidents of anybody knocking anybody's ears down. I would say that the majority of us were farmboys. We had some people from New York City. We had some colored people from Chicago. We had some Jehovah's Witnesses, some Mormons. They believed altogether different than we did. The camp was interdenominational. There were a lot [of groups]. They had their own meetings, usually during the week at night. We had people in camp who didn't belong to any church. They were political objectors who didn't believe in any kind of war.

During the summer we worked on the dam 24 hours a day in three eight-hour shifts. We worked around the clock because the summer was short, and the work needed to get done. Our job was to clear the basin for the lake. The basin had to be cleared of trees and as high as the water would eventually reach. Everything had to be cleared and the lake bottom trimmed out and all the usable logs hauled off. It was a new experience, because none of us knew anything about building a dam. Of course, we had the government foremen furnished by the Bureau of Reclamation to direct us when we were out on project. They started all the new guys out doing what they called "cleaning up the bedrock." We dug down below the ground, down to rock, and then we had to sweep all the crevices and get out all the dirt and loose gravel and everything and then clean up all that loose dirt. Boy, that was a tedious job. That part of it was discouraging. We dug into the hillsides into a kind of slivery, scaly-looking rock. Then we would drill into the [exposed] rock and the drilled place would be [injected] with something called "grout"; it was a mixture of water and cement which would fill the crevices and cracks to do away with any seepage. That's why we had to clean out the rock.

After a couple of weeks, I got on the dynamiting crew. This crew worked about eight miles above camp at a separate rock quarry where we blasted down rock and crushed it for use on the dam. We hauled the broken rock back to the camp where there was a big rock crusher. The rock would be dumped in there and be crushed to bits. But before this could be done, somebody had to do the dynamiting. So the COs would drill holes into the quarry rock, and we would put dynamite in there. The dynamite came in sticks. My job was to stuff the dynamite sticks in the holes. You would put that down in the hole very carefully. You had a wooden spike, and you would tap the dynamite sticks down, and, on the last stick that went into the hole, a detonating cap would be placed. You would stick a sharp spike into the end of last dynamite stick, put the detonating cap in there, and pull the paper back over. There were some wires, and you would bring the wires out and string the wires out for quite some distance. Then you would holler, "Fire in the hole," and everybody would get under cover. The wires connected to a little electrical box; you pushed that [button] down, and it blew. That's what it took to blow out the chunks of rock so we could load it.

Sometimes we went to work with that dynamite sitting in the back of the truck, between twenty to thirty guys in the back of the truck, but that wasn't the dangerous part. The detonating caps were what were really dangerous. We all managed though. We never did have an accident with the dynamite, not one. The only accident that we had came when we were clearing trees where the water was going to be. All the trees had to be cleared out of this area, and, while we were doing this, one person broke his leg and one person was killed. The person who was killed drove a bulldozer. He was pushing a dead tree with the 'dozer, and the tree toppled over backwards and killed him.

After the dynamiting job, I got a truck-driving job. I got promoted quite often, which was good. I liked that. After the truck-driving job, I got an easy job, a grease monkey's job on one of the big shovels, and then, after that, I got on the bulldozers. I was on a bulldozer for about two and a half years. We didn't actually work on the dam much in the winter. It was all clearing work in the winter. We worked eight hours, no matter how cold it got. The ones who drove the crew trucks were out early in the morning. At a certain time, we lined up the trucks. Then we all got on our trucks, and we went to cut wood and haul it back to camp.

In the summertime, we had a little time off in between shifts. When we had time off, there was fishing and horseshoes and volleyball. A lot of guys played cards and dominoes and checkers on their time off in the evenings. We would read, and we had a library. We had radio. In the winter there was ice skating and hunting. We had singing in the camp choir. Ministers came in from different churches to hold services, but not very often. It was pretty remote. There was a little country store three miles up, and we went up there quite often. We'd go to town once in awhile. You could get a pass for a weekend. If you had the money and if you had transportation, you could go to Mount Rushmore, or you could go see the Needles or the Badlands. But I had very little money. The only money I had was what came to me through the church and through my friends. My parents and my future wife sent me money to help me get by too.

Approximately five hundred men served in the camp during the more than three years of its existence. All in all, there were a lot of trees cut and hauled, and there were tons and tons of cement laid to make that dam. In February of 1946, they transferred us to Colorado Springs. They were not completely finished in Hill City, but there were just little things left to do. It was, well, in the final phase, when we were transferred out. In Colorado, we made diversion ditches and cutoff gates to divert water runoff. It was a lot of shovel work, handwork. It didn't really appeal to me. I was only in Colorado Springs for two months when I got my discharge in April of 1946. I worked three years, five months, and nineteen days. I had it down to the hour.

I wouldn't take a million dollars for the experience I had. I felt like it was something I had to do. It was always in our family that it was wrong, wrong to kill anybody, wrong to go to war; it was absolutely wrong. That just got stuck in my craw to where I wouldn't shake it, and I still think it's wrong. I sure do. I was doing what I thought was right; that was the main thing. If everything could come down to the point to where it says in the Bible, "Love thy neighbor as thyself," all the world's problems would be over. You know that you don't love anyone more than you do yourself, so if you could love somebody else like you love yourself, that would solve the problems.

## Harry Martens

In May 1945, while I was at Clear Spring, Maryland, Civilian Public Service Camp 24, unit 4, I applied to be transferred to a "guinea pig" unit. I had been in conservation work camps where I had been a cook and helped some with forestry and soil conservation, but I felt that I wanted to do something that would help people directly. I was thinking that I wanted to do service valuable to saving human life rather than taking human life, which was what the war was all about. Somewhere, maybe it was on a camp bulletin board, I found information that asked for volunteers willing to be human subjects in a medical experiment to begin in June at Pinehurst, North Carolina. I signed up. I was nineteen years old at the time and didn't think much about the risk. For this particular project, they were looking for men who were young and healthy. I was accepted and soon reported to the Holly Inn in Pinehurst, a small town in North Carolina.

I spent the months of June, July, and August 1945 in confinement in room 324 on the third floor of the Holly Inn. The experiment was conducted by the U.S. Surgeon General's office on the mysterious disease called atypical pneumonia. The duration of the project was to be about three months, depending on the condition of the "guinea pigs" at the end of that time. Fifty-one boys volunteered for this project, eight of whom served as attendants. Their job was to take care of the needs of the other fellows after they were placed in confinement. Before we were sent to confinement, one day was spent in orientation. A doctor told us how the experiment would be conducted and what was expected of the participants. Then the head nurse explained the procedures for exposing us to the pneumonia and gave us a tour through the laboratories and the rooms where cages and cages of white mice were kept. Each guinea pig had a cage of white mice assigned to him and the mice were inoculated with the virus taken from the volunteers each day. The sick and dead mice were then used to find out what caused the illness and find a possible cure.

That same day, we all were escorted to our separate rooms, where we would stay for the duration of the experiment. The only times we left our rooms were on the two days that we were exposed to the disease or if one of us required hospitalization. After a couple of days of observation and various health checks, we were escorted to an isolated place in the woods where several white tents were set up. We went into a tent one at a time with an attendant who took us to a doctor or nurse who exposed us to the "germs"—the mysterious bacteria or virus that was being studied. The germs were taken from throat scrapings of soldiers who were suffering from atypical pneumonia in the military hospital at nearby Fort Bragg. We were exposed by a mixture of the germs and gaseous nitrogen that was blown into our throats. As we inhaled through our mouths, the doctor or nurse would spray a shot of the gas down our throats; this was done probably eight or ten times. We were given this treatment on two different occasions—on the second day and again about halfway through the experiment.

The room I was confined to was quite large, maybe twenty by twenty feet with a bathroom, one double bed, and a chest of drawers. Double windows faced the backside of the hotel so there wasn't much to see. The daily routine was much the same each day. Breakfast was served on a steel tray; it was slid through the door on the floor and the door quickly closed. This was the way we got our noon and evening meals also. When I'd finished eating, I'd set the tray near the door and an attendant would reach in and pick it up. Before breakfast, a nurse would come in and take my temperature, pulse, and blood pressure and a sample of blood from my finger. If I was not feeling too well, a doctor might come in with the nurse. Anytime a doctor, nurse, or attendant came in, they were dressed the same—white pants, white jacket, white cover on their head and a mask over their face.

The first weeks went by slowly, but, as time went along, I got adjusted to being by myself and improvised or made up things to do to pass the time. One thing that helped a lot was a small radio that Uncle Fred Hamms had sent along with me. When I was home on furlough and getting ready to leave for Pinehurst, his family felt sorry for me and they brought their small radio to me. I returned it to them after I was released from the project. We were allowed magazines or books if we requested them. The request might take a day or two while the books were sterilized so as not to bring any germs into the room. The same was true of mail. I liked to read, and I nearly completed reading the Bible all the way through while I was there. I ordered several model airplane kits [and I built the planes]. Then when I finished one, I'd open a window, and watch it fly and finally crash. This led to making other models to see which kind would fly the best and longest.

More of my time was taken up in leather work. I had learned to do this nearly two years earlier at the Civilian Public Service camp in Downey, Idaho. I made billfolds, coin purses, and other things. Another thing I did was put my bed in the middle of the room and walk round and round for exercise. This helped, but my feet would swell up, probably from lack of use. We were allowed to have our windows open first thing in the morning. Then guys would holler out to each other and pass on a little news. Another thing we all had in our rooms was a telephone for in-hotel use only. Since I didn't have time to get acquainted with very many of the guys, I called very little. If I called anyone, we'd share news we'd gotten in our letters or discuss the war news we heard.

As a result of the exposure, some of the fellows got pretty sick, some mildly sick, and others had only a few days where they didn't feel good. On the days I felt bad, I received treatment by the doctors and nurses in my room. I became sick but I was never sick enough to be taken to the hospital. Sometimes the doctors or nurses would come in and kid us about our assigned cage of mice all having died the night before; the joke was that we might just end up the same way the mice had. It helped to have a good sense of humor. If I'd been older, I might have been more frightened.

When volunteers were ill, every effort was made to treat us at the inn, because to take us to the hospital would, of course, alter the experiment. I don't recall hearing anything about anyone who went to the hospital, but we weren't given many details at all. I know that no one died during the experiment. The way the experiment was run wasn't secretive, but, in a way, it was. None of us were supposed to know about the condition of the others, because the doctors didn't want to take the chance that our thinking along those lines might have an influence on a person's own condition.

As the time of our release came closer, the more intense the examinations and care of us became. Anyone with any fever or other symptoms was advised that he would have to stay until he was fully recovered. I don't know how many had to stay, but a few did. The day of our release we were given a schedule with a time we were to appear at the town barbershop for a haircut.

We were taken down to the barbershop six at a time. It wasn't easy to recognize a friend, since, by that time, we all had long hair and sometimes a beard. Most of the men I wouldn't have known anyway. Our train tickets and food vouchers were ready for us to pick up the next morning. Everyone got extra days off to spend at home, or wherever, before reporting to his next assigned camp. We also were given a letter from the doctors stating we were to be given every consideration as we traveled by train in case we got sick on the ride. During the war, the trains were always overcrowded with a lot of military men as well as civilian passengers. I felt all right and enjoyed my trip back home, except for the fact I couldn't get my shoes on. My feet were swelled up until I got home.

After spending my recuperation time at home, I reported to camp number 33 at Fort Collins, Colorado, September 1945. I was not allowed to go on another human guinea pig experiment.

When the United Nations Relief and Rehabilitation Administration began relief programs for war-torn and developing countries, men who were drafted and served in Civilian Public Service wanted to help, but by law, CPS volunteers could not leave the country. With a transfer from CPS to the CPS Reserve, the conscientious objectors could become eligible for the overseas projects to rebuild industry and agriculture left devastated by the war. Several projects involved transporting livestock to Europe to help revive agriculture. I volunteered for one of them and was selected to tend livestock on a ship that crossed the ocean carrying 841 mules and 37 horses to postwar Greece.

We sailed on the SS *Park Victory* from the port of Houston on March 10, 1946, and arrived at Piraeus, Greece, on March 26. The ship had been outfitted with stalls on the top deck and two lower decks to accommodate the hauling of livestock. The guns were removed from their turrets to provide space for stacks of hay. The ship's crew was composed of about forty men, and thirty men made up the livestock handling crew. We were often referred to as "oceangoing cowboys." In addition to the thirty cowboys, there were two veterinarians on board. It turned out that one of the other animal tenders on the ship with me was a Mennonite CO from Oklahoma.

The government of Mexico contributed the mules and horses that made up the cargo bound for Greece. The mules had been rounded up out of the mountains of Mexico and loaded directly on the ship. To say they were wild is not a good enough description. They were mean and wild. Each man was assigned about three or four stalls, which held thirty to thirty-five animals each. We were responsible for feeding hay to the animals, hanging buckets on the stalls' top rails, filling the buckets with water, and later removing and storing them until the next chore time. The deck also had the be swept and washed daily. Our chore times were from 6:00 to 7:30 a.m. and 4:00 to 5:30 p.m. Other duties included stacking and restacking hay if the ocean was rough, participating in fire drills, life jacket and life raft drills, and going on night-watch duty.

Those unbroken mules had our respect. They were stronger than the horses and would kick and bite like crazy. As the days went by, the hay in the bottom of the pens began to build up. In time, the mules could jump the rails from pen to pen, and they would crowd together, leaving some of the pens empty and others packed. When a mule became seasick, he would lie down and usually was trampled or kicked to death. On several occasions, I helped the veterinarian inject saltwater into a mule's veins to put him out of his misery. It took as many as sixteen men to heave a dead mule overboard. Total casualties for the sixteen days were twenty to twenty-two animals, all buried at sea.

The ship's crew was composed of men of many nationalities, some of whom could speak very little English. The captain may have been Norwegian. This mix of personalities proved quite interesting, and on several occasions, dangerous. Several fights broke out during the voyage. At one mealtime, one man came chasing another through our mess hall and attempted to stab whim with a butcher knife. I don't know if this was a continuation of the same argument or not, but a day or two later one fired a gun at the other, the bullets hitting the steel walls near where we were eating the noon meal. Added to this mix was the terrible problem of seasickness, which happened to us as well as the mules. During stormy periods the ship would roll from side to side. Seasickness was less when the ship would pitch end to end. The direction of the storm would dictate which way the ship tossed.

On reaching our destination, instead of unloading our cargo at Piraeus, we sailed to the port of Kavalla in northern Greece and unloaded about half of the mules. We then returned to Piraeus and unloaded the other half. The livestock attendants were not allowed to offload the animals. The wild mules had never been handled before, so it made an interesting sight to see the Greek longshoremen try to manage them. A few mules broke out onto the deck and jumped overboard, and others broke and ran after they were unloaded onto the docks. Amazingly, the Greeks retrieved the mules from the ocean by rowboat and gathered the other escapees together so that few, if any, mules were lost.

While in port we were assigned watch duty, and when the captain saw fit he would give us shore leave. The ravages of war lay all around: bombed-out buildings, burned train cars and engines, remains of all sorts of aircraft, and crippled and poor humanity. This was the result of World War II, but now Greece was in the midst of a civil war, which just added to its misery. Probably the most heartrending sights were the many children wandering around in tattered clothes and begging for food, money, or anything of value which could be traded for their needs. Early in the mornings or evenings we would have to step over these children as they lay on dirty sacks or papers in the doorways and entrances to buildings. When we asked them why they were there, they said they had no homes or parents. They followed us everywhere we walked, often reaching into our pockets while begging.

It wasn't long before our work foreman announced that the SS *Park Victory* was being hired by the British government to make two shuttle trips in the Mediterranean Sea for UNRRA. We would be hauling donkeys from the island of Cyprus to Greece. Anyone who objected to this would be sent back to the United States. How or when, we weren't told—so we agreed to stay on. We sailed for Larnaca, Cyprus, and arrived there the next day. In three more days, we were loaded and ready to leave for Salonika (Thessalonica) and Piraeus, Greece. This load contained 971 donkeys and enough barley chaff in large bags to feed the animals. The second shuttle trip also began in the port of Larnaca, Cyprus, and consisted of 700 donkeys destined for Patras, Greece.

During our travels around the Mediterranean, we saw some memorable things. At the times we were given shore leave, we saw the Parthenon, Acropolis, and Mars Hill in Athens. On the island of Cyprus, we visited the Church of St. Lazarus and the tomb of Lazarus. We passed by the isle of Patmos in the Aegean Sea, crossed the Corinthian Canal, and stopped in the town of Corinth. In northern Greece (Macedonia), we traveled by British army truck to the town of Philippi. Here we were shown the remains of the Philippian jail where Paul and Silas were imprisoned and the river where Lydia was baptized (Acts 16). Other cities mentioned in the Bible that we visited were Thessolonica and Neapolis.

The entire trip, from the time we left Houston, was conducted under wartime regulations, which meant no ship's lights were allowed to be on at night. Also, for our safety, our routes in the Mediterranean Sea were restricted to those areas where the mines had been swept. The captain and his officers had possession of the maps, so we were unaware if or when our ship was off course.

We also were not aware at the time that drinking alcohol may have played a part in our ship's troubles, but later that concern was voiced. As it happened, we once went aground off the coast of Cyprus, then ran into a submarine net, and then finally struck a submerged German mine on April 30. This happened at 7:10 a.m., just after most of the cowboys had finished feeding and watering the animals and were waiting for their own breakfast. First came a tremendous, loud sound. The ship seemed to go all directions at once. Large steel loading booms crashed to the deck, all lights went out, and men scrambled for their life jackets. There was no electric power, so we could not receive orders over the intercom, but our survival drills served us well. We all proceeded to our assigned fire stations or lifeboat stations while getting into our life jackets. The first officer informed us what had happened, and life rafts and lifeboats were lowered into position. When the emergency power came on, the radios sent out an SOS asking for help, but other ships in the area refused to come to our aid because of the mines, so the captain chose to proceed for the port of Patras at about five knots speed. It took until late evening to arrive at the port, which was a distance of about thirty miles. Our two rear holds were nearly filled with seawater. The rear holds were where a lot of the ship's machinery was located. We probably wouldn't have made it much farther. Divers inspecting the hull the next day reported a rip of about eight feet by thirty feet.

The cargo of seven hundred uninjured donkeys and the remaining feed was unloaded. After four days, all us cowboys were loaded onto three army trucks and transported 140 miles to Athens. We spent eight days waiting for transportation back to the United States. The SS *Marine Shark*, a troopship, was anchored in the harbor and loading Greek refugees bound for the United States. This was our transportation back to New York harbor. We arrived on Memorial Day, were discharged from the ship, went through customs, and found a place to stay at the Seaman's Hotel, where sailors and merchant marine personnel stayed while in port. I went from New York to New Windsor, Maryland, and then to Oklahoma. I received my discharge in August of 1946. Then I met Viola Kliewer, and, after a two-year courtship, we were married on August 24 1948. Viola and I stayed in Oklahoma—farming and ranching. We raised a family of four children. Two are in California and two in Oklahoma. We cowboys never heard of the fate of the SS *Park Victory*, but we were told there were two options: tow it to drydock in Italy for repairs or tow it out to sea and sink it. I think the latter option became its fate. As for the human guinea pig experiment, we were told we would receive some of the results, but we never did. [The tests proved the disease is caused by a virus (Silbey & Jacob 1952, 144)]. In the years that have passed, I've had no ill effects from the experiment that I know of. Recently, there was a fifty-year reunion of the oceangoing cowboys, but I did not attend.

# CHAPTER 9

# Learning vs. Learning in German

It was harder for my folks to send us
to high school than for a lot of people
now days to send their children to
college.

—*Norman (Shorty) Unruh*

The question of education was an issue of primary concern to Oklahoma Mennonites. Because the Anabaptist tradition called for informed
choice of adults seeking membership and a ministry of the laity, the
congregations of the Mennonite settlers, like all Mennonite groups,
including the more conservative Amish, considered the ability to read
the Bible vital. Beyond that, the Mennonites recognized their need to
understand economic and political issues external to the group. While
the Amish and "conservative" Mennonite groups continue to this day
to support the idea that formal education beyond the elementary
grades is unnecessary, by far the greatest number of Oklahoma Mennonites supported the advancement of education. (An exception in
Northwest Oklahoma is the Church of God in Christ—Holdeman—
Mennonites who send their children to public schools only through
eighth grade.)

The Mennonite groups in Northwest Oklahoma who strongly
supported education—for the most part, Mennonite Brethren and
General Conference churches—were both composed largely of immi-

grants from Russia. For them, education was a powerful instrument capable of perpetuating or destroying the values and traditions of their religious community (Juhnke 1975). Overall, the Russian Mennonites viewed education as an enhancement of economic opportunities and a source of reification of the group's historical identity (Urry 1983a). In Russia, the Mennonite schools had been a mark of cultural superiority over the peasants in the surrounding area (Juhnke 1975). The Mennonites had almost complete control over their own schools, and the schools were known for their quality of instruction. For many years, there was no interference from the Russian government regarding curriculum; consequently, the Bible and German both were important subjects of study (Smith 1927).

In Russia, school and church may have been closely connected, but in Oklahoma, it was soon evident that conditions were very different. Maintaining independent educational institutions was a great expense, and qualified teachers were difficult to find. Whereas a well-funded and staffed separate educational system provided superior education in Russia, the small and, in many instances, impoverished Mennonite communities and isolated congregations in Oklahoma faced tremendous obstacles in organizing church schools.

Not long after the run, in many of the more populated areas of the outlet, neighbors began to gather informally to set up schools for their children, and rural schools sprang up in townships across the newly plotted territory. Constructed from logs or sod, most were built with donated labor and supplied with books the parents had brought from their previous homes (Gibson 1984). Mennonite parents actively supported the development of these schools, and, in actuality, some small, one-room public schools in the rural districts existed as de facto Mennonite schools, since all the children attending were children of Mennonite immigrants.

Free public education had been initiated by the first territorial legislature in 1890. Although funds were not adequate, the accessibility of public schooling was, in theory, extended to all when the Cherokee Outlet was opened. This included Mennonite families. In reality, little support, financial or otherwise, trickled down from the territorial legislature. But the public school situation began to improve with the advent of statehood (Gibson 1984). In 1907, the first Oklahoma legislature established a textbook commission, a state superintendent of public instruction was elected, and plans to create a uniform school system got underway. The public schools were taught in English, but this was not as much a point of contention to the Oklahoma Mennonites as might have been expected.

German was spoken in Mennonite homes and used exclusively in church services; nevertheless, by the turn of the century, many Mennonites had stopped considering the English language a threat to their identity. They saw it instead as a prerequisite for necessary communication (Juhnke 1975). Most Mennonites recognized the practicality of learning English and the difficulties involved with private education, yet many Mennonites hung onto the idea of religious education for their children, and a number of German schools were organized. The schools were usually taught in the congregation's church building or in a member's home. The curriculum centered on Bible study, German language instruction, reading, writing, and arithmetic. There was no uniformity of texts. In fact, often there were very few texts; neither were there any uniform qualifications or standards of performance required of teachers. Lack of finances and problems with attendance and with retaining teachers caused the schools great difficulty. They often had trouble remaining open on a daily basis throughout the term of the school year, and sometimes the school year was as short as three months. This was, in part, because the children, except during the winter months, were needed at home to help on the family farm. Public schools faced many of the same problems and public school financing was meager, but the German (Bible) schools faced even greater financial and organizational difficulties.

The German schools—Mennonite parochial schools—were never a viable alternative to public education. On the other hand, public education was insufficient for Mennonite youth. Mennonites outside Oklahoma founded schools for specific purposes—to make their history and identity clear, to counteract the influence of the larger society, and to train their children to serve as reconciling people. Likewise, Oklahoma Mennonites sought to combine religion and education (Hertzler 1971). Many of the German schools were never intended to supplant public education but were organized to augment what Mennonite children learned in public school. In some areas of Northwest Oklahoma, public schools cooperated by opening their facilities to Mennonites after hours or during the summer for supplemental instruction in German and religion. In other areas or at other times, a day-long church service and Sunday school became a way to offer German language instruction and religious teaching to the youth of the church (McKee 1988a).

In the years after statehood in 1907, the German schools gradually disappeared and public elementary schools increased in importance as the method of educating the majority of Mennonite children. But even when most Mennonite children were taught in public schools, education to preserve the Mennonite faith and way of life free from outside control persisted as a prominent concern of Mennonites in Oklahoma. In certain Russian Mennonite settlements parents were reluctant to send their children to public high schools. As one church member explained, "Not that the education part stood in their way, but the environment in these public schools was not edifying; besides that the Mennonites had all settled in rural districts." The parents felt it unnecessary to the future of young farmers to go to the expense and inconvenience of secondary education (Unruh 1973, 25).

The overarching problem centered on how to provide strong basic education and strong religious training at the same time (Juhnke 1975). The Mennonite response to the issue of proper education for their children worked its way out in an informal and unarticulated compromise that developed gradually over the years, largely because of financial necessity. For the primary grades, Mennonites would use state-supported schools. Public schools also would be acceptable for secondary education, but Mennonites established their own church-related secondary schools and colleges to serve their membership.

The Mennonite Brethren Academy at Corn (outside the boundaries of the Cherokee Outlet) was established in 1902 to provide religious training and general education at the secondary level. The school at Corn enrolled children of parents living within the boundaries of the old Cherokee Outlet and throughout Oklahoma. It is still operating today. In 1911 the Meno Preparatory School was opened (McKee 1988b) by the General Conference. The school was located in Meno, a town founded on the day of the famous run. In 1911 it was a thriving farming community, with a large population of Mennonite farm families living in the surrounding countryside. The Meno school was begun as a day and boarding school, providing Bible and German language instruction. By 1917, it had become the Oklahoma Bible Academy. Incorporated and governed by a five-member board of directors, the academy in 1934 was accredited as a four-year high school with seventy-eight students, a dormitory, and a classroom building. During the 1930s and 1940s, postsecondary education in Christian leadership was provided through a three-year matriculation of three successive six-week Bible courses taught by faculty and invited lecturers (Presenting the OBA 1941). Young men and women in their late teens and early twenties attended the Bible classes held in January and February of each year, where they were trained as lay leaders and teachers in their local congregations.

For decades, enrollment at the school fluctuated. The school had sixty-six students during the 1941-42 school year (Presenting the OBA 1941). Eventually, the postsecondary Bible training sessions were eliminated. Enrollment probably dropped to its lowest in the mid-1950s, but mostly it hovered between fifty and sixty students. In the early 1960s a new gymnasium was built, and a controversy arose regarding the appropriateness of placing OBA students in competition with students from nonparochial schools. As it turned out, the girls' and boys' basketball teams competed successfully with public school teams and made it to the state playoffs several times. In 1971, eighty-two students and nine teachers made up the school (New Hopedale Mennonite Church Historical Committee 1989). Then in the late 1970s, a burst of interest in private education sent non-Mennonite parents, frustrated they said by the lack of discipline and low levels of achievement in the public schools, in search of alternative education for their children. OBA offered a no-frills curriculum that concentrated on the basics and a no-nonsense atmosphere. Enrollment jumped as parents from Enid, now grown to a city of nearly fifty thousand, found the thirty-minute commute to Meno an easy trade-off when they considered the value of the Christian educational environment to be found in the tiny hamlet. By then a four-lane highway connected towns, east and west, and OBA was no longer a boarding school. The curriculum was expanded to include grades seven through twelve. The influx of new students altered the profile of the student population from almost exclusively Mennonite to more affluent urban students, more often from Christian fundamentalist or mainstream Protestant backgrounds than from Mennonite homes.

As OBA grew, Meno no longer served as a geographic center for the school, and in 1983, the campus was relocated to Enid. By 1992, the school was housed in a new structure of contemporary design, which included several classrooms, a gymnasium, a commons area, and offices. Enrollment had risen to 162. This included 7 international students who attended OBA as part of a working relationship between the school and the students' home church in Korea. As part of the international educational exchange, an OBA school administrator traveled to Korea, where he conducted a ministry for the church through educational seminars and speeches. Relocating the school in an area with a larger total population base and established Mennonite congregations, drawing students from several different communities, and, in more recent times, encouraging enrollment of non-Mennonite students has helped the school grow and attain financial security.

The move into Enid was not accomplished without conflict, however. Objections were, for the most part, not based on the relocation of the school itself or the growing numbers of non-Mennonite enrollment. Tension, instead, developed among different groups of the school's supporters over changes in the way the school was financed and the type of theology taught. For the most part, farm families and some of the older generation of supporters wanted to keep the school in Meno. Others welcomed the modern new facilities and urban setting but resented the hard-cash influence that accompanied the more urbane constituency. Coincident with the move came a switch from the rural, local, low-budget support dependent largely on individual and family gifts of time, labor, and some money to more up-scale financial planning based on tax-deferred and tax-deductible donations and tuition revenue. This conversion seemed to cut out a certain segment of school supporters and alumni. To that group, running the school had become more business than religion, with less value given to in-kind contributions.

In addition, some of the more traditional leaders among the General Conference Mennonites who originally founded the school saw the relocation as the beginning of a move to "water down" Mennonite teaching. Eventually, the traditionalists acquiesced, most of them gracefully, but the move was not accepted by everyone involved with the school. Some supporters withdrew, some new people offered support, and some changed the amount or kind of support they donated. On the other hand, some who were discontented when the move was first made are now among the school's most ardent supporters.

Ultimately, a decision was made to include some non-Mennonite members on OBA's independent board of directors, a change that broadened the base of financial and public support for the school. Those with Mennonite background, however, continue to dominate the makeup of the board. The student population broadened as well. In 1998 students at OBA represented 32 different religious denominations, 7 international students were in residence, and enrollment had grown to 217 (Caldwell 1998). The school facility completed in the mid-1980s was completely paid off, the school boasted a new assembly hall and a fine new music department, and fund raising was underway for a new advanced-learning-center building that would double the size of the science labs and double the school's computer technology. The curriculum included arithmetic, language arts, social studies, and physical education, but Spanish had been substituted for German since it was requested by more students and parents. Students in each grade had a one-hour Bible lesson each schoolday, and they attended chapel once a week. There, selected students took part in leading worship, and all students heard from a cross section of local ministers who were invited to speak.

Despite the dramatic changes at the school—in new facilities and location, in enlarging the number of grades taught and the number of students in attendance, in student demographics, in curriculum content—the overall influence of Mennonitism at OBA remains. Although the current head administrator is a Baptist, several of the school's twenty teachers are of Mennonite background. The General Conference still supplies two representatives to the governing board of the academy and, in 1995, of the ten other seats on the board, five were occupied by members of Mennonite General Conference and Mennonite Brethren churches. Support for the school is widespread among area Mennonites, and the general public associates the school with the Mennonite faith. Nevertheless, because they do not live near enough or cannot afford the tuition or for other reasons, many Mennonite children attend public schools.

Although the early years for both the Meno and the Corn academies were difficult, the greater financial security of the later years and the continued conservative fiscal as well as educational leadership enable the schools to provide students with a strong curriculum in religion and academic courses and a variety of qualified teachers. Over the years, the emphasis that the Russian-Mennonite culture historically placed on education has resulted in two stable church-related secondary schools in Oklahoma. In addition, two Mennonite colleges—Bethel, founded in 1887 at North Newton, Kansas, and Tabor, founded in 1908 at Hillsboro, Kansas—have drawn students from Oklahoma since their establishment.

Mennonites traditionally placed great emphasis on education to preserve their culture, and secondary schooling in Christian education still provides religious and academic training for some students. But over the years, out of financial necessity, there has been a shift in two major educational traditions. The first shift was away from values that favored Mennonite educational institutions to the exclusion of public education. The second was the shift away from emphasis on German language instruction. Accepting and justifying public schooling in English and was one break from tradition that altered the closed system of Mennonite community life. Friendships with non-Mennonite classmates; a broader, nonsectarian curriculum; and the influence of extracurricular activities were also acculturating influences on Mennonite children educated in public schools. Throughout the years, the shift in priorities that opened Mennonite congregations to public education also opened families to the larger world outside the Mennonite community.

## Walter and Ruby Regier

Walter and Ruby Regier have been married for many years. Walter taught for a short time at the Oklahoma Bible Academy before entering the ministry and pastoring churches. Ruby is a graduate of the academy. Her job, the time-honored role of a preacher's wife, was to take care of Walter and their two sons and to help him out with his ministry in any way she could. They are in retirement now after many years of service to the church. They had lots of time, and they had many memories to share about Christian education.

Walter and Ruby are quiet people, and with me, politely reticent. They are precise in their speech and patient in their explanations. They are kind to each other, and although they never outwardly displayed affection, there is a certain romance in their relationship that can be read by any observer. In anticipation of my interview, Walter had gathered a few materials for examination: a school yearbook from the early 1940s, a four-page pamphlet that contains "eight facts about the Oklahoma Bible Academy," and a few other papers. Their recollections of church schooling reveal the ways in which Mennonites adapted in order to preserve their religious community during and after the years of global conflict. The interview fell quite naturally into the structure set by the pamphlet, "Facts about the OBA."

*1. The OBA stands for the inerrant Word of God, the virgin birth and deity of Christ, the Blood atonement, and the pre-millennial return of Christ.*

WALTER:    I was asked to teach in OBA in 1940. I came to teach history, and I also was asked to help with the athletic program. The reason that OBA started, primarily, was because our young people didn't have an opportunity to go away to college or a university. Their parents, however, were eager that their children receive some Bible training. The interest was strong to have Bible training, and the church desired it as well. As a result, the school was started.

Now it's interesting to see that these students became acquainted with the Scriptures, the Bible, enough so that they could serve in their churches later on. We didn't realize it so much at the time, but we've noticed that in some of the area churches, most of the leaders have come from OBA. That is, many of the area church leaders are former students, individuals who once attended OBA. I don't mean that they all became Sunday school teachers, but many have become active in the work of the church, some very active.

I remember many of the students I taught. The boys' quartet is listed here. [Walter shows photographs of the young men and points each one out as he talks.] We still see some of them occasionally. Smith, you see here, is a missionary in Ecuador, and Buller is out in Dallas where he works with a Christian organization that helps raise money for our group, and Penner is a worker in Hesston, Kansas, in a factory there. He has a job in the office. Here the fellows are shown again as a singing group.

*2. The school was begun over twenty years ago to provide sound educational facilities uninfluenced by evolutionary or modernistic tendencies.*

WALTER:    OBA was a boarding school. There was one large building which was used as a dormitory. One of the teachers was in charge of the ladies [female students], and I was in charge, for two years, of eight or ten boys. That was during the week. On the weekends, many of students would go home. That depended on how far the students were from their homes. Some came from Inola, which was quite a distance, and some from Kansas. Those that were within ten miles of Meno would usually go home every weekend.

I was almost one of the students. Most were about my age. There was not very much difference between us. The school had a program lined out. The students got up about seven o'clock and had breakfast around eight. Classes started at nine as a rule. We just had four classrooms in the building. One was the auditorium, one was the library which held a classroom, and another two classrooms were in the basement. After class, from four until six, the program pertained to the athletics at the school. The activity worked itself in games and sports. We had a number of inside games. We didn't have any gym or organized football. After the scheduled activities, the boys would like to continue playing basketball outside. The athletics were primarily for the boys. I don't think the girls got as much exercise or didn't think they needed as much as the boys did at that time. The students had their own fun time. Even though they needed to be in their rooms with their books, they weren't tied to just being quiet all the time.

During the supper hour from six till eight, the program was mostly a social time, with the boys and the girls together. Devotionals were also included as part of the instruction. Devotionals were held in the evening. We always had a prayer before the evening meal, but the devotional time was . . . I believe it was divided from the girls in their activities. The girls probably adhered to it more regularly than the guys. But we [the male teachers and boys] had devotional in the evening as well . . . probably more at the close of the evening time, at ten o'clock.

There was church Wednesday night. We were required to go. At eight o'clock on other nights was what we termed "study time." During that time, it was individual study for students in their rooms. I'd have the privilege to share in what they were doing and sometimes answer some questions that they had concerning their schoolwork. At ten o'clock the lights were supposed to be out, and the morning began again at seven. Saturday was pretty much open and the guys would look for jobs to earn a little money—wash cars or something—to have some spending money for themselves. But the jobs were only for those who were unable to go back home for their weekend.

*3. During 1941–42 the total enrollment was 66 [excluding the short-term Bible course]. Of these, 44 were from Oklahoma, 12 from Kansas, 9 from Texas, and 1 from California.*

WALTER:    According to the report that I'm holding in my hand here, there were sixty-six students. In addition to that, there were about twenty-five other students who came in for six weeks of study. The six-week Bible term was taught in January and February. The school was well staffed for the sixty-six full-term students, but it was not staffed as well for the Bible courses.

Things were transpiring as time went on. The students were facing the draft. Most of them were close to it, close to the age for registration. And I think we as teachers were agreed: We would simply share the teachings of the Scriptures pertaining to peace and leave the individuals to make their own decisions. We wanted them to feel responsible for their own decisions, whatever they decided to do. I don't recall that we had any pressure put on us pertaining to the draft. I hope I can explain how it was. I guess I didn't feel, back in 1942, that the students were facing the draft. But, in fact, I faced it myself. I was granted a [deferment] due to my physical condition. Because of a heart condition I had, I didn't stay very long at OBA. I entered the work of the church. I went into the ministry in '42. Most of World War II was really [fought] after I left OBA. Now there are many experiences involving Mennonites during the First World War which were quite gruesome.

*4. In 1931 there were two teachers; now there are five. All know Christ as their personal savior and are anxious to lead those entrusted to them into a closer walk with Him.*

WALTER:    Oh, at OBA I enjoyed getting close to the young people and seeing the youth respond. I just leaned to the youth. I had some older students in class. They were students who hadn't finished high school with their age group, and they wanted to finish high school. I very much enjoyed those students.

The fondest experiences I had in teaching were the times when we had open sharing. Open sharing time happened once a week at school. At open sharing, the students were invited to share some things that they liked and some things that they didn't like, and teachers were also able to share their own interest in the kids' interests. I remember sharing experiences—a trip to the World's Fair in '39 was one. [Experiences such as the World's Fair] were some of the things to which the students could relate by listening to the radio. The World's Fair was quite unique for us, for the boys. As young people, we weren't able to have many first-hand, unique experiences. But we all just wanted to get out and do something. We had an opportunity to discuss this in groups and also with individuals.

I enjoyed that two years at OBA teaching history and taking care of some of the athletic programs. But I discovered I wasn't able to really do justice with the athletic program because of the heart condition I had. So I used the teaching experience as a beginning in Christian work. My wife, Ruby, had graduated from OBA two years before, in 1939. After graduation, she was connected with the mixed quartet at the Zoar Mennonite Church in Goltry, Oklahoma, and ofttimes these singers would come and share public programs at OBA. It was at OBA that I got acquainted with her.

RUBY:   We met at a party. The school often held parties where they'd invite all the young people from all the area. He was teaching at OBA, and I attended the party. In those days, we used to play these "swinging" games, and that's how we met.

WALTER:   "Last Couple Out" was the name of the game. She sprained her ankle—that one did.

RUBY:   Yes, I sprained it, I fell and sprained my ankle And I think you picked me up, and we met.

INTERVIEWER:   How is Last Couple Out played?

WALTER:   You begin with a row of people, two people together. And one of the players calls "shots." She'll say or he'll say, "Last couple out," then the last couple has to come out of the row and go around the leader. If you go around the leader without being caught, then you can keep your partner, and you're allowed to go back in the front of the row, keeping the same couple. Now, if you didn't like the person you're coupled with, then you didn't . . .

RUBY:   You didn't want to run so fast.

WALTER:   And then she sprained her ankle.

RUBY:   I sprained my ankle.

WALTER:   And her sister was to be married the next Sunday.

RUBY:   And I was bridesmaid for my sister the next Sunday, and I could hardly wear my shoe.

INTERVIEWER:   So were you running with Walter when you sprained your ankle?

RUBY:   Oh, no. In fact, we had just barely met. Remember?

INTERVIEWER:   So you wanted to get rid of the other guy so badly that you sprained your ankle? Is that it?

RUBY:   I probably was just running too fast. Well, . . .

*5. Since 1941 OBA is a member of the Evangelical Teacher Training Association, having gained the recognition of the major Bible schools of our country.*

RUBY:   My parents believed in Christian education. It was mostly the Christian aspect of the high school that was the reason they sent us children there. I went to public school in Goltry for the first two years of high school. My parents couldn't afford to send each of us all four years, but we children were each able to attend OBA for two years. We wanted to go. We just really enjoyed it. We didn't like it when we had to go to public school.

The boys and girls received the same education at OBA. I took courses in American history, medieval history, Oklahoma history, geometry, and algebra. I took a year of German, but the way they taught German was to learn the words, the meanings of the words. You didn't learn to converse, and I missed not being encouraged to speak the language. My parents spoke Low German, and this was High German that we were being taught. Oh, I talked Low German at home. I can't anymore though. But I can still pick up a song written in German, and I can read the words even now.

WALTER:   As part of the instruction, in the middle of the morning, there was time set aside for chapel. At chapel, the teachers usually would have a short devotional. Local church leaders were invited to help with the morning chapel, to be in charge. The pastors came from Enid and the surrounding areas. That way the school was really connected closely with the churches of the area. Mostly, the connection was with the Mennonite churches, but some of the other churches participated too, and some students were from other churches. That didn't make any difference.

RUBY:    When I was at OBA, we had chapel every day, and once a week we had separate chapels—one for the boys and one for the girls. Those chapels were held on Friday afternoon. At the separate chapels, students were asked on a rotating basis to give the program. The regular chapel, on the other days, was mostly devotions and singing led by the teachers.

WALTER:    You know, you had to do a "special-incentive" chapel.

RUBY:    Yes, I remember, one time my friend and I were asked to sing a duet in the chapel. We took a song, and we translated it into Low German and sang it. [This would have been the reverse of church tradition, which required High German to be used in services, with Low German reserved for use at home.] They liked it. We did a lot of crazy things.

When I was in school, from four in the afternoon on we could do anything we wanted to till supper time.

INTERVIEWER:    And what did you do then?

WALTER:    You'd watch the boys play ball.

RUBY:    We did watch the boys play, but we'd also walk to the stores, because it wasn't very far. At that time there was quite a little downtown [in Meno]. There were businesses—some implement and other shops, a grocery store, and there was also a drugstore. That was where we liked to go.

*6. Besides the high school course, there is being offered a full 120-hour (3-year) Bible course designed to equip the student for any kind of Christian service.*

WALTER:    The school also offered certificates for a three-year term of three six-week-long Bible course sessions taught yearly during the winter months, beginning usually just after the start of the new year. These sessions were taught to students who either had finished high school or were not interested in continuing their high school. There were a few of those students. However, most of the students who came for the course were high school graduates. Most of the students came for the purpose of increasing their Bible knowledge, to help them teach Sunday school classes and do other service in their local churches in a better way. The students came from various churches. Most of the visiting professors were brought in from Kansas, and some were from more distant places. Dr. Warkentine, who was one of the teachers [Walter points to the man's photograph as he thumbs through an old yearbook], was a pastor, an associate pastor, at my home church in Newton [Kansas]. He was a Bible teacher at Bethel College. He also taught German during the sessions.

RUBY:    My parents wanted me to go on with my education. They wanted to send me to college, but they just didn't have the money. So I never did get to go to college. I think OBA provided me just as good an education as I would have received in a public school. However, we all got this extra Bible education with our schooling, and I think that was probably the most important benefit of OBA. But it wasn't all school. We had time to play too.

*7. The school is equipped with a school building in which there is a small but useful library and a dormitory of fifteen rooms, besides additional rooms for men available at neighboring homes. Running water and laundry facilities are provided.*

RUBY:    I was there in the years of '37 and '38, '38 and '39. Actually, the fun time of the day was the time we spent in the dorm. There might have been fifteen or twenty of us girls altogether. There were three of us in one room, and we had single beds, and it was really crowded, but we had a ball. I lived just ten miles away, but I stayed in the dorm during the week. On the weekends, if we'd have a snow blizzard or some other bad weather, we'd just have a ball on the weekend, you know, it was really fun. Otherwise, we went home every weekend. In the evenings we would sometimes get together in the recreation room. When I was staying in the dorm, we didn't have radios. Our people didn't listen to that kind of thing. Plus, we girls didn't really need the radio in those days. We just had a good time otherwise. We played games, not card games. We played checkers and dominoes and games like that. But mostly we just visited—girl talk. We visited a lot!

The first year that I attended OBA, we cooked for ourselves. Each of us had a separate place to do the cooking. At mealtime, we went down into the big basement below the dorm, and there we had curtains to mark off our own little kitchens. We each brought food from home to cook in our little kitchens. We just had so much fun. We had a stoves, just little ones, as I remember. I think they must have been more than just a simple hot plate. They were larger than that. They were like a Coleman burner. They ran on kerosene, I believe. I don't think there would have been gas or electricity available at that time. We also had an icebox.

The second year we had cooks to do the cooking, and that year we took turns helping the cooks make things. We'd fix salads, like apple salad, and for this dish, one of the girls always brought the dressing from home, homemade dressing. It was so good. I suppose our parents must have sent meat along for us, I just can't remember everything.

WALTER:    Potatoes.

RUBY:    Yes, we usually cooked potatoes and made gravy. We cooked the typical Mennonite meals.

*8. Financially the school is dependent upon the prayers and gifts of its friends. The tuition covers only part of the expenses.*

RUBY:    I would definitely say that OBA is worth [the cost of tuition]. The school is definitely worth the money that people put into it. There are many people who really can't afford OBA, and, yet, they do . . . they do send their children. I feel that attending the school is a valuable thing. I know my parents had to sacrifice to send us, even though the tuition wasn't nearly as great as it is now.

INTERVIEWER:    Do you think OBA is the same kind of school as it was when you were there?

WALTER:    It's different than it used to be. It's . . . I don't know just how to say it. It just seems as if the way they do things now is . . . maybe I can use the word "updated." It was really simple, you know, when we were there.

INTERVIEWER:    It's not simple anymore?

RUBY:    OBA is a very nice, large facility today. The school provides a really good music program too.

WALTER:    When the school was moved into Enid, they lost some of the participants [the school's traditional supporters]. On the other hand, they gained many new students from the Enid area. The move made it possible for the school to go forward.

Before the move, we had to seek out some people, to share with them that the school was not making progress at Meno. It was difficult [in some years] to keep it going, to attract enough students, to hire and retain teachers and so forth. The people who opposed the move felt that they would lose the Mennonite heritage, I guess. And it has, to a certain extent, happened, but actually there are at least four or five of the teachers [presently at OBA] who are associated with the Mennonite church. Not all of the teachers are. You wouldn't expect that today. I guess nonresistance is another one of the things the teachers don't stress as much, but they do stress it some. I think the school taught German for a couple of years, but they won't teach it every year. This doesn't mean that German is never going to be taught again. The students, however, will get more help with Spanish or French today. It's good to know the students will learn their languages, but our Christian schools are not restricted to teaching only German.

What the school is really interested in is having teachers make the Scriptures practical, and they do really well along those lines. Chapel is held once a week. In a large school like that, the administration has to work the program so there is time for each of the classes needed in the curriculum. The superintendent does really well to adjust the classes to serve all the different types of students who attend there now. The students learn to appreciate each other, to appreciate those from different backgrounds.

# CHAPTER 10

# The Legacy

The old German men would say, "A devil's stick is on top of the house." But if you wanted, you could hide your TV antenna in the attic, you know.

*—Eugene Karber*

The post–World War II era accelerated the social and cultural break in the Mennonite community begun by World War I. From World War II onward, the forces of change expanded exponentially and impacted directly on farming as a way of life, on Mennonite social activity, and on church organization. Technology ushered in a different world. The retooling of postwar industry brought refrigerators, electric ranges, vacuum cleaners, toasters, and other modern conveniences—including indoor plumbing—into farm homes (Todd and Curti 1961). Farmers had prospered during World War II. Farm production nationwide increased 28 percent (Perrrett 1973, 404). More and far more powerful farm implements that could handle more-complicated and strenuous tasks became available after the war. Tractors of less that fifty horsepower became obsolete (Hurt 1991). Self-propelled combines with large grain tanks streamlined harvesting. Tractors to pull the combines and trucks to follow alongside them were no longer needed. The work required fewer people and was less physically demanding.

The advanced equipment allowed women to participate in more farm-work outside. Inside the home, labor-saving devices freed women's time, time many put to use in helping with farm record keeping, which became more and more complicated over the years because of government regulations and more-advanced systems of tracking production. Science and technology continued to boost wheat production.

Altogether, improved varieties of seed wheat, improved soil and water conservation, increased mechanization of farming, an expanding national economy, and continuing price supports, all opened the way for Oklahoma farming to enjoy the postwar prosperity that swept across the country. Federal farm price supports begun during the 1930s under the Roosevelt administration continued, while vacillating markets for farm products and Department of Agriculture policy created a crop allotment system that encouraged farmers to concentrate even more than in the past on their wheat crop (Smith 1966, 97; Strange 1988, 131). Northwest Oklahoma wheat production soared, emerging as the single greatest source of farm revenue. Eventually, most farm endeavors in Northwest Oklahoma—including feed-grain production, hay making, and cattle raising—came to revolve around the needs and constraints of producing wheat.

A strong farm economy held postwar until 1948 (Isern 1982, 31). The 1950s saw years of below-average rainfall. These and other problems were battled by the federally funded county agricultural stabilization and conservation districts that carried out, extended, and refined a wide range of programs begun during New Deal days. Cover crops were planted and rangeland allowed to rejuvenate through a deferred grazing plan. Terraces were built to better utilize rainfall and slow soil erosion, and help was provided to control competitive plant growth (weeds) along farm roads and in fields. To supplement flood control and provide for livestock, water wells were dug and farm-pond dams constructed (Two hundred twenty-six county farms 1959).

Experimentation and development in livestock breeding, agronomy, fertilizers, insect and plant disease control, and cultivation at land grant universities also contributed to increased production and promoted larger farming operations. A modern farmer may select from literally hundreds of varieties of wheat seed. Kansas State University and Oklahoma State University have been recent leaders in new wheat seed development (Schovance 1995). Turkey Red, the hard winter wheat of the Russian Mennonites, has been replaced as a distinct classification, by other, far more sophisticated varieties. In the early 1990s, Karl 92 a was prevalent variety, but it was superseded in the mid-1990s by the popularity of 21-63, 21-80, and Agseco (Schovance 1995). These highly bred varieties phase through what is roughly a four- to five-year cycle as new strains gain popularity, come to be planted extensively, then, due in part to their saturation of the environment, begin to lose their effectiveness. The longer and more extensive a variety's use, the more susceptible it becomes to rust, tan spots, and other foliage disease. At some point these highly engineered varieties lose potency and are replaced by other, still newer strains. The successive advances in varieties continue to yield more disease- and weather-resistant, fuller, larger, and more protein-enriched heads of wheat. As great as these advances in new seed types are, until the late 1990s all evolved directly from hard winter wheat, and almost all the strains of hard red winter wheat developed in the past century have originated from those choice grains from Asia brought to America by the farmer-immigrants.

In 1990, Oklahoma was the nation's second largest producer of hard red winter wheat, surpassed only by Kansas (Lilley 1990). It was third in 1992, with 5.2 million acres of wheat harvested. Eight counties of Northwest Oklahoma produced more than 45 million of the 128 million bushels of wheat harvested. Garfield, Grant, and Kay were the top-producing counties in the state, with Garfield totaling a little over 9 million bushels (U.S. Department of Commerce 1992). All types of hay made up the next-largest segment of Oklahoma farm production, with 2.1 million acres.

Across the United States, early-day Mennonite farmers were successful because they understood how to make things grow and how to stay out of debt (Swierenga 1983, 91). Although that still goes a long toward success, it takes more than being a good, debt-free land manager to be a successful farmer these days. From the 1960s into the 1990s, unstable commodity markets at home and abroad and an uncertain national farm program shaped as much by political pragmatism as by economic circumstance have operated to the disadvantage of small farmers and those wanting to enter the business. Across the board, inflation moved ever upward through the first nine decades of the twentieth century, affecting the cost of land, of equipment, and of other products farmers need to purchase. From the mid-1980s into the 1990s, however, land values decreased, while the price of wheat usually held well below four dollars a bushel, creating marginal profits for small farms and generating opportunities for still-greater expansion of the bigger operations. Today, young people and others just starting out can little afford the cost of what few parcels of farmland come onto the market. It is also difficult to buy the expensive combines engineered with the latest technology and equipped with air conditioning and compact disc players, or the large tractors that cost more than $100,000. Moreover, many farmers are now college-educated and computer-networked; they program their machinery and consult CPAs.

The traditional emphasis on solid financing and the understanding of how to make things grow remain essential; yet perhaps an even more vital skill in farming at the turn of the century is understanding how federal farm policy works (Strange 1988, 135–65). For the last half of the cnetury, the ability to cut through the maze of farm programs, select the most advantageous, and manipulate program options and regulations for personal advantage was often the difference between "make" and "break" in Northwest Oklahoma farming. These conditions and the simple fact that since the opening of outlet there has been no new, untilled land to accommodate new farm operations meant the demise of the small, single-family farm. Selling a farm, on the other hand, because of the overall increase in land values, has often allowed an aging farm couple to retire to town in comfort. The conditions that worked to discourage small, single-family farming have in

turn stimulated the growth of large-land, family-corporate, and corporate farming (Strange 1988, 56–78). In Northwest Oklahoma the
result has been megascale farming and agribusiness. A farming operation that covers fifteen hundred acres of pasture and wheat today is
considered somewhat modest. There are farms much larger. In the
economic shakedown of the past quarter century, many farmers lost
the struggle to hang on to a family farm; but among those who hung
on, many were able to move up the ladder through land acquisition,
obtaining land and allotments through leasing farmland owned by
others. Although size may not always result in success, size has become
a prerequisite to success.

Some farms in Northwest Oklahoma still exist as traditional one-
owner, family farms. Others are operated by partnership or by individual farmers who farm their own land and, in addition, the land of
absentee owners. Still others, mostly smaller farms, are operated as
a side interest. They offer supplemental occupation for individuals
whose main source of income is not from farming. There is not a great
deal of public shareholder ownership of agricultural properties in
Northwest Oklahoma. Of the farms that lie in what was once the
Cherokee Outlet, many are operated by family-owned farm corporations. A major benefit of these corporations, which are usually composed of two or more generations of one family, is the tax advantages
provided by the corporate structure (Harris 1960, 27–75). Mennonites, as part of the total population of farmers, can be found participating in each of the types of farming arrangements.

As farms have grown larger, the farm population has grown smaller.
Rural population has been decreasing in Northwest Oklahoma since
dust bowl days. The 1940 census showed a decline in Oklahoma farm
population for the first time, from the all-time high of 213,325 in 1935
down to 179,687. World War II further reduced the U.S. farm population by 15 to 20 percent (Perrett 1973, 404), and the war virtually
eliminated the hired hand (Perrett 1973, 404). In 1970, across
America, the farm population totaled only 4.8 percent of the total
population (Norton, et al. 1993, 928). The trend of farm youth and

farm population overall to relocate from rural to urban areas accelerated (Beegle and Johnson 1982). and continues to this day.

One of the most striking features of modern Mennonitism is the high degree of urbanization of a group that once was completely rural. Through the years, a good many Mennonite men and women, like a good many of the farm population in general, abandoned farming for life in urban areas. The largest concentrations of Mennonite people in Northwest Oklahoma today are found living in and near Enid, a city with a population of 45,000-plus, and in Fairview, the seat of Major County. Nationwide, about 20 percent of Mennonites are farmers (Hostetler 1983). The minister of the Mennonite Brethren church in Enid, which has both urban and rural members, estimated that in 1988 about 15 out of the 370 members of his congregation were actively engaged in farming. The trend of migration from farm to urban areas is ongoing, and this overall trend includes youth and family migration to areas outside the state.

Not all farm skills have proved useless in the modern labor market. The reputation of Mennonite farmers, their propensity for hard work and their tenacity, has opened doors to urban employment for Mennonite men. Rural Mennonites have brought various types of skilled craftsmanship to the urban workplace with success. Mennonite carpentry skills, in particular, are in high demand. Adept Mennonite carpenters are sought after for the high quality of their work and their attention to detail. Urbanization has also required employment of Mennonites in other jobs totally unrelated to farming.

Historically, Mennonites relied on education as an enhancement to church life. Education was also viewed in part as an economic benefit because it was thought that the knowledge gained stimulated agricultural innovation. As urbanization demanded of Mennonites the ability to compete in a skilled-job market, the emphasis on education became increasingly more important. In recent years, a large number of Mennonites have sought higher education to prepare themselves to enter the workforce in areas that require technical skill and professional training (Epp 1977). Education and urbanization also have provided opportunities for the entry of Mennonite women into the working world, although there are no available statistics to document their exact numbers in Northwest Oklahoma. Nationwide, 56 percent of Mennonite women were employed in the workforce in 1989 (Kauffman and Driedger 1991).

Individual Mennonites today work at any number of different jobs. The genealogical records of one Mennonite family show that from the 1940s to the present, members have been employed as farmers, secretaries, teachers, nurses, and public school administrators. A commercial artist, a welder, a cook, and a corporate manager, represented as well (The genealogy of Peter R. and Katherina Theisen Brandt, 1845–1978). Urbanization, a multiplicity of occupations, and a more affluent standard of living characterize the modern Mennonite community. More extensive education, diversified occupations, affluence, have all contributed to and reflect the acculturated lifestyles of Mennonites in Northwest Oklahoma in the later half of this century.

This twentieth-century progression dramatically changed the Mennonite churches. Gradually, most times imperceptibly, but occasionally over the protest of the older generation of Mennonites, the taboos placed on members that enforced nonconformity withered almost completely away. But old customs, firmly entrenched, were difficult to put aside. The 1948 Resolutions of the Conference of the Mennonite Brethren Church of North America retained among many admonitions the following: Sisters, both single and married, should not appear in church or at family worship without the proper head covering; a remarried, though once-divorced person, might not become a member until the death of the "guilty party" [divorced partner]; members should stay away from circuses and theaters; members should not hold office or take any part at the polls; sisters should not preach nor take part in discussions in business meetings of the church. Activities such as visiting saloons, selling tobaccos, and creating humorous writings in newspapers or magazines were also forbidden (Conference of Mennonite Brethren 1948).

Despite the many sanctions observed by local congregations and edicts passed by the national conferences, assimilation into the larger society gradually occurred. Marriage of members to non-Mennonites increased. Mennonite women cut their hair and put on earrings and lipstick. Mennonite men cut their beards and shaved their faces. Some of the final conflicts were over dancing, attending movies, and watching television. At some point in time came the realization that the rules of conduct that separated Mennonites from the larger community were interpreted by those outside the church as not necessarily a sign of faithfulness to the teachings of Christ. Instead, Mennonite rules for personal grooming and abstinence from the amenities of modern life were considered by most in the larger population to be merely harmless, amusing eccentricities. The more critical in the established society found the Mennonites' restrictive lifestyle to be slightly foolish. This was nothing new, since outsiders in the past had repeatedly poked fun at the reclusive ways of the Mennonites and found their lifestyle humorous. Somewhere along the line, though, Mennonites began to poke fun at themselves and agree with the larger community that some of the old traditions had served their usefulness.

Change came at no certain turning point. Mennonite codes of conduct and social taboos were intermittently broken and slowly forgotten. Eventually it became impossible to distinguish members of General Conference and the Mennonite Brethren churches from the mainstream population in Northwest Oklahoma. [Differences existed between General Conference and Mennonite Brethren members in the rate of their acculturation, but these differences were relatively small (Kauffman and Driedger 1991).] From the 1960s to the present, the appearance and manner of living of these Mennonites has conformed to that of the public in general. In style of dress, in grooming, in work, in social activity, there is no longer any appreciable difference. To the majority of contemporary Mennonites, the old church rules that prohibited participation in social activities with non-Mennonites and prescribed a certain type of behavior and style of dress now seem quaint relics of a far-removed past.

Although Mennonite doctrines today still discourage alcohol and tobacco use and unhealthful dietary habits, some Mennonite men and women can be found who indulge in moderate alcohol consumption; there are members who smoke cigarettes, and overeating is a sin more often talked about than resisted. The transition from the wearing of prayer caps to cover their heads, to leaving their braided and coiffed hair uncovered, to bobbing their long hair, to coloring it paralleled for Mennonite women the transition from floor-length dresses with sleeves to the wrist to "active wear" that includes comfortable slacks and shorts. In earlier times Mennonites refused to dance but now their children attend proms. Most Mennonite colleges permit dancing on their campuses (Kauffman and Driedger 1991), though there is still some opposition to dancing, mostly in rural churches, because it is said to lead to inappropriate behavior that leads to even more inappropriate behavior.

Mennonites today are no longer withdrawn but are enmeshed in public life at all levels of interaction. In earlier times Mennonites refused to attend "picture shows." Today they visit shopping malls where they see movies, and many of their homes have complete media centers that include radio and television sets, videocassette recorders, and compact discs players. Mennonites move in mainstream society, and almost all participate fully in the material world of consumer goods and services. The world of the modern Mennonite revolves around business ties, civic associations, leisure activities, and, for some, even country club memberships. Current political issues and societal problems centering on the proliferation of nuclear weapons, on environmental pollution, on the plight of the homeless, on abortion, on divorce, on high crime rates, and on family and educational concerns impinge on Mennonite life. Yet the rates of alcohol consumption (Currie et al. 1979) and divorce (Driedger et al. 1983; Kauffman and Driedger 1991) are still far lower among Mennonites nationwide than among the general population. Personal problems viewed as social problems and other pressing public concerns have been addressed in recent Mennonite publications for church members

(Bergen 1988; Epp 1989; Witmer 1989) and from the pulpits of Mennonite churches in Northwest Oklahoma.

The extent of material wealth, acculturation, and assimilation into the economic and political structure of Mennonite society has not gone unnoticed by the church leadership. Much attention by Mennonite scholars, church officials, ministers, and local congregations has been devoted to reflecting on the changes in Mennonite life (Hardwick 1974; Hostetler 1986; Hostetler 1987; Epp 1977; Driedger and Kauffman 1982; Kauffman and Harder 1975; and others). As early as 1955, the Western District of the General Conference began to present programs aimed at the situation. "How to Live the Abundant Life" and "The Christian in Business" were the topics of just two of the meetings concerned with Mennonites' attitudes toward materialism and social ethics (Haury 1981).

From the beginning of the movement, the physical and social isolation of the early churches in Europe and later in America and certain doctrines of Mennonitism fostered an independence among individual congregations. That independence found expression among branches of the church and among congregations. Differences in theology separated branches; theology, however, was certainly not the only distinguishing boundary between churches. During their years in Oklahoma, individual congregations developed their own peculiar characteristics as local circumstances affected general instructions from the larger church associations. Often the complexion of congregation was colored by the personality of its pastor. The tone and makeup of the congregations frequently were altered with the arrival of a new minister. Visible differences among congregations could be seen by Mennonites outside their own groups.

In addition, disputes arose occasionally within congregations and sometimes led to a congregation's formal withdrawal from its larger subgroup. For example, the Saron Mennonite church in Orienta established in the late 1890s as a part of the General Conference withdrew in 1989 and became an independent church. The Saron church is affiliated with the Fellowship of Evangelical Bible Churches formerly

THE LEGACY

known as the Evangelical Mennonite Brethren. The Zoar church, also General Conference, begun in Goltry around 1911, withdrew from the General Conference in 1963. There also were splits in congregations that formed new churches. The Bethel church was begun when a group of General Conference Mennonites in Enid broke away from Enid's Grace church in 1937. From time to time there were disputes in the New Hopedale church in Meno that led members away from the main body of that church. In 1954, a split in the New Hopedale church resulted in some members forming the Grace Chapel. Among other General Conference churches, the Grace church in Enid, established in the mid-1930s, merged with Bethel in Enid in 1958 (Haury 1981).

Through all this, the two Church of God in Christ groups (Holdeman) at Fairview and Pleasant View, dating from 1895 and 1893, respectively, persevered. To a large degree these churches have practiced their religion within a closed community and continue to hold themselves separate from outside society. Their combined membership totaled approximately 250 in 1995.

Despite the differences among the Mennonite subgroups and differences in and among Mennonite congregations, several general trends developed during the 1960s. Four of these ongoing trends have continued to influence Mennonites through the 1980s and into the 1990s. They are the influence of Protestantism, fundamentalism, evangelism, and the peace movement.

The influence of Protestantism in the organizational life of the church, beginning as early as the establishment of Sunday schools at the turn of the century, has continued into the late twentieth century. Protestantism as an overall influence on the Mennonite churches can be seen in changing membership perspectives. Ongoing changes taking place in the structure of the group can also be associated with the influence of Protestantism. In adapting to the mode of efficiency in administration of church activities that Protestant denominations practiced, the various Mennonite subgroups began to set standards for church organization in the years that followed World War II. After the war, almost all Mennonite churches were able to salary a full-time pastor. As pastors came to be full-time employees of the church, it was expected that they would have had training at seminary for their calling. Even as the Vorsänger was replaced by a song leader in the 1930s, the song leader in many of the larger churches was replaced by a paid choir director in the 1950s and 1960s. The developing pattern of professionalism among the laity was mirrored in the paid employment and standardization of training for the ministry.

Along this line, consolidation of churches occurred in the larger towns. A new Fairview Mennonite Brethren church saw substantial growth after it was created in the merger of the old North Fairview church and South Fairview church in 1951 (Epp 1962). Subsequently, an ambitious building project was undertaken during the early 1980s that resulted in a large new building that houses a sanctuary, educational rooms, restaurant-size kitchen, auditorium, and a congregation estimated at more than five hundred. The North Enid Mennonite Brethren church, in existence since 1897, was a rural church located outside the city. It was joined in 1960 with the Enid City Mennonite Brethren church. The two groups combined and relocated to a new building with a large sanctuary and classrooms at the time of their merger in 1960.

Some churches grew larger from mergers, and some declined in members. At a higher level of organization, the regional and national structures of the Mennonite subgroups tended to grow steadily larger and more complex. Boards and committees, conferences and organizations took more responsibility for the work of the denomination. By 1974, there were seventy-two inter-Mennonite organizations (Kraybill 1978). Only three of those predated 1940, and many have been added since (Kauffman and Driedger 1991). Denominational leadership became more prominent and was tied to the local congregations in a variety of ways, including ties through the ministers, conference meetings, and church publications. The Christian Leader and The Mennonite are two publications that continue, along with other specialized publications, to be produced by Mennonite organizations (Jacquet 1989).

Another trend, the declining age at baptism, continued well into the mid-twentieth century. The age of baptism dropped steadily over the years, from baptism of men and women in their mid-twenties, which was customary in the early 1900s, to the present custom of baptism sometime during the early teen years (McKee 1988a). The ceremony of foot washing largely disappeared over the years, as did many other Old World church traditions. The system of men and women sitting separately in church services ended for one group when a new church building was erected. When the Mennonite Brethren congregation near Enid decided to move to a new church house, the building was designed and constructed with two main entries. But before the congregation relocated to the new building, their pastor suggested that families might want to sit together in the new church. The congregation accepted his proposal; men and women entered the new church through either door, and the segregated seating custom ended at the time the new church building opened.

In times past, Mennonite farmers worried about their crops. Damage from flooding, hail and fire was unpredictable, and a destroyed crop meant an entire year's work lost. But buying crop insurance—or other types of insurance, for that matter—was strictly prohibited. Mennonites believed that they should rely on God's will alone to protect them from the perils of nature. Those ideas also have been revamped. The current listing of financial agencies sponsored by Mennonite associations numbers twenty-nine insurance organizations (Kauffman and Driedger 1991). Mennonite Mutual Aid, Inc., the largest of the organizations, insures its own brotherhood with programs for health and life insurance and retirement pension funds and investment programs.

Women, once excluded from the formal, decision-making processes of the churches, now are allowed a vote in church meetings—not that they did not always have some influence over the direction of church policy. In many Mennonite marriages, discussions between husband and wife on topics to come before a vote of the church patriarchy had long been customary. Papa and Mama would talk over church policy and talk out church problems within the confines of the home. Then Papa would carry the vote to the church meeting. The enfranchisement of women legitimatized the behind-the-scenes input a number of women had and offered an alternative in those instances when consensus on the way the husband would cast his ballot was not forthcoming.

There were other revisions of time-honored church traditions. The authoritarian structure of the church was broadened to allow for more congregational participation in leadership roles (Hostetler 1987). The wider base of participation opened some of the churches to receive women as deacons, and women were asked to speak at meetings and to teach Sunday school classes of teenagers and adults. In the past, women had not spoken during services, and their teaching had been limited to the instruction of small children. The entry of women into the decision-making levels of the church structure, however, has been slow, and many women today still decline or are not offered opportunities for formal leadership positions in their local congregations. A 1991 survey that included General Conference and Mennonite Brethren found that about three-fourths of all those questioned favored women serving as deaconesses (Driedger and Friesen 1995, 492). Yet only 45 percent of men and 37 percent of women approved of ordaining women as ministers of congregations. When the men's and women's responses were compared, more males thought it appropriate for women to hold recognized positions in the church than did the women themselves (Driedger and Friesen 1995, 492). This survey showed little change in opinions from a national survey of Mennonites conducted in 1989 (Witmer). In that study only 33 percent of Mennonite women said they approved of women conducting church ordinations, while three-fourths of both male and female respondents approved of women serving as deaconesses in the churches (Kauffman and Driedger 1991).

Still other data show that about half of Mennonite spouses identify their marriages as husband-led and only one-third as equalitarian.
Patriarchal marriages are not viewed as less satisfying than egalitarian
(Kauffman 1994); both husband-led and equalitarian marriages were
rated about the same on a marriage-relations scale. All this does not
mean that feminism has not worked its way into Mennonite thinking
nationwide. Mennonite women writers publish regularly in church
publications. But the concept of Mennonite feminism is very different
from mainstream feminism. For example, a recent academic article
by Wilma Ann Bailey (1994, 247) cites Hagar, the servant woman who
survived in exile, as an alternative role model. Bailey argues that it is
not enough for the world to merely replace powerful Caucasian men
with powerful Caucasian women, but that true equality requires the
affirmation of all people and is built on servitude as an alternative
approach to society's dominant norms.

The key values of the church that originally stressed withdrawal
from the world have been irretrievably altered. A move toward an
interpretation that emphasized service programs, missions, and work
to relieve the suffering of the world, which had been present in the
churches for many years, became more noticeable after World War II
(Hostetler 1987). More time and effort was devoted to growth and
outreach as an aspect of church life. This shift in emphasis contributed
to the development of a more complex organizational structure
among the various congregations of the different Mennonite subgroups. Youth camps, retreats, and intergroup meetings became
popular (Haury 1981; Forty Mennonites 1959). In 1958, the Fairview
Mennonite Brethren church hosted a three-day conference that drew
some two hundred delegates representing Mennonite Brethren
churches west of the Mississippi (Fairview Church 1958) Local, state,
and special conferences also drew crowds (City M.B. Church 1959;
Training Meetings 1958), and the yearly Oklahoma conventions of the
General Conference were well attended. A huge tent was set up to
provide extra seating and shade for members during outdoor meetings held each summer. The tent was moved around from year to year

as the meeting site changed and was used until 1959 when the meetings began to be held in air-conditioned auditoriums or public school gymnasiums (McKee 1988b).

Tent meetings and revivals were popular among Mennonite congregations during the 1950s (M. B. Church 1957; Saron Mennonite Church 1957). The mass revivals of Billy Graham and local and national ministries of radio personalities also drew a following among Mennonites. So too do the televangelists of more recent years (Hunter 1983). Fundamentalism, the primary direction of many of the revivalists' messages has appealed to a sizable number of Mennonites, with influence being stronger in some churches than others. Certain aspects of Mennonite faith—authority of the Scriptures and personal conversion of adult believers, for example—coincide with the theology of fundamentalism (Haury 1981; Hostetler 1987). The fundamentalist message that places heavy emphasis on the virgin birth and stresses the second coming of Christ has also been strongly voiced by Mennonites in Northwest Oklahoma. Many Mennonites have joined with fundamentalists in believing that the religious foundations of America are threatened by the teachings of the "modernists" or those who, in more recent years, have been termed "secular humanists." Fundamentalist literature is popular with this group. Christian magazines and books, biblical reference material, and other inspirational reading material have come to be used by a sizable number of Mennonites, as is literature produced by mainstream Protestant publishing houses. *The Upper Room* and *Daily Bread*, periodicals of daily devotions, have circulated among church members for many years. Christian music produced by fundamentalists with a down-home, country-and-western sound is popular. The music is played in Mennonite churches and listened to by individuals on radio and recordings.

Certainly not every aspect of fundamentalism coincides with Mennonitism. Historically, many doctrinal differences existed. A wide division separated Mennonites and fundamentalists over the peace issue. Mennonites shied away from the nationalistic and militaristic themes present among fundamentalist teachings (Kauffman and

Driedger 1991). There were other differences too. Whereas emotion-alism played a central role in conversion for fundamentalists, partic-ularly in revival settings, Mennonites presented sober sermons and temperate revival sessions that focused on Bible teaching and virtuous living. Mennonites were, after all, quiet people, historically *die Stillen im Lande*, not given to emotionalism. The Mennonites of Northwest Oklahoma did not embrace fundamentalism in its totality; however, the co-optation of certain fundamentalist doctrines indicates the influ-ence of other religious groups on Mennonite theological orientation (Haury 1981). What is important to the social development of Men-nonites in Northwest Oklahoma is the adaptation of one doctrine associated with fundamentalism in particular —evangelism, which has played a major part in the continuing viability of most Mennonite churches and Mennonites as a religious-ethnic group.

Evangelism is associated with the revival movement of the 1950s that actively "brought in souls" and enlarged membership, but its influ-ence has been wider in scope. In addition to gaining new members, it has changed the direction of Mennonite church life. For centuries Mennonites practiced separatism. They withdrew into closed religious communities. On relocating in Oklahoma, Mennonite congregations expanded to accept many who were of dissimilar ethnic backgrounds and, later, those who married into the faith. But recruiting members from the outside society was not a primary concern of the group, and some congregations, mostly those found in rural areas, still do not seek to enlarge membership by recruiting from the outside commu-nity. But urbanization forced a scattering of Mennonite individuals and families. Many found themselves in towns and cities where there were no Mennonite congregations. In addition, the youth began to drift away from the church. By mid-twentieth century, not all Men-nonite young people were choosing to remain in the church of their parents. Those who relocated away from their home churches did not always have, or seek, the opportunity to worship with another Men-nonite congregation. In Northwest Oklahoma, evangelism, especially in the larger communities, helped the Mennonite churches survive.

It brought in new members and broadened the base of monetary and personal contributions to the church, but beyond that, it loosened the tightly knit, in-group social life of the church and opened it to broader association with the public at large.

There are still some who play the "Mennonite game," tossing surnames back and forth to trace lineage and establish an individual's identity. The turf continues to be church social events, but the play has lost its edge, the competitors grown old or disinterested. The importance attached to Unruh, Jantz, Schmidt, or other prominent Mennonite family names has faded over the years, as evangelism has broadened the scope of the church. By its basic nature, evangelism— the sharing of the gospel with others—necessitated an increased inter- action with the public at large. Not all, but many, Mennonite churches began to be of service to those in the community surrounding the local Mennonite churches (Haury 1981; Hostetler 1986, 1987).

Another reorientation in thinking among many Mennonites that has brought further interaction with the community at large is the extension of the peacemaking concept. This came in part from changes in the draft law precipitated by the involvement of U.S. troops in Korea (Moskos and Chambers 1993). In 1952 new provisions pro- vided COs a wide variety of service opportunities in government and nonprofit organizations in charitable, health, welfare, education, and scientific work. Inductees were not allowed to serve in their own communities but could serve abroad, and they were allowed pay for their work (Keim and Stoltzfus 1988, 139–46). In 1973, the draft itself came to an end, replaced by an all-volunteer armed forces. Even as conscientious objection to war became more widespread during the 1960s and 1970s, the central focus of the peace mission of the church shifted away from nonresistance as a form of group protest to war. Instead, emphasis was directed toward programs of service to suffering people. The Mennonite Relief Fund and a variety of other charitable programs organized through the Mennonite Central Com- mittee, the general association of Mennonite churches, have built up the religious and cultural identity of the group while at the same time opening up contacts for peaceful development worldwide. Further, during the return to "normality" in the years after World War II, many local churches, especially those of the General Conference, formed peace committees to reinforce education among their membership about nonresistance and to encourage peace witness.

The various Mennonite churches cooperate and work together today in many organizations, notably the Mennonite Central Committee, but also in educational projects and charitable activities. In Northwest Oklahoma two benevolent activities bring together the inter-Mennonite associations and have been particularly effective as service projects. Each has grown out of historic Mennonite traditions. One of these is the meat-canning project, which has roots in the communal butchering of times past. Throughout the year, Mennonites gather at appointed locations to process sides of beef. When the canning project first began, meat was obtained through the donation of local beef from Mennonite farms, but today the meat is purchased. The bulky canning equipment used in the process is trucked from site to site by a trained crew who supervise the volunteers they meet at each location.

The meat-canning project provides food for those less fortunate. In Northwest Oklahoma the project began after World War II. In 1963, ten thousand pounds were canned over a three-day period in Fairview. Seventeen head of cattle were purchased from the area and processed at a locker plant in Fairview. Then volunteers helped operate a truck-mounted canning unit dispatched from Akron, Pennsylvania. The beef canned in Fairview was sent first to Newton, Kansas, then on to Pennsylvania and from there was shipped abroad to Mennonite distribution centers (Mennonites Can 1963).

The second large-scale project undertaken by Mennonites in Northwest Oklahoma is the annual relief sale. Once held at the Major County fairgrounds in Fairview, it was moved to the Enid Convention Center in 1998. The sale includes an auction of handmade quilts; hand-crafted grandfather clocks, trunks, and children's toys; new and used farm equipment and major appliances; and other items. While the auction is going on, Christmas decorations, green plants, some art and craft items made by local Mennonites, and some items made in Mennonite missions throughout the world are sold from booths.

The project is an opportunity to raise money for Mennonite peace and relief programs and an opportunity for the group to reify its ethnic heritage. It is a family reunion, a major social event, and a bargain-hunter's paradise. Holdeman Mennonites, dressed plain, men in full beard and women capped in black, work together with General Conference Mennonites and Mennonite Brethren who wear colorful clothing. If the weather turns bad, most everyone, except the Holdeman, wears jeans and a warm coat. Men's and sometimes women's choral singing and religious services open the festivities. Mennonite literature explaining the use of the proceeds is on display. Ethnic foods—including New Year's cookies, Verenika, German sausage and sauerkraut, zwieback, peppernuts, and many other kinds of baked goods—can be purchased and eaten at long tables set up near the auction arena. Tacos and hamburgers are also served. A group of auctioneers spell each other during the one-day sale, held traditionally on the Saturday after Thanksgiving. The auction is attended by hundreds of people. It brings together all the Mennonite branches in the area and, has netted as much as eighty-five thousand dollars (Cox 1988).

The large numbers of Mennonites who have participated in some form of Mennonite Central Committee service illustrate the extent to which these multiple programs have pervaded Mennonite congregational life. Thousands more have served voluntarily in MCC thrift and gift stores, mediation services, prison visitations, sewing circles, food bank, and many other types of activity. This laypeople's service movement, especially through the work of MCC, has become an important and widely known arm of the Mennonite churches (Kauffman and Driedger 1991).

In the 1960s the Mennonite Central Committee established offices in Washington, D.C., and in Ottawa, Canada, to promote the denomination's peace and religious efforts. The offices were opened over the objections of some Mennonites in both countries who feared such political action was not in keeping with the Mennonite ethic (Kauffman and Driedger 1991). But over the years, the offices have gathered increasing support from a large majority of the general membership (Kauffman and Driedger 1991). Alternative service was provided Mennonites during the Korean conflict and the Vietnam War, and some Mennonite men took advantage of the opportunity to serve their country in this way. But even during the Vietnam War, when the numbers of those claiming conscientious objector status for other than religious reasons increased dramatically and the percentage of the general public opposed to hostilities in Vietnam climbed, the numbers of Mennonites who chose service in the military apparently was about the same as in World War II.

The peace initiative, once a personal and group vow of nonresistance to violence in any form, has become, in the 1990s, a multidirectional effort based, for the most part, on the cooperation of all Mennonite groups to bring comfort to victims of misfortune. While the meat-canning project and the relief sale are projects organized and carried out locally, individual commitment of time and effort at the sites of major disasters such as floods and hurricanes are also representative of the modern Mennonite peace ethic. The question of service in the military, a major focus of the religion, has become a matter of personal choice for Oklahoma Mennonites.

At the end of the twentieth century, numerous well-attended churches are located in the growth centers of Northwest Oklahoma. Churches in the rural communities that are losing population are losing church members too. General Conference churches are located in Ringwood, Meno, Medford, Enid, and Deer Creek. Large congregations of Mennonite Brethren are in Enid and Fairview. The Zoar independent church is located in Goltry and the Saron independent church is in Orienta. Two groups of Holdeman Mennonites, one at Fairview and the other at Goltry, also remain active.

The Anabaptist doctrines of adult baptism, fellowship through partaking of communion, and devotion to the example of Christ's life remain the religious foundation of the Mennonites. Symbols of ethnicity, German foods, ceremonial holidays, and religious rites preserve time-honored traditions within the church family. World service through charity and community service through personal commitment reflect the intentional efforts of the Mennonite Church to interact purposefully in contemporary culture. The secular world is the social world of Mennonites. The Mennonites of Northwest Oklahoma no longer remove themselves from society. Unlike the early settlers who withdrew from public life, most Mennonites today participate fully in the world they share with everyone else.

## *Elda Wiebe Martens and Henry Martens*

Elda and Henry Martens live on the edge of town, just off the main highway that leads into Fairview, Oklahoma. Their house is located behind Henry's machine shop and across the way from a larger, older, two-story house that was once their home and now belongs to one of their sons. Elda and Henry are outgoing people. They appear to be happy, always on the go, involved with other people, and optimistic. Elda and Henry spend their time with things big and small that somehow, in some way seem almost always to have some connection with their church. Their day rarely begins at nine and never ends at five. Their world is a seamless existence that mixes children and parents and business, small-town life and travel to faraway places, the social, the political, and the religious all together in an up-front, out-and-out oneness that pulsates around the clock, across the seasons, and through the years. Elda and Henry find plenty to do. Theirs is one out of many contemporary Mennonite family stories. The excerpts below come from a tape-recorded interview made in their home one evening.

> HENRY:    I was born in 1924. Then, everyone around here, like me, was raised on a farm and went to a country school. We were expected to grow up and make a living by farming.

ELDA:    Then everyone came home from World War II, and we found out soon that there wasn't enough room for everybody [in farming].

HENRY:    Well, in addition to that, by the time the war was over, we had all seen so many other things. We understood the world a little better. And after we returned home, we recognized that life didn't end because we didn't farm. There were other things for us to do after the war. In the Fairview community today, there are all kinds of businesses that are owned by Mennonite people.

ELDA:    For us Mennonites, though, farming played such an important part in our past. Giving it up said something about the passing of that part of our great heritage. We farmed, and we didn't ever think we would do anything but farm. But when it came about in one way or another that we weren't able to continue farming, we simply did other things. It's hard to conceive, to imagine, the huge change that technology has brought—technology. Everybody says, "Oh, the economy has ruined the family farm," but it wasn't the economy. It was the development of the bigger machinery. Technology defeated the family farm. It wasn't all the fault of the economy. The tractors became bigger and more powerful, so that people could farm more land. The combines became bigger too, and more efficient, and they could cut the wheat faster. [Henry and I] are just not very sympathetic to the idea that the economy ruined the family-farm business.

HENRY:    During and right after World War II, there weren't four people around here who weren't in the business of farming. I remember when there was a house with a farm family living in it on every quarter section of land in the county.

ELDA:    A few years ago, HENRY and I decided to count the people in our church who make their living strictly by farming. We counted only those who do nothing but farm. You know, there are people in our church who farm and teach school and people who farm and work at construction and those who farm and do still other types of work. But when we counted only those who farm for a living, we found there were thirteen. And that's out of a congregation totaling more than five hundred. So the number of people who make their living by farming has changed dramatically. Where there was once a house on every quarter section, now there are many, many entire sections of land that have no houses on them, no one living there. In fact, it's rare to see a section with a house on it anymore.

INTERVIEWER: What other changes have you seen in Mennonite life?

ELDA: Oh, changes in our church. The church made, possibly, one of its biggest changes during the midst of World War II. That was when we gave up our German language in the church. We were forced to.

HENRY: Well, we weren't forced to, but if we had gone ahead and continued to use German in our services, we would have had a few more problems.

ELDA: There was a great deal of pressure to give up speaking the German language. The trouble was all because we were fighting the Germans in the war, because the Germans were our enemies. It was a very, very difficult time for our older people. A good many of them spoke only German. In fact, I never heard Henry's mother pray in English. Henry and I didn't talk English ourselves until we started to school. We both learned to speak in German.

As we went through school, though, we spoke English, and we never talked German in our married life, in our home. That is, not unless we wanted to say something to each other about the kids and not have them listen. But I remember all the old German songs, and I still sing them, and I can still read the German Bible too. We can still speak German well enough. In fact, we've had young people who have lived in our home as part of the Mennonite Central Committee training program, and we were able to speak German with them. Three were from Europe and one from El Salvador. The first one who arrived came from Switzerland. He could use only four English words when he got here. They were "yes," "no," "frankfurter," and "milk." And that's the way he got along on his trip, and he came all the way from Pennsylvania to Oklahoma City on the bus. He spoke the same dialect in German that Henry and I had grown up with. As it turned out, we learned German instead of him learning English, because he didn't want to speak English and we did want to talk German.

I think that Henry and I are some of the younger people in our church who understand and read the German Bible. But we didn't teach our kids, and now our children are almost mad at us, because we didn't give them the opportunity to learn German as a second language. At the time, though, with people other than our church folks, speaking German was made to be such a terrible thing.

Another thing that was not a popular thing here in Major County was to take the peace stand. There was a lot of . . .

HENRY:    Animosity. We had animosity here but not much.

ELDA:    Around the time of the war, people would egg our churches and they would egg our houses.

HENRY:    They egged our house.

ELDA:    When they egged the church, the church folk went out to wash it off quick, but we never confronted anyone. When it was all said and done, some of the people who did the egging are some of our best friends now. That is a really wonderful thing about it all.

What were some other changes? Well, we remember that whenever a prayer was said, both of our grandmothers always covered their heads. It's something that comes from Scripture— that women should cover their heads. I remember how my grandmother would just untie her apron and pull it over her head very simply if someone should start to pray. She didn't run get an hat or cap or anything like that; she would just cover her head. I'd say that was another change—the way women stopped covering their heads. Of course, some of our Mennonite people today interpret that Scripture to mean that women should have their heads covered at all times, and that's why they wear the prayer caps, and I have no problem with it. That's just something we don't feel is necessary. Wearing a prayer cap is something that we don't do. We don't wear hats or any head covering now [for religious reasons]. Basically, our grandparents always dressed conservatively, but as far as dressing differently from most people, they really didn't ever dress differently. Yet there was a time when we women wouldn't have gone to a Wednesday night prayer meeting without a hat on. I guess I would say that was a carryover from the practice of head covering.

INTERVIEWER:   What stopped it the practice?

ELDA:   When Jackie Kennedy came out with that big bouffant hairdo! After that, it just didn't make sense to wear a hat.

HENRY:   Actually, the women started not wearing hats when they started cutting their hair and that was around the time of World War II.

ELDA:   Henry's mother would have never have thought of going to church without a hat.

HENRY:   She wouldn't go to town without a hat.

ELDA:   She wore a very stylish hat, not the little prayer cap. When those older women passed away in the 1960s, that was the end of wearing hats. Another thing about my grandmothers . . . they didn't like short dresses on little children. So each season [when I was a child], my mother made me a grandma dress to wear on Sunday afternoons when we went to visit. My family would rotate visits between grandmothers. We'd visit one grandmother one Sunday the other the next. The dresses I wore were always longer on Sundays than other days. This was so my grandmothers wouldn't have to admonish my mother about my skirt length. In spring, my mother would make me a summer grandma dress. In the winter, she would make another. It was really kind of silly, when I think back on it. But the fact that my mother respected my grandmothers' wishes is also important. Doing what my mother did says something to me about respect, but it really had nothing to do with religion. You know, the way I dressed was not a sin; but my mother respected my grandmothers enough that she would go to all that trouble. Today, I don't think that my daughter-in-law should make her girl's shorts a little longer just for me.

INTERVIEWER:    People tell me you're involved in the meat-canning project.

HENRY:    The Mennonite Central Committee instigated the program. They saw a need for a common thread that would unite Mennonites to work together for people who were suffering all over the world. That was right after the war and the meat was canned mostly to be sent overseas. Actually, the first time meat was canned in Fairview, it was canned right here [at the Martens place], in 1946.

ELDA:    The canning took place in a new [machine] shop his brother David had recently built. His brother offered the building, and the group accepted his offer. [Volunteers] moved out the tractors and cleaned up the new shop for the canners, and that's how the project began at Fairview. In the early days there were two Mennonite canners. It takes three men now. They travel all across the country with the canning equipment from the MCC on the back of a truck, making stop after stop at Mennonite churches where people turn out to help can meat that will be given to hungry people.

HENRY:    First we butchered the cattle here. [In other years,] the canning was moved to several different farms. They did it wherever they could find a place. There would be four or five or six whole beefs to can each time the canning operation came to town. The canners were clean and sanitary then, but now it's a different process. That was before meat was inspected. [Inspection of all meat to be consumed is now required by federal law.] After we were no longer able to butcher our own cattle for canning, for many years we bought sides of beef that were federally inspected.

ELDA:   The first canner was somewhat crude. It was just a little thing with one kettle in it. I guess it was an old cast-iron kettle at that time. That first old canner and its crew came from Heston, Kansas. The first year [1946], the cattle were slaughtered right here on the yard. It took more time to can then because the volunteers had to do their own killing, cutting, boning, and everything. I suppose it took fifty people. You have to remember, at that time people did their own butchering at home, so they knew what they were cutting. They chunked the meat. In those days, the volunteers would line up on either side of long tables. They would stand by the tables and cut. There were always those who knew what to do. They made sure the pieces were the right size.

HENRY:   And that the bone got cleaned all right. All that was before it was cooked.

ELDA:   Now we use ground meat. It turns out that we can buy meat cheaper already ground, so we [Mennonites from area churches] buy the meat, and we donate the labor. Last year, our son John drove a big refrigerated truck to Liberal, Kansas, and got the meat for this area. Our son brought thirty thousand dollars' worth of meat for canning in Oklahoma. Chickens are canned by volunteers too, but not here in Fairview. Canning used to take longer than now and was much more work.

HENRY:   In this area, we do canning in the spring. Of course, the crew cans nine months out of the year, but the canner is taken up north first. It's a three-man crew, usually an older man and two younger men. Often the older one of the canners will be someone who has done the work for years, but the other two are usually young men who volunteer to help for a period of time. These young people volunteer to work for MCC for a specified length of time. I don't know how much it is they are paid now, but they only get so much. It's a very meager allowance. They also get their room and board. The three MCC workers bring the canner truck into town. There is a big pressure cooker on the truck. The meat is cooked and put into cans and then they pressure-cook it to seal the cans. For the last several years the canning has been done southeast of town at the Church of God in Christ, the Holdeman church.

ELDA:    The Holdeman are Mennonite people. The women wear the little black hats, and the men wear beards. They had a fellow in their church who was able financially to donate money to build a big building right next to their Christian school. It's just a big metal building. They use it for a gym; but when meat-canning time comes, it is used to can meat. The man who gave the building—who built it—definitely saidthat the building should be used for canning. They made arrangements for a big door so the canners could be moved in and out, and they also arranged for the waste disposal to be easier. But other than that, there is no special equipment in the building.

HENRY:    We [the Martens and their church, the Fairview Mennonite Brethren congregation] are not involved with the canning as far as being in charge. That's the Holdeman church. The Holdemans have very little to say [the reference here is that Holdeman people are quiet in manner], but they are very handy on the meat canning.

ELDA:    The labor is still all done by people from the churches. The different denominations of Mennonites around here work here together on that.

HENRY:    Anymore, they've got it down to an art.

ELDA:    It's much simpler today than it was the first year.

HENRY:    But it hasn't changed all that much. Now we have stainless-steel kettles. The canner truck also has a big grinder and a big saw, but they don't use them anymore, although it's just been the last couple years that they haven't used the grinder.

The cloth aprons are gone. Now you are required to wear a hat and gloves and apron and they are the plastic throwaway kind.

ELDA:    Of course, the cans still have to be washed, and they have to be labeled, and they have to be marked, and then, when they're filled and sealed, they have tobe hauled to Newton, Kansas, which is our MCC central headquarters.

HENRY:    It's a long workday. We start at four in the morning and quit about ten at night. There are evening shifts and day shifts. What we're doing most of the time is washing those cans and labeling and numbering them.

ELDA:    Breakfast is served, and the different churches each volunteer to bring in the other meals during the day. The canner usually stays in one place about three days. It's still a lot of hard work.

INTERVIEWER:    What's the finished product?

HENRY:    Well, we tasted some and we didn't like it.

ELDA:    It's just that the meat isn't seasoned. Joyce, our daughter, was involved in a mission [serving as a MCC volunteer nurse stationed in Bangladesh, Pakistan, and Africa for eight years], and when we visited her [in Bangladesh], we opened a can. She and the other Mennonite workers were eating the canned meat. The MCC gave each person a small allowance and their room and board. That's the only time I have ever seen the canned meat being used. [The meat was not distributed to the people of Bangladesh because of religious proscriptions]. Henry and I didn't think it was that good, but I know if we had been real hungry. . . .

HENRY:    It was good. It just wasn't spiced right. That's all. If you fixed it the way we prepare meat, it would taste good.

ELDA:    The reason for this [lack of seasoning] is that some of the people who get the meat are real particular about the meat they eat. You see, we can't afford to do separate canning just for the special tastes of each group of people. [Because the religion of some people prohibits eating beef, chickens are also canned for distribution.] For that reason, the meat isn't seasoned at all.

It's an interesting sidelight that one of the most prized possessions of the Bangladesh people—something they almost had to guard with their lives—were the tin cans that the meat came in. I think it was the two-pound cans that were so popular. The people would just scramble for those cans. They could not eat the meat because of their religion, but they sure wanted the containers it came in. Our daughter said that if [her superiors] ever wanted to give something really nice to the local workers, they would let them have one of those cans. To the Bangladesh people, it was a very prized possession. Over here, a big tin can? You see them all the time.

The cans aren't marked in any special way, so you can't tell where they were processed. They just all are marked a yellow label that says, "In the name of Christ."

HENRY:    And the cans are numbered.

ELDA:    Yes, every can has "In the name of Christ" and a number on it.

HENRY:    I think that in Newton [Kansas, the headquarters for the canning project] they know where each can came from.

ELDA:    Yes, they have a record. The MCC workers in Newton take one can from each batch processed and keep it separate from the others. They watch those cans to check for spoilage. After a certain length of time each test can is opened and checked. That way they keep an account of all the cans processed at every location and know that all of it is good. It's the job of one volunteer at every canning site to be sure to keep one can from every batch that goes into the canner separate from the other cans and label it to be sent to Newton. We have a system of watching and selecting the cans for Newton.

Today, much of the canned meat is used in the United States, in soup kitchens and for disaster-relief purposes and in community food pantries. In urban areas, in Oklahoma City, and

Wichita, wherever there's a need. At one time, the meat was strictly for war-torn countries overseas. That's another big change that we see. We see now that there are others, not in war-torn situations particularly, but in needful situations. The MCC is very active in the United States.

INTERVIEWER:   How did the Mennonite relief sales begin?

HENRY:   Actually, the first sale was in 1921 in California. But they didn't continue it.

ELDA:   There weren't any more until after World War II. There have been sales for forty-five years in other states, and there are thirty-eight different sales in the United States and Canada. There are sales in Kansas, Missouri, and Washington. We've had the sale here for years, and I organized the first one [in 1978]. [The sale is no longer necessarily held in Fairview.] The sale was my dream, and I do not want to take the credit for it . . . but I can't help it. I was on the [Major County] fair board at the time. So, it was easy for me to say, "We've got the facilities." That's really why it started at Fairview, because it was easy to start, and we had a good workforce here, which is very important. Our church is fairly large, and we had the Church of God in Christ Mennonites and the Orienta church nearby to help, too. Maybe we didn't do it right the first year, but it worked and it's worked ever since. If you have a lot of people each do a little bit, it's possible. The Kansas sale raised half a million dollars this last year, and that makes us look very little. Ours is just two or three thousand in attendance. It's quite an undertaking to organize, but it works. When people donate, you kind of have to take what they give.

HENRY:   We do have a rule. We say, 'If it's not good enough for you to buy for yourself, don't bring it. We don't want it." Our relief sale isn't a garage sale. It's an auction.

ELDA:   Every year we have a feature quilt. Each church makes one quilt square and donates it to the sale, then we quilt those squares all together and that makes the feature quilt. The feature quilt brings between twelve hundred and twenty-four hundred dollars at the auction. We organize several different projects similar to that that we all can participate in. So far, the most any quilt brought at our sale is four thousand dollars. The size and the color determine the price. What's most popular are quilts made up in whatever colors are being shown in the stores right now.

HENRY:     Well, workmanship has something to do with it.

ELDA:     Oh, yes, it does, it does. You don't need seven or eight sixteen hundred-dollar quilts for the sale, because it's obvious that people who can pay sixteen hundred to two thousand dollars for a quilt probably don't need it. They're just wanting to make a contribution, which is commendable, and we need those people, but we need eighty-, ninety-, and one-hundred-dollar quilts, too, just the practical, cover-up type. I always say that you need to have some low-dollar quilts for families who need quilts, people who need a quilt to cover with and to wash when they are soiled, a quilt that you can put on a child's bed.

Every year I think, the quilt market is saturated. I think, "Who on earth is going to buy all these quilts?" and the sale day comes and there are 140 quilts hanging there, and the auction begins, and they're sold. Of course, I know there are lots of people who buy because they are interested in helping other people. We don't feel the sale is necessarily a dollar-for-dollar return on man-hours invested, but an opportunity to serve. I know my friend and I [who work together on a quilt each year] could have never done anything with our two hands that would have generated twenty-five hundred dollars. But that's what one quilt did. I look at it as an opportunity for me to do something with my hands that will profit someone else, because I don't hold down a regular job. Some people can't understand why other people don't just give their money to the MCC. They say, "Why go to all the trouble, if someone wants to donate twenty-five hundred dollars, why not let that person give it?" And that's one way of thinking, but, on the other hand, it was a thrill for me to know that I could do something for a purpose. To make that quilt and sell it was a thrill for me. I had the opportunity to multiply my gifts, or whatever you want to call it. And I think other people feel the same way. The same way with baked bread and peppernuts (a very small, hard cookie). A little cookie is not a big deal, but it's an opportunity to serve. And food is actually what sells best.

HENRY:   Sausage, liverwurst, bread, peppernuts. Some of the cooking is Russian and some Polish. Our own parents were Dutch and came from Holland. Grandpa Martens came from Russia.

ELDA:   Crafts don't sell as well as they did years ago. I wish crafts sold better, but I think they're not popular because there are so many other arts and crafts festivals now. Plus, anyone who likes that kind of thing is doingit at home.

I think the economy plays a part in what sells. If I had forty dollars that I wanted to spend at the sale as a contribution and I went there with two children, I probably wouldn't buy an . . .

HENRY:   Afghan for forty-five dollars.

ELDA:   I'd probably buy peppernuts for the kids to eat. I'd probably buy sausage and try some of the New Year's cookies that they fix there at the sale and get my kids and wife some Russian pancakes. I'd eat dinner and visit and then go home. If you've only got so many dollars, why spend it on an afghan?

INTERVIEWER:   Is the sale open to the public or just for Mennonites?

ELDA:   Well, more Mennonites come than others. It's kind of a Mennonite reunion. We want other people there. In Oklahoma, we have lots of Mennonite people who are Mennonites because they have joined our church. People think that you have to be born Mennonite to be a Mennonite; but, that's not true.

We are all sinners saved by grace. It happened that we chose to belong to the Mennonite Church, just the same as the Baptist

Church. People are sometimes surprised that I would say that, because they think that to be a Mennonite you have to be born a Mennonite.

[Overall], I think being careful is important [to Mennonite life]. I'm not talking about being stingy, but being careful with things, taking care of things and making things reach and living within your means. Henry and I have tried to teach that to our children, and I don't think we've done too bad in that area. But young people today don't learn it like we learned it. We grew up in the depression era.

There are so many people out there in the world and so many opportunities to serve. I'm not one to think that everything should be done in Africa or India. Right here in our town, there are people who are hurting. I don't know that I've done so well in this—extending friendship and living what we were taught.

HENRY:    I would like to be remembered for what I do, for what I do for other people. They don't have to do for me. I've always been service-oriented. I've always worked among the public. I would like to be remembered for helping the community.

ELDA:    And not because that is part of our religion, because it isn't.

HENRY:    No.

ELDA:    You do it because . . .

HENRY:    You do your part and a little more, and it sure won't hurt you any.

# CHAPTER 11

# The Challenge

Die Stillen im Lande

Mennonitism has undergone a tremendous transformation in the past century. Beginning in 1893 when the Cherokee Outlet was opened for settlement, many German-speaking Mennonite immigrants crossed into Oklahoma from Kansas. Other Mennonites came from the other plains states and from the eastern states to establish homesteads and churches in Northwest Oklahoma. Today the great-grandchildren of those Mennonites have moved from poverty to prosperity, from nonconformity to integration, from closed congregations to open worship, from nonresistant pacifism to proactive peace initiatives. As a group the Mennonite Brethren and the General Conference Church members interviewed for this study have seen their congregations transformed from the outside, and, perhaps more importantly, the membership has transformed itself from the inside.

The development of the group through more than one hundred years of life in Northwest Oklahoma reflects the integrated nature of their religious and social organization. When the Mennonites arrived in Oklahoma, their strong group ties were undergirded by three basic principles: (1) church doctrine and purpose, (2) a distinct and elaborate history, and (3) a self-sufficient community network. The Mennonites of Northwest Oklahoma were able to survive the experience of discrimination, violence, and imprisonment that accompanied their peace stand during World War I and the resurgence of discrimination against them during World War II. While their neighbors, the Holdeman Mennonites, held to separate communities, Mennonite life for the group studied, Mennonite Brethren and General Conference Church members, was transformed from a farm-based, closed culture to an urbanized culture following two world conflicts.

Because social life is always a process, sustaining viability depends on a group's ability, despite ever-present change, to build and maintain distinctive boundaries between itself and the larger world. Communication based on frames of reference individuals inside and outside a group hold about the group is one form of boundary. In adapting to change, the Mennonites of Northwest Oklahoma redefined the way they express their religion to themselves and the larger world and in doing so have shifted the boundaries of their group life.

In accounting for group life in the past and present, the preceding narrative, and accompanying personal interviews reveal the important frames of reference and demonstrate shifts in the manner of their expression. The stories of many people were involved in putting this book together. Although the discussions ranged widely from individual to individual, commonalties of theme in the responses were greater than differences. The accounts lay open Mennonite history and current group practices in a comprehensive and verifiable narrative.

The boundaries that distinguish these Mennonites today are invisible and are language-based. In some ways, frames of reference have been transformed from the past. For example, those interviewed explained Mennonitism as compatible with, rather that at odds with, mainstream America. In other ways, the frames have remained the same; what has been altered—reframed—is merely the way the group presents itself or communicates with the larger society. Transformed or no, the frames reaffirm subtle boundaries that distinguish the group from society at large. For Mennonite society in Northwest Oklahoma, two major frames of reference help the group both to interact with the larger society and to maintain its own identity. These frames are the values of nonresistance and separatism.

The frame for nonresistance, a primary descriptor and marker of Mennonite identity, currently is expressed in terms of "the peace stand." In the past, nonresistance was more often voiced as rejection of militarism (Frances 1955; Hostetler 1986; Kroeker 1954). Furthermore, past conflicts with mainstream society that once were evident are now minimized. Change coming from the larger society—for instance, the advent of the "all-volunteer" armed services—has loosened the wedge between mainstream society and the Mennonites' stand on pacifism. However, Mennonites have also reframed their peace position. The conflict with the larger society over military service was termed in individual interviews with Mennonites as "not like in the past." Nevertheless, prevailing public opinion was assessed by those interviewed as linking Mennonitism with pacifism in a negative way, thereby perpetuating historic tensions between Mennonites and the larger society. In the interviews, the concept of nonresistance as a stand for peace was offered to mitigate this tension, and nonresistance often was justified by the elaboration of another Mennonite doctrine—individual interpretation of biblical teaching. For instance, one person said, "I know of one of the men in our church who was in the army. . . . But with my own children, there was a very strong feeling, very, very strong so that they would not have been in the military at all. That's my own. I can't speak for the other families." Another person explained, "Peace is still a very prominent part of the Mennonite culture and faith; however, there is more freedom now. If somebody wants to join our church, we can't say, 'Well, we can't accept your position.'"

Others spoke of nonresistance as a "peace initiative," referring to the humanitarian mission of the church. These accounts usually involved narration of personal or family involvement in one of many altruistic projects sponsored by the interdenominational Mennonite Central Committee. These include aid to war refugees, agricultural help to developing countries, and programs to assist people with mental illness. The majority of those interviewed had participated directly in at least one major Mennonite program, ranging from disaster relief for flood victims to building and repairing homes for those in need of housing. Thus, nonresistance was reframed as positive action in a way that could be sanctioned by society at large rather than as unequivocal rejection of mainstream mores.

Shifting the frame for nonresistance from a group norm prohibiting violence against another person to individual choice in demonstrating nonresistance has opened options for upholding the belief. The options are usually one or more of the following: service in the military, service as a conscientious objector, and the promotion of peace through good works. Despite these changes, nonresistance remains a basic value of the group. At the time of the interviews, all the respondents together could name only one Mennonite member who had entered any kind of military service in the past decade.

The second major frame of reference used to explain Mennonite life is separatism, and that value, too, was conceptualized by those interviewed as different from the past. In general, individuals have transformed their primary frames of reference to encourage integration with those outside the Mennonite community. Mennonites justified their acculturated lifestyles as being "more positive" approaches to Christianity. "When I think of the bondage that some people are in about those kind of things [avoiding TV or dancing], it is so sad to me," said one woman. Consequently, talk often centered on Mennonitism as a distinctive way of life that is not only attainable in the secular world but is actually a duty demanded of the Christian. This justification preserves the religious dictate of separatism while simultaneously affirming interaction with the larger society.

Transformation in the view of separatism also is associated with church membership. Historically, Mennonite ethnicity was passed down from generation to generation by endogamous marriage and by church membership granted adults upon their confession of faith and baptism. Although activities that reify Mennonite heritage—the teaching of ethnicity in worship, common foods, and in-group charitable activities—have not been neglected, in recent years the impact of fundamentalism and Protestantism, among other influences, has prompted group expansion through evangelism. But this activity is problematic to some extent: Welcoming everyone reverses the exclusive church relationships that discouraged outsiders, or *Englische*, in the past; furthermore, identification of the group as a religious body negates the ethnic history of the group. The words of one ethnic Mennonite illustrate the dissonance and difficulty encountered in defining the relationship: "Since we have gone over to the English [language use], we have other people that don't have our kind of names in church, so there's been a change. Mennonites used to feel kind of like the children of Israel—stay with your own people, don't get mixed up with these other people." A convert expressed the duality this way: "I would say our church is a very big melting pot. . . . Although they're hanging onto the culture and they should—I think that's important—probably a third of the church come from different backgrounds."

As the quotes above illustrate, reconciliation of the dual status of membership presents different problems to different categories of Mennonites. On the other hand, both converts and ethnic members view the church as an extended family. Phrases such as "The Mennonites are a very close-knit people," "They are extremely helpful to each other," "Church is almost a second home," "It's a conviction of individuals to be exemplary in life, to care for one another" were voiced. Doctrinal themes of sin, forgiveness, salvation, right living, and the importance of strong, nuclear family units serve as agreed upon guideposts of everyday activity and frames for group bonding for all Mennonites regardless of membership status. In addition, in-group bonding is cultivated through reframing of the group's past. The history of persecution for their beliefs, with which all Mennonites can identify, comes forward as a bulwark of Mennonite identity in the accounts, rather than an emphasis on setting group boundaries through German language use and a separate culture.

Even though there is not complete consistency among members regarding the interpretation of nonresistance and separatism, the idea that ongoing frames of reference may endure despite a lack of complete internal consistency is supported in the stories collected here.

The frames of reference that uphold Mennonite society in Northwest Oklahoma offer a range, albeit limited, of interpretation that allows for group-identity maintenance despite internal and external pressures for change. The longevity of the Swiss nation despite language and cultural divisions is another example of the strength of such ties (Smith 1992). The Mennonites' frames of reference establish a boundary of what the group is not. The frames, to those inside the boundary, situate Mennonitism as not militaristic, not permissive, not ahistorical. To those outside, Mennonitism is viewed as neither a completely exclusive group nor a threat to social order.

Through the interviews, two-sided barriers of group-boundary maintenance were shown to exist between Mennonites in Northwest Oklahoma and their larger social world. From outside the boundaries, Mennonitism appears to be moving toward assimilation. From inside, Mennonitism looks to be holding a line behind which cultural traits may be nurtured and practiced. Overall, the current frames of reference used by group members incorporate change by allowing Mennonitism to be viewed from either side of the group boundary as a religious and an ethnic affiliation with a long and rich history and traditions of its own. The basic tenets of nonresistance and separatism remain cornerstones of Mennonite faith, even though the Mennonite ethic has been reframed or transformed through written and oral communication to focus on these essential values somewhat differently. Despite this, the overall conception of group life continues to rest on the same fundamental principles—religious beliefs, a unified history, and a strong fellowship of believers—that the group brought with them from Russia. In reality, the framing processes of Mennonite identification are far more complex than this analysis reveals. Further study of the forces that shape Mennonite society is needed, as is research to more clearly define the processes of communication involving framing, vocabularies of motive, and group-boundary maintenance for religious-ethnic groups of European ancestry.

The history, events, and circumstances the group has experienced transcend a century of Mennonite life in Oklahoma. Complex historical, economic, political, social, and psychological forces have shaped the contemporary Mennonite identity in subtle and forceful ways. Mennonites frame their heritage as that of German-speaking Russian immigrants who came to America looking for a home and religious toleration. They survived economic hard times and the elements of nature to build a community of faith on the Oklahoma plains. Of particular attention in accounts of their past is the Russian Mennonites' contribution of innovative farming practices and, most importantly, their part in introducing a new strain of wheat to the recently opened frontier. World War I was a threat to the basic beliefs of Mennonitism and to Mennonite society itself. As Mennonites recall this period, they describe it as a great watershed.

Mennonites believe that others conceive of them as traitors during World War I, while they see themselves as victims of malice and unjust imprisonment. They see themselves misjudged as disaffected cowards during World War II. In their view, conscientious objectors made real and beneficial contributions to the welfare of others. They hold to the image of Mennonite farmers as directors of sophisticated agribusinesses that have helped make Oklahoma a national leader in wheat production. But these images of Mennonites are not ones typically held by the general public. Moreover, none of these images that Mennonites hold of themselves have been emphasized in general histories of the era. They are, however, the resolute articulation of the Mennonites' understanding of their common experiences.

In telling the stories of their past, Mennonites continually test old ideas and institutions and create new ones. Some traditional and unique forms of church life live on in modern context. Among them are quilt making, meat canning, the yearly relief sale, and other celebrations that cut across denominational ties of Mennonites. Nonresistance, not overlooked, is expressed as a personal choice for peace initiatives and humanitarian aid to suffering people worldwide.

Concerned with the dangers of secularism and the problems of the peace stand in a world that grows increasingly more violent, most contemporary church members nevertheless hold that assimilation and acculturation are an advantage to Mennonitism. It appears, though, that as hard as the old times were, the new times may be harder. With the ascriptive Mennonite identity of the past now largely a nonvisible ethnicity, group ties are without visible means of support. The processes of group identity are always in flux. The Mennonites live with no guarantee that the boundaries of their society will withstand unknown future threats to their faith.

We leave the Mennonite story at the dawn of a new century, knowing only that nothing is locked in the past. Individuals continuously recollect and interpret the present, and narration reframes experience into knowledge. Once called "the quiet in the land," Mennonites now find that communication has become the principal indicator and sustainer of their religious and group life. Recounting the development of the Mennonites in Northwest Oklahoma demonstrates the great power of language and perception. Through the stream of memory, historic challenges can be mastered, old wounds closed, and reconciliation sought—both for the storyteller and for those who listen.

# Mennonite Churches in Northwest Oklahoma

| CHURCH | TOWN | COUNTY | DATES |
|---|---|---|---|
| MENNONITE BRETHREN | | | |
| Coy | Coy | Woods | 1912–15 |
| Enid City<br>Developed from<br>North Enid,<br>1925–26 | Enid | Garfield | 1926–present |
| Lahoma | Lahoma | Garfield | 1901–23 |
| Lookout | Lookout | Woodward | 1905–12 |
| Medford | Medford | Grant | 1896–1910 |
| North Enid<br>Merged with<br>Enid City, 1960 | Enid | Garfield | 1896/97–<br>present |
| North Fairview<br>(Nord Houffnungsfeld)<br>Merged with<br>South Fairview, 1951 | Fairview | Major | 1896–present |
| Ringwood | Ringwood | Major | 1920–28 |

| | | | |
|---|---|---|---|
| South Fairview (Süd Houffnungsfeld) Merged with North Fairview, 1951 | Fairview | Major | 1896–present |

## GENERAL CONFERENCE MENNONITE (Western District)

| | | | |
|---|---|---|---|
| Bethanian | Coy | Woods | 1905–16 |
| Bethel Broke away from Grace, 1937 Joined, 1947 | Enid | Garfield | 1937–58 |
| Deer Creek Joined, 1901 | Deer Creek | Grant | 1899–present |
| Friedensau | Perry | Noble | 1898–1935 |
| Grace Joined, 1938 | Enid | Garfield | 1935–present |
| Medford Joined, 1898 | Medford | Grant | 1897–present |
| New Hoffnungstal (New Hopedale) | Meno | Major | 1904–present |
| Saron Withdrew, 1989 | Orienta | Major | 1897–present |
| West New Hopedale | Ringwood | Major | 1948–present |
| Zion Joined, 1902 | Lucien | Noble | 1898–1912 |
| Zoar Withdrew, 1963 | Goltry | Alfalfa | 1911–present |

| KRIMMER MENNONITE BRETHREN* | | | |
|---|---|---|---|
| Medford | Medford | Grant | 1918–23 |

| (Old) MENNONITE CHURCH | | | |
|---|---|---|---|
| German Springs | German Springs | Kay | 1895–1920[†] |
| Milan Valley | Jet | Alfalfa | 1897–1941 |
| Newkirk | Newkirk | Kay | 1906–1910[†] |

| CHURCH OF GOD IN CHRIST, MENNONITE (Holdeman)[‡] | | | |
|---|---|---|---|
| Fairview Mennonite | Fairview | Major | 1895–present |
| Pleasant View | Goltry | Alfalfa | 1893–present |

Source: Goertzen 1990; Kuschel 1989; Haury 1981; Erb 1974; Koehn 1992.

* Outside the Northwest Oklahoma area, Krimmer churches were located in Hooker, Texas County, 1906 to 1926, and in Weatherford, Custer County, 1897 to 1936.

[†] The exact date of church dissolution is not certain

[‡] Outside the Northwest Oklahoma area, Holdeman churches were located in Paul's Valley, Garven County, 1898 to 1902, and in Chickasha, Grady County, which was founded in 1902 by families from Paul's Valley.

# Bibliography

Alba, R. D. 1988. The twilight of ethnicity among Americans of European ancestry: The case of Italians. In *Ethnicity and race in the U.S.A.*, ed. R. D. Alba, 134–58. New York: Routledge.

Alba, R. D. & M. B. Chamblin. 1983. A preliminary examination of ethnic identification among whites. *American Sociological Review* 48:240–47.

Ammerman, N. T. 1987. *Bible believers: Fundamentalists in the modern world*. New Brunswick, NJ: Rutgers University Press.

Anderson, R. A. 1994. *Peace was in their hearts*. Watsonville, CA: Correlan Publications.

Bailey, W. A. 1994. Hagar: A model for an Anabaptist feminist? *Mennonite Quarterly Review* 68:219–28.

Barclay, H. B. 1967. The plain people of Oregon. *Review of Religious Research* 8(3):140–65.

Barone, M. 1990. *Our country: The shaping of America from Roosevelt to Reagan*. New York: Macmillan.

Barth, F. 1969. *Ethnic groups and boundaries*. Boston: Little Brown.

Beegle, J. A., and N. E. Johnson. 1982. The rural American people: A look backward and forward. In *Rural society in the U.S.: Issues for the 1980s*, eds. D. A. Dillman and D. J. Hobbs, 58–69. Boulder, CO: Westview Press.

Bekker, J. P. 1973. *The origin of the Mennonite Brethren Church*. Hillsboro, KS: Mennonite Brethren Historical Society.

Belk, F. R. 1975. Migration of Russian Mennonites. *Social Science*: 17–21.

Bender, H. S. and C. H. Smith. 1964. *Mennonites and their heritage: A handbook of Mennonite history and beliefs*. Scottdate, PA: Herald Press.

Bergen, K. 1988. *Palestinian women* (Women's Concerns Report No. 78). Akron, PA: Mennonite Central Committee.

Board of Christian Literature. 1984. *Meet . . . the Mennonites*. Hillsboro, KS: Author.

Boldt, E. P. 1979. The plain people: Notes on the continuity and change. *Canadian Ethnic Studies* 11:17–28.

Boldt, E. P. and L. W. Roberts. 1979. Mennonite continuity and change: A comment on Rodney J. Sawatsky. *Canadian Journal of Sociology* 4(2): 151–54.

Bush, P. 1993. Military service, religious faith, and acculturation: Mennonite GIs and their church, 1941–1945. *Mennonite Quarterly Review* 67:261–82.

Caldwell, D. 1998. Personal interview.

Chandler, R. 1970. The Mennonites: Pioneer nonconformists. *Christianity Today* 14:44–46.

City M. B. Church will host conference. 1959. *Fairview Republican*, July 16.

Combs, J. E., and M. W. Mansfield, eds. 1976. *Drama in life: The uses of communication in society*. New York: Communication Arts Books.

Conference of the Mennonite Brethren Church of North America. 1948. *Resolutions*. Hillsboro, KS: Mennonite Brethren Publishing House.

Cooley, C. H. 1962. *Social organization*. New York: Schocken Books. Originally published 1909.

Coon, R. 1988. Being a peace church makes a difference. In *Growing faith: General Conference Mennonites in Oklahoma*, ed. W. McKee, 145–56. Newton, KS: Faith and Life Press.

Cox, A. 1988. Fairview: Mennonite sale nets $85,000. *Enid Daily News and Eagle*, November 28.

Crosby, A. W., Jr. 1976. *Epidemic and peace, 1918*. Westport, CT: Greenwood.

Currie, R., L. Driedger, and R. Linden. 1979. Abstinence and moderation: Mixing Mennonite drinking norms. *Mennonite Quarterly Review*, 53(4): 263–81.

Cuzzort, R. P., and E. W. King. 1976. *Twentieth century social thought*. New York: Holt, Rinehart & Winston.

Dale, E. E. 1949. *Oklahoma: The Story of a state*. Evanston. IL: Row, Peterson & Company.

Davis, D. K., and S. J. Baron. 1981. *Mass communication and everyday life*. Belmont, CA: Wadsworth.

Defrange, A. 1988, June. A separate peace. *Oklahoma Today*, 12–19.

Denzin, N. K. 1970. *The research act*. Chicago: Aldine.

Driedger, L. 1968. A perspective on Canadian Mennonite urbanism. *Mennonite Life*: 147–51.

———. 1975. Canadian Mennonite urbanism: Ethnic villages or metropolitan remnant? *Mennonite Quarterly Review* 47:225–44.

———. 1977. The Anabaptist identification ladder: Plain urbane continuity in diversity. *Mennonite Quarterly Review* 51:378–81.

———. 1983. Changing Mennonite family roles: From rural boundaries to urban networks. *International Journal of Sociology of the Family* 13:63–81.

———. 1988. *Mennonite identity in conflict*. Queenston, Ontario: Edwin Mellen Press.

———. 1993. From martyrs to muppies: The Mennonite urban professional revolution. *Mennonite Quarterly Review* 67:304–22.

Driedger, L., and G. Church. 1974. Residential segregation and institutional completeness: A comparison of ethnic minorities. *Canadian Review of Sociology and Anthropology* 11:30–52.

Driedger, L., and D. N. Friesen. 1995. Mennonite women in pastoral leadership. *Mennonite Quarterly Review* 69:487–505.

Driedger, L., and P. Jacob. 1973. Ethnic identity: A comparison of Mennonite and other German students. *Mennonite Quarterly Review* 47:225–44.

Driedger, L., and J. H. Kauffman. 1982. Urbanization of Mennonites: Canadian and American comparisons. *Mennonite Quarterly Review* 56:269–90.

Driedger, L., R. Vogt, and M. Reimes. 1983. Mennonite intermarriage: National, regional, and intergenerational trends. *Mennonite Quarterly Review* 57:132–44.

Driedger, L., M. Yoder, and P. Sawatsky. 1985. Divorce among Mennonites: Evidence of family breakdown. *Mennonite Quarterly Review* 59:367–82.

Dueck, A. J. 1995. Mennonites, the Russian state, and the crisis of brethren and old church relations in Russia, 1910–1918. *Mennonite Quarterly Review* 69:453–71.

Dyck, C. J., ed. 1967. *An introduction to Mennonite history: A popular history of the Anabaptists and the Mennonites*. Scottdate, PA: Herald Press.

———. 1981. *An introduction to Mennonite history: A popular history of the Anabaptists and the Mennonites*, 2d ed. Scottdale, PA: Herald Press.

Eaton, J. W. 1952. Controlled acculturation: A survival technique of the Hutterites. *American Sociological Review* 17:331–40.

Ediger, M. 1984. *Mennonites in American society*. ERIC Document Reproduction Service No. ED 248178.

Eller, C. 1991. *Conscientious objectors and the Second World War: Moral and religious arguments in the support of pacifism*. New York: Praeger.

Engbrecht, D. D. 1985. The Americanization of a rural immigrant church: The General Conference Mennonites in central Kansas, 1874–1939. *Dissertation Abstracts International*. Doctoral dissertation, University of Nebraska.

Epp, F. E. 1962. *Mennonite exodus*. Altona, Manitoba: D. W. Friesen and Sons.

Epp, F. H. 1977. *Mennonite peoplehood: A plea for new initiatives*. Waterloo, Ontario: Conrad Press.

Epp, J. L. 1989. *Shelter, housing, homelessness* (Women's Concerns Report No. 84). Akron, PA: Mennonite Central Committee.

Erasmus, C. J. 1981. Anarchy, enclavement, and syntropy in intentional and traditional communities. In *Persistent peoples: Cultural enclaves in perspective*, eds. G. P. Castile and G. Kushner, 192–211. Tucson: University of Arizona Press.

Erb, P. 1974. *South central frontiers*. Scottdale, PA: Herald Press.

Fairview church will be host to M.B. conference. 1958. *Fairview Republican*, July 31.

Fiftieth anniversary of the First Mennonite Brethren Church. 1947. Unpublished manuscript. Enid, OK: First Mennonite Baptist Church.

Fine, G. A., and S. Kleinman. 1979. Rethinking subculture: An interactionist analysis. *American Journal of Sociology* 85(1):1–21.

Flynn, G. O. 1993. *The draft, 1940–1973*. Lawrence: University of Kansas Press.

Forty Mennonites to attend Ark. camp. 1959. *Fairview Republican*, August 6.

Francis, E. K. 1948. The Russian Mennonites: From religious to ethnic group. *American Journal of Sociology* 54:101–7.

————. 1955. *In search of utopia: The Mennonites in Manitoba*. Glencoe, IL: Free Press.

Fretz, J. W. 1977. The plain and not-so-plain Mennonites in Waterloo County, Ontario. *Mennonite Quarterly Review* 51:377–85.

Gans, H. J. 1979. Symbolic ethnicity: The future of ethnic groups and cultures in America. In *On the making of Americans: Essays in honor of David Riesman*, eds. H. J. Gans, N. Glazer, J. R. Gusfield, and C. Jenks, 193–220. Philadelphia: University of Pennsylvania.

Genealogy of Peter R. and Katherina Thiesen Brandt, 1845–1978. Unpublished manuscript of family history.

Gibson, A. M. 1984. *The history of Oklahoma*. Norman: University of Oklahoma Press.

Gittinger, R. 1939. *Formation of the state of Oklahoma*. Norman: University of Oklahoma Press.

Glaser, T., and A. Strauss. 1967. *The discovery of grounded theory: Strategies for qualitative research*. Chicago: Aldine de Gruyter.

Glazer, N., and D. P. Moynihan. 1975. *Ethnicity: Theory and experience*. Cambridge, MA: Harvard University Press.

——, eds. 1970. *Beyond the melting pot*. Cambridge, MA: Joint Center for Urban Studies of The Massachusetts Institute of Technology and the President and Fellows of Harvard University.

Goertzen, P. 1990. Chronology of Mennonite Brethren Churches. Unpublished manuscript. Tabor College, Center of Mennonite Brethren Studies, Hillsboro, KS.

Goffman, E. 1963. *Stigma: Notes on the management of spoiled identity*. Englewood Cliffs, NJ: Prentice-Hall.

——. 1973. *The presentation of self in everyday life*. Woodstock, NY: Overlook Press.

——. 1974. *Frame analysis: An essay in the organization of experience*. New York: Harper & Row.

Gonos, G. 1977. "Situation" versus "frame": The "interactionist" and the "structuralist" analyses of everyday life. *American Sociological Review* 42(6): 854–67.

Gordon, M. M. 1964. *Assimilation in American life: The role of race, religion and national origins*. New York: Oxford University Press.

Greeley, A. M. 1972. *The denominational society*. Glenview, IL: Scott, Foresman.

Green, D. E. 1977. Beginnings of wheat culture in Oklahoma. In *Rural Oklahoma*, ed. D. E. Green, 56–74. Oklahoma City: Oklahoma Historical Society.

Hale, D. 1980. *The Germans from Russia in Oklahoma*. Norman: University of Oklahoma Press.

Hardwick, R. S. 1974. Change and continuity in two Mennonite communities: The effects of urban and rural settings. *Dissertation Abstracts International*, 4606A. Doctoral dissertation, University of Virginia.

Harris, M. 1960. Farm family corporations *Proceedings of the North Central Land Tenure Research Committee Seminar*, 27–75. Ames: Agricultural Law Center of the College of Law, State University of Iowa.

Hart, L. H. 1988. Arapaho and Cheyenne meet the Mennonites. In *Growing faith: General Conference Mennonites in Oklahoma*, ed. W. McKee, 14–37. Newton, KS: Faith and Life Press.

Hartzler, J. S. 1922. *Mennonites in the world war: Nonresistance under test.* Scottdale, PA: Mennonite Publishing House.

Haury, D. A. 1981. *Prairie people: A history of the Western District Conference.* Newton, KS: Faith and Life Press.

————. 1988. The hard road to Oklahoma. In *Growing faith: General Conference Mennonites in Oklahoma*, ed. W. McKee, 1–13. Newton, KS: Faith and Life Press.

Heatwole, C. A. 1974. Religion in the creation and preservation of sectarian culture areas: A Mennonite example. *Dissertation Abstracts International.* Doctoral dissertation, Michigan State University.

Hein, J. 1974. Review of a Mennonite drama: The Anna Barkman story. Unpublished manuscript.

Hertzler, D. 1971. *Mennonite education: Why and how?* Scottdale, PA: Herald Press.

Hershberger, G. F. 1951. *The Mennonite Church in the Second World War.* Scottdale, PA: Mennonite Publishing House.

Hiebert, C., ed. 1974. *Brothers in deed to brothers in need: A scrapbook about Mennonite immigrants from Russia 1870–1885.* Newton, KS: Faith and Life Press.

Horowitz, D. L. 1975. Ethnic identity. In *Ethnicity: Theory and experience*, eds. N. Glazer and D. P. Moynihan, 111–40. Cambridge, MA: Harvard University Press.

Hostetler, B. S. 1986. Midcentury change in the Mennonite church. *Mennonite Quarterly Review* 60:58–83.

————. 1987. *American Mennonites and Protestant movements.* Scottdale, PA: Herald Press.

Hostetler, J. A. 1980. *Amish society.* Baltimore: Johns Hopkins University Press.

————. 1983. *Mennonite life.* Scottdale, PA: Herald Press.

Hostetter, C. N. 1997. *Anabaptists-Mennonites nationwide USA.* Morgan, PA: Masthof Press.

Hunter, J. D. 1983. *American evangelicalism*. New Brunswick, NJ: Rutgers University Press.

Hurt, R. D. 1991. *Agricultural technology in the twentieth century*. Manhattan, KS: Sunflower University Press.

Huxman, S. S. 1993. Mennonite rhetoric in World War I: Lobbying the government for freedom of conscience. *Mennonite Quarterly Review* 67:283–303.

Isern, T. D. 1982. *Custom combining on the Great Plains*. Norman: University of Oklahoma Press.

Jacquet, C. H., Jr., ed. 1989. *Yearbook of American and Canadian churches*. Nashville, TN: Abingdon Press.

Jenkins, C. A. 1986. Mennonite values and farming practice: Proscription and prescription in disequilibrium. *Dissertation Abstracts International*. Doctoral dissertation, Kansas State University.

Johnson, B. H. 1977. Pilgrims on the prairie: Rural life in Oklahoma Territory. In *Rural Oklahoma*, ed. D. E. Green, 6–21. Oklahoma City: Oklahoma Historical Society.

Juhnke, J. C. 1975. *A people of two kingdoms: The political acculturation of Kansas Mennonites*. Newton, KS: Faith and Life Press.

————. 1980. General Conference Mennonite missions to the American Indians in the late nineteenth century. *Mennonite Quarterly Review* 54:117–34.

————. 1989. *Vision, doctrine, war: Mennonite identity and organization in America, 1898–1938*. Scottdale, PA: Herald Press.

Kauffman, E. G. 1931. *The development of the missionary and philantropic interest among the Mennonites of North America*. Berne. ID: Mennonite Book Concern.

Kauffman, J. H. 1977. Boundary maintenance and cultural assimilation of contemporary Mennonites. *Mennonite Quarterly Review* 51:227–40.

————. 1994. Power and authority in Mennonite marriages. *Mennonite Quarterly Review* 68:500–23.

Kauffman, J. H. and L. Driedger. 1991. *The Mennonite moasic: Identity and modernization*. Scottdale, PA: Herald Press.

Kauffman, J. H., and L. Harder. 1975. *Anabaptists four centuries later: A profile of five Mennonite and Brethren in Christ denominations*. Scottdale, PA: Herald Press.

Keim, A. N. and G. M. Stoltzfus. 1988. *The politics of conscience*. Scottdale, PA: Herald Press.

Koehn, D. 1992. Personal interview with business manager, Church of God in Christ, Mennonite, Moundridge, KS.

Koehn, P. 1949. History of New Hopedale Church, Meno, Oklahoma. Unpublished manuscript.

Kohn, S. M. 1986. *Jailed for peace: The history of American draft law violators 1658–1985*. Westport, CT: Greenwood.

Krahn, C. 1949. *From the steppes to the prairies: 1894–1949*. Newton, KS: Mennonite Publication Office.

Kraybill, D. B. 1978. *Mennonite education: Issues, facts, and changes*. Scottdale, PA: Herald Press.

Kroeker, D. 1988. Social times of true communion. In *Growing faith: General Conference Mennonites in Oklahoma*, ed. W. McKee, 137–44. Newton, KS: Faith and Life Press.

Kroeker, M. E. 1954. Mennonites of Oklahoma to 1907. *Dissertation Abstracts International*. Master's thesis, University of Oklahoma.

———. 1989. Die stillen im lande: Mennonites in the Oklahoma land rushes. *Chronicles of Oklahoma* 67(1):76–97.

———. 1994. "In death you shall not wear it either": The persecution of Mennonite pacifists in Oklahoma. In *"An Oklahoma I had never seen before,"* ed. D. D. Joyce, 80–100. Norman: University of Oklahoma Press.

Kurokawa, M. 1969. Children in a changing society. *Canadian Review of Sociology and Anthropology* 6(1):15–35.

Kuschel, T. 1989. Personal interview with pastor of Grace Mennonite Church, Enid, OK.

LaGumina, S. J. 1981. *The immigrants speak*. New York: Center for Migration Studies.

Lambert, C. R. 1983. Dust, farmers, and the federal government. In *Hard times in Oklahoma*, ed. K. D. Hendrickson, Jr., 66–84. Oklahoma City: Oklahoma Historical Society.

Liebow, E. 1967. *Talley's corner*. Boston: Little, Brown.

Lilley, B. 1990. Pasta is not Oklahoma born. *Enid Daily News and Eagle*, May 27.

Lingeman, R. R. 1970. *Don't you know there's a war on?* New York: G. P. Putnam's Sons.

Maines, D. R., W. B. Shaffir, and A. Turowetz. 1973. Leaving the field in ethnographic research: Reflections on the entrance-exit hypothesis. In *Fieldwork experience: Qualitative approaches to social research*, eds. W. B. Shaffir, R. A. Stebbins, and A. Turowetz, 261–81. New York: St. Martin's Press.

Marzolf, A. H. 1992. Pietism and the German-Russians. *Heritage Review* 22(3):3–10.

M. B. church to hold revival. 1957. *Fairview Republican*, April 25.

McKee, W. 1988a. Customs and convictions in the churches. In *Growing faith: General Conference Mennonites in Oklahoma*, ed. W. McKee, 112–36. Newton, KS: Faith and Life Press.

—————. 1988b. Working together in the Oklahoma convention. In *Growing faith: General Conference Mennonites in Oklahoma*, ed. W. McKee, 157–201. Newton, KS: Faith and Life Press.

McKee, W., R. R. Coon, and D. Kroeker. 1988. Churches growing in faith. In *Growing faith: General Conference Mennonites in Oklahoma*, ed. W. McKee, 38–92. Newton, KS: Faith and Life Press.

Mennonite Brethren Publishing House. 1960. *Century of grace and witness.* Hillsboro, KS: Author.

Mennonites Can 10,000 pounds of beef to feed hungry abroad. 1963. *Fairview Republican*, March 21.

Morgan, H. W., and A. H. Morgan. 1977. *Oklahoma: A bicentennial history.* New York: W. W. Norton.

Morris, J. W., C. R. Goins, and E. C. McReynolds. 1986. *Historical atlas of Oklahoma.* Norman: University of Oklahoma Press.

Moskos, C. C., and J. W. Chambers. 1993. *The new conscientious objection: From sacred to secular resistance.* New York: Oxford University Press.

Nash, G. D. 1979. *The Great Depression and World War II: Organizing America, 1944–1945.* New York: St. Martin's Press.

National Service Board for Religious Objectors. No date. CPS guinea pigs. Washington, DC: National Service Board for Religious Objectors.

New Hopedale Mennonite Church Historical Committee. 1989. Unpublished manuscript. Author.

Newman, W. M. 1973. *American pluralism: A study of minority group and social theory*. New York: Harper & Row.

————. 1978. Theoretical perspectives for the analysis of social pluralism. In *The Canadian ethnic mosaic: A quest for identity*, ed. L. Driedger, 40–47. Toronto: McClelland & Stewart.

Norton, M. B., et al. 1993. *A people and a nation*. Boston: Houghton Mifflin.

Novak, M. 1971. *The rise of the unmeltable ethnics*. New York: Macmillan.

Orienta Saron Mennonite Church to observe 60th anniversary. 1958. *Fairview Republican*, November 27.

Pacifist view hard for young men to accept: War creates problems and heartaches for Mennonite clergymen and families. 1942. *Daily Oklahoman*, February 16.

Park, R. E. 1967. *On social control and collective behavior*. Chicago: University of Chicago Press.

Pearson, J. and J. Pearson. 1980. *No time but place: A prairie pastoral*. New York: McGraw-Hill.

Perinbanayagam, R. S. 1985. Carbondale: Southern Illinois University Press.

Perrett, G. 1973. *Days of sadness, years of triumph*. New York: Coward, McCann & Geoghegan.

Peters, H. 1968. Martensville: Half-way house to urbanization. *Mennonite Life* 23:164–68.

Plett, C. F. 1985. *The story of the Krimmer Mennonite Brethren Chruch*. Hillsboro, KS: Kindred Press.

Presenting the OBA. No date. Meno, OK: Oklahoma Bible Academy.

Rasmussen, W. D., and G. L. Baker. 1986. The New Deal farm programs: The myth and the reality. In *The Roosevelt New Deal: A program assessment fifty years later*, ed. W. J. Cohen, 201–20. Austin: The University of Texas.

Redekop, C. 1974. A new look at sect development. *Journal for the Scientific Study of Religion* 13:345–52.

————. 1982. Mennonite displacement of indigenous peoples: An historical and sociological analysis. *Canadian Ethnic Studies* 14:71–90.

Redekop, C., and J. A. Hostetler. 1977. The plain people: An interpretation. *Mennonite Quarterly Review* 51:266–77.

Reimer, G.E., and G. R. Gaeddert. 1956. *Exiled by the czar*. Newton, KS: Mennonite Publication Office.

Remple, D. 1973. The Mennonite commonwealth in Russia: A sketch of its founding and endurance, 1789–1919. *Mennonite Quarterly Review* 47:8–54.

————. 1974. The Mennonite commonwealth in Russia: A sketch of its founding and endurance, 1789–1919 (concluded). *Mennonite Quarterly Review* 48:259–308.

Rippley, L. J. 1976. *The German-Americans*. Boston: Twayne.

Roark, M. O. 1979. Oklahoma territory: Frontier development, migration, and culture areas. *Dissertation Abstracts International*. Doctoral dissertation, Syracuse University.

Rohrs, R. C. 1981. *Crossroads Oklahoma: The German-American experience in Oklahoma*. Stillwater, OK: College of Arts and Sciences Extension.

Rose, M. 1988. Migration and ethnic persistence: A study of a rural Mennonite church. *Mennonite Quarterly Review* 62:167–76.

Royce, A. P. 1982. *Ethnic identity: Strategies of diversity*. Bloomington: Indiana University Press.

Saron Mennonite church to conduct week's revival. 1957. *Fairview Republican*, November 11.

Sawatsky, R. J., 1978. Domesticated sectarianism: Mennonites in the U.S. and Canada in comparative perspective. *Canadian Journal of Sociology* 3(2):233–44.

————. 1987. *Authority and identity: The dynamics of the General Conference Mennonite Church*. North Newton, KS: Bethel College.

Schovance, E. 1995. Unpublished interview with W. B. Johnston Grain Company agronomist.

Schramm, W. 1983. The unique perspective of communication. *Journal of Communication* 33:6–17.

Schutz, A. 1967. *The phenomenology of the social world*. Evanston, IL: Northwestern University Press.

Sibley, M. Q., and P. E. Jacob. 1952. *Conscription of conscience*. Ithaca, NY: Cornell University Press.

Smith, A. D. 1992. Chosen peoples: Why ethnic groups survive. *Ethnic and Racial Studies* 15(3):436–56.

Smith, C. H. 1927. *The coming of the Russian Mennonites*. Berne, IN: Mennonite Book Concern.

————. 1957. *The story of the Mennonites*. Newton, KS: Mennonite Publication Office.

Smith, N. 1966. Farm programs and the family farm. In *What's ahead for the family farm?* eds. Agricultural Committee of the Greater Des Moines Chamber of Commerce and Iowa State University Center for Agricultural and Economic Development, 97–102. Ames: The Iowa State University Press.

Snow, D. A., and R. D. Benford. 1988. Ideology, frame resonance, and participant mobilization. *International Social Movement Research* 1:197–217.

Snow, D. A., et al. 1986. Frame alignment processes, micromobilization, and movement participation. *American Sociological Review* 51:464–81.

Sowell, T. 1981. *Ethnic America: A history*. New York: Basic Books.

Sprunger, M. S., ed. 1986. *Sourcebook: Oral history interviews with World War One conscientious objectors*. Ester Bergen interview. Mennonite Central Committee.

Strange, M. 1988. *Family farming: A new economic vision*. Lincoln: University of Nebraska Press.

Stucky, H. J. 1973. *Century of Russian Mennonite history in America*. North Newton, KS: Mennonite Press Inc.

Suderman, M. W. 1987. *Homestead memories*. Copyright held by author.

Swierenga, R. P. 1983. Agriculture and rural life: The new rural history. In *Ordinary people and everyday life: Perspectives on the new social history*, eds. J. B. Gardner and G. R. Adams, 91–115, Nashville, TN: American Association for State and Local History.

Tannen, D.,and C. Wallat. 1987. Interactive frames and knowledge schemas in interaction: Examples from a medical examination/interview. *Social Psychology Quarterly* 50:205–16.

Terkel, S. 1970. *Hard times: An oral history of the Great Depression*. New York: Pantheon Books.

————. 1984. *The good war: An oral history of World War Two*. New York: Pantheon Books.

Todd, L. P., and M. Curti. 1961. *Rise of the American nation*. New York: Harcourt, Brace & World.

Toews, J. B. 1962. *Lost fatherland: The story of the Mennonite emigration from soviet Russia, 1921–1927*. Scottdale, PA: Herald Press.

————. 1967. *Lost fatherland: The story of the Mennonite emigration from Soviet Russia, 1921–1927*. Scottdale, PA: Herald Press.

Toews, P. 1986. The long weekend or the short week: Mennonite peace theology, 1925–1944. *Mennonite Quarterly Review* 60:38–57.

Training meetings slated by M. B. church group. 1958. *Fairview Republican*, January 16.

Two hundred twenty-six county farms participated in conservation program. 1959. *Fairview Republican*, February 19.

Tyson, C. N. 1977. The Oklahoma agricultural experiment station. In *Rural Oklahoma*, ed. D. E. Green, 56–74, Oklahoma City: Oklahoma Historical Society.

Umble, D. Z. 1990) Mennonites and television: Applications of cultivation analysis to a religious subculture. In *Cultivation analysis: New directions in media effects research*, eds. N. Signorielli and M. Morgan, 141–56. Newbury Park, CA: Sage.

———. 1996. *The telephone in Old Order Mennonite and Amish life*. Baltimore: Johns Hopkins University Press.

*United States* v. *Butz et al.* 1918.

U.S. Bureau of the Census. 1989. *Statistical abstract of the United States*. Washington, DC: U.S. Government Printing Office.

U.S. Department of Commerce Bureau of the Census. 1992. *Oklahoma cencus of agriculture*. Washington, DC: Author.

Unruh, A. 1973. *The helpless Poles*. Copyright held by author.

Urry, J. 1983a. "The snares of reason"—Changing Mennonite attitudes to "knowledge" in nineteenth-century Russia. *Society for Comparative Study of Society and History* 21:306–22.

———. 1983b. Who are the Mennonites? *Mennonite Quarterly Review* 24: 241–62.

———. 1989. *None but saints*. Winnipeg, Manitoba: Hyperuion Press Limited.

Warner, M. E. 1985. The maintenance of continuity in a religious ethnic group. *Dissertation Abstracts International*, 462736. Doctoral dissertation, University of California, Berkeley.

Weinstein, L., A. De Man, and L. Almaguer. 1988. Purpose in life as a function of religious versus secular beliefs. *Perceptual and Motor Skills* 67:335–37.

Wenger, J. C. 1949. *Glimpses of Mennonite history and doctrine*. Scottdale, PA: Herald Press.

Wheat farming in wartime. April 25, 1942. *Business Week* 660:81.

Wiebe, D. V. 1974. *They seek a country*. Freeman, SD: Pine Hill Press.

Wiesel, B. B. 1977. From separatism to evangelism: A case study of social and cultural change among the Franconia conference Mennonites, 1945–1970. *Review of Religious Research* 18:254–63.

Wilson, N.J. 1977. Oklahoma and midwestern farmers in transition, 1880–1910. In *Rural Oklahoma*, ed. D. E. Green, 21–36. Oklahoma City, Oklahoma Historical Society.

Witmer, L. E. 1989. *Restored hope* (Women's Concerns Report No. 84). Akron, PA: Mennonite Central committee.

Yancey, W. L., E. P. Ericksen, and R. N. Juliani. 1976. Emergent ethnicity: A review and reformulation. *American Sociological Review* 41:391–401.

Yoder, M. L. 1985. Findings from the 1982 Mennonite census. *Mennonite Quarterly Review* 59:307–49.

# Index

Employment. *See* Labor

Engine repair, 98

English language, 270; in church
services, 120, 171, 191; in public
schools, 229; separatism and, 286

"English" people, 68

Enid, OK, 50, 72, 77, 171, 178, 187,
189, 190, 191, 257, 267; air force
base, 196; Mennonite population,
252; Oklahoma Bible Academy, 232,
245; relocation of Ediger family to,
88; World War II anti-Mennonite
activities, 200

Enid City Mennonite Brethren church,
258

Enid Convention Center, relief sales at,
265–66

Epp, J. B., 44

Erb, T. M., 60

Ethnic group formation and
continuation, 6, 8, 9, 282–83,
286–87, 289

Ethnicity studies, 6–7

Evangelical Mennonite Brethren,
256–57, *(map)* 2

Evangelism, 257, 263–64, 286

Excommunication, 67

Extended family, 17, 68

"Facts about the OBA" (pamphlet), 236

Fairview, OK, 42, 50, 51, 60, 178, 188,
205, 209, 267; meat-canning project,
265, 273; Mennonite population,
252; old settlers day (1933), 44–45;
relief sales, 265, 278

Fairview Mennonite Church, 51, 257,
258, 261

Family, commitment to, 17, 18, 51, 66

Family farming, 250, 251, 269

Farm Credit Act, 177

Farm income, 175, 179, 195

Farming, 17, 288; in Colorado, 71; and
community life, 65; in early
twentieth century, 79–80; in Great
Depression, 178–79; mixed farming,

80, 175; in Nebraska, 70; New Deal
legislation and, 176–77; by
Oklahoma settlers, 39, 43, 51–52,
57, 59, 65–66, 72, 73, 78–79; in
post–World War I era, 75, 175–76;
in post–World War II era, 190,
247–52, 269; pre–World War II,
189, 195, 196; in Russia, 25–26; as
supplemental occupation, 251,
269–70; in Texas, 71; in World War II
era, 190. *See also* Wheat farming

Farm machinery and implements, 81–82,
98, 102–7, 111, 173–75, 247, 248,
269; cost of, 250

Farm population, 251

Farm prices, 176, 179, 195

Farm workers, World War II: military
deferments for, 202–4, 210; shortage
of, 196, 201–2

Father, authority of, 66

Federal Council of the Churches of
Christ in America, 197

Federal farm policy: New Deal
legislation, 176–77, 195, 248;
post–World War II, 248, 250

Feed crops, 43

Fellowship of Evangelical Bible
Churches, 256–57, *(map)* 2

Feminism, 261

Fertilizers, 106

Fire guard, 56

Firewood, 98

First Amendment, U.S. Constitution,
112, 113, 115, 198

First Mennonite Brethren Church, North
Enid, OK, 60

Flannelgraph, *158*

Floods and flood control, 43, 71, 248

Foot-washing ceremony, 259

Fort Leavenworth, KS, 118–19, 122,
133–37

*Frame Analysis* (Goffman), 8

Framing, 8–9, 14, 16, 17, 283–88

Freedom of religion, in America,
112–15, 198

Sand plums, 53
Santa Fe Railroad, 51
Saron church, Orienta, OK, 60, 170, 256, 267
Sawatsky, R. J., 7
Schmidt, Leonard, 209; Civilian Public Service experience of, 210–17
Schools. *See* Education
Secondary education, 230–34
Secular humanists, 262
Seed drill, 81, 96
Seed money, 51
Seibel, Reverend, 77
Selective Service Act of 1917, 118
Selective Training and Service Act of 1940, 197, 198, 200–206
Self-identity, 6, 13, 16, 112–13, 166–67
Self-reporting, of interviewees, 12
Separatism, 7–8, 16, 21, 24, 25, 64, 65, 67–68; and group identity, 283, 285–87; in post–World War I era, 172–73; in post–World War II era, 254, 257, 261, 263, 268; renewal of, 167
Siemens, Helen Paukratz, 184–88
Siemens, John (son of John K.), *152*
Siemens, John K., 77, 184–88
Simplicity, practice of, 64, 112
Slaughtering, 65
Small-farm operations, 250, 251, 269
Smith, A. A., 172
Smoking. *See* Tobacco use
Social Security Act, 177
Society of Friends. *See* Quakers
Sod houses, 52, 54, 56, 57
Soft winter wheat, 85
Soil conservation programs, 177, 248
Song leaders, 63, 171, 258
South America, 34
South Dakota, 33, 34; Civilian Public Service camp, 211–16
South Fairview church, 60, 258
Soviet Union, 180–84
Spanish, instruction in, 234
Sports. *See* Athletics and sports

Spring wheat, 85
Steam engines, 81, 102
Strauss, A., 14
Sunday schools, 257
Sweeney's School of Mechanics, Kansas City, 98
Swimming, 173
Swiss Mennonite colonists, 36

Tabor College, Hillsboro, KS, 189, 234
Taxation, 24, 25, 64
Teacher education, 231
Technology, 247–48, 269
Telephones, 173–74; German-language conversations, in World War I era, 116–17
Televangelists, 262
Television, 254, 255
Terkel, Studs, 5
*Teutonia* (ship), 31
Theology. *See* Mennonite theology
Thomas, Elmer, 200
Threshing, 100–105; machines, 81, 100; stones, 81
Tinker Field, Midwest City, OK, 196
Tobacco use, 173, 255
Tonkawa Reservation, 37
Topeka, KS, 31, 41
Tractors, 102, 174, 175, 247, 250, 269
Turkey, 39–40, 181 & n, 185
Turkey Creek (N.W. OK), 55
Turkey Red wheat, 42, 83–87, 249
Tydings, Sen. Joseph, 202

Ukraine, 180
United Nations Relief and Rehabilitation Administration (UNRRA), 206–7; Civilian Public Service Reserve, relief work by, 221–26
*United States* v. *Butz et al.* (1918), 132
Unruh, Pete, 119
Unruh, Simon, 119
*Upper, Room, The* (devotional periodical), 262
Urbanization, 252–53, 263